WHISPERS
IN THE WIND

Communications
from an
Ascended Master

Laura Peterson

Sun Valley Publishers
El Cajon, California

Cover by Edward Peterson.
Diagrams by Dave Francis.
Text design and layout by Silvercat, San Diego, California.

**Publisher's Cataloging-in-Publication
(Provided by Quality Books, Inc.)**

Peterson, Laura
  Whispers in the wind : communications from an ascended master / Laura Peterson. -- 1st ed.
  p. cm.
  Includes bibliographical references.
  ISBN 0-9671815-0-X

  1. Peterson, Laura.   2. Aureal (Spirit)
3. Spiritual biography.   4. Spirit writings.
I. Aureal (Spirit)   II. Title

BF1301.P48   1999 133.9'3
                              QBI99-500472

Printed in the United States of America

Have you not heard the subtle **whispers in the wind** *that bear a message just above the threshold of your hearing; a feeling that permeates the air about you, a silence that penetrates your realm of noise?...Or, perhaps, a knowing that stirs somewhere deep within your being, that earth and all upon her surface is moving into an experience like none other within man's span of knowing?*

Aureal

Contents

Aureal...

Who persistently leads me into other dimensions of consecious awareness.

When my footsteps falter as the way seems difficult, his love and patience are always there leading me on.

It is through the guidance of this ascended one that I have come to realize all truth resides in this great sea of mind surrounding us; that it provides all the answers to any question we might ask, if we will listen.

It is from his caring and nurturing of me to become his channel that the concepts in Whispers *has become a reality and his words, as he requested, may reach my people.*

Acknowledgments

It is not possible to name all who have so enthusiastically contributed to the writing of this book. First, however, I am indebted to my wonderful and loving parents who would not live to see the book's fulfillment.

To my husband, Larry, and three children, Eugene, Edward, and Karen, I offer my deepest gratitude for their patience and understanding when I demanded quiet time in my communication with a being they could not see nor hear.

To my editor and dear friend, B. J. Mulvey, whose skill and devotion to endless hours of editing I am deeply grateful.

To Lynda Busdosh, who enthusiastically waited for the finish of each chapter as she read and critiqued the unfinished manuscript.

Rev. Robert Frost, author of Chapter Nine, who provided profound understanding of my spontaneous adventures in "Hyperspace" when I could find no earthly map to guide my way.

Charles Beharka, whose scientific understanding led me on the path to finding the ultimate black hole.

There are so many people who encouraged me to compile my mystical experiences in book form. Among them are Ethel Allen, who patiently listened as I related the latest of my adventures.

For their dedicated participation in helping to design and map out the book, I am grateful to Dave Francis and my son, Edward Peterson, for the graphics that give expression to concepts where words are not adequate.

Overview

Reflections

Crimson bougainvillea and cocoa palms sway in rhythm to the warm, gentle breeze that caress the beach. The rain, gently falling on the palm thatched roof, captivates my senses. It seems a lifetime ago and a world away from my home in California, but in reality it was only hours since I left San Diego for this last outpost of civilization, my brother's native home on a private beach south of Puerto Vallarta.

I just completed teaching a course sponsored by San Diego State University entitled "Exploring Psychic Phenomenon," though I would have preferred to call it "Beyond The Fourth Dimension."

I came to this Mexican paradise at the suggestion of my brother to document the strange and tantalizing experiences which have occupied more than 50 years of my life. It has taken me these many years to understand and make sense of these paranormal adventures so that I can describe their nature with an adequate degree of perception.

It is not only my experiences that seek the written page, and the years of intense research in an attempt to reconcile these cosmic journeys with traditional modes of understanding. It is the multitudes of questions from my students, demanding sincere and reasonable answers, that consume my attention now.

I relate the age-old mysteries of man as I perceive them, and suggest some startling challenges that await us in these last days of the twentieth century and the first years of the twenty-first. I do not have all the answers and the story I tell comes from my own perspective as I continue to travel further along this uncharted path.

It has been a long journey. Since 1954, I traveled a path few have gone before. With no map to guide my way, I felt like a cork adrift on a stormy sea, unaware I was part of a plan in which others would also play a vital role. Oblivious that I was not alone, but would be carefully, patiently guided and led by an Ascended One, a being of Light, whom I call Aureal. (pronounced Ah-rul).

The terrain I travel cannot be found in the geographical areas of earth. It is a journey into expanded awareness; dimensions of reality beyond time and space, into planes overlapping our own. It is a voyage to the home of beings—guardians of mankind, who at this time in our evolution train some of us for their channels. "It is time now our words must reach your people," they proclaim.

∞

This book seeks to answer questions that, so far, have defied solution. It explains, from my perspective, some age old mysteries of man in the light of current scientific knowledge.

This is a challenging story that requires from the reader an open-mindedness and a willingness to investigate the more abstract realms of being, and to penetrate beyond the veil that shrouds the reality of who and what we really are. It is not my intent to change your belief system, only to bring an optimistic message of hope and joy for the future of humankind and earth.

In this turbulent time of dramatic changes and uncertainty, it brings an optimistic message.

Within each chapter, at least one major concept is explored. Like pieces to a gigantic cosmic jigsaw puzzle, they come together in the final chapters to explain one of the most profound, exciting and optimistic events of this coming new age. At this current, vital time in the history of mankind, the most awesome, fantastic predictions of modern-day seers and ancient prophets are merging with current scientific discoveries.

∞

It is here, on this remote beach where the trade winds gently cool the air under the palapa's thatched roof, that I delight in the solitude so necessary for my given task. It is here that I am organizing the multitudes of strange and exotic adventures my life has known.

A little breeze ruffles the ferns along the edge of the terrace, bringing me back to the realities of my jungle surroundings. A small Indian fishing boat slowly disappears in the mists lying over the water. Evening will soon replace the last fading light of day, and night in the jungle can be very dark. With one candle to guide my pen, I begin:

It has been a long journey as I travel a path few have gone before. With no map to guide my way, I feel like a cork adrift on a stormy sea...

I am a psychic, a clairvoyant channel, sometimes called a mystic. I have not always been of this nature. This is an account of my journey through a warp in space/time into other realms of conscious reality. It is a documentary of my years of intensive scientific research to understand the cosmic voyage.

∞

Though His words were beyond my comprehension, from that time forward He patiently led me through the warp that separates His plane of brilliant white light from ours of earth. The journey into progressively expanding realms of consciousness had begun. It was a journey of mystical origin that would continue through the years, leading me progressively beyond our three dimensional perceptions into realms of conscious realities beyond earth. What I experienced radically altered my preconceived notions regarding the nature of our reality and the universe in which we live.

Where did I come from?

PART 1

Search for
Realities beyond
Time and Space

I

AUREAL
The Awakening

I have been before time was. I have walked among you in the flesh. I have also been before the forming of Earth. Who am I? I am of you as you are of me. We are an energy essence—a particle of that from which all is. I have traveled the path before you, acquiring the light of knowing along the way. I have no beginning and no end, only moving forever toward the greater light of knowing.

You ask my purpose. My purpose is no different from your own. We are the created. We are the creator. There is no energy essence beyond our own. Do you understand? The God you worship is yourself. It cannot be otherwise. You are puzzled and uncertain of the truth I tell? There is but one essence growing, expanding, dividing, loving—just one. That which we and all things are is ongoing and self perpetuating.

*I come from a plane of life only a frequency away from
yours. I and my brothers are very real. You and your people will
come to know this.*

*You are my channel. I want of you an equal partner. I will
take you with me in the fullness of your consciousness into other
dimensions of reality. The way will be long and difficult and you
may not want to follow.*

It was 1954, a balmy, warm midsummer day, that He came.
I had just reached the pinnacle of success in my career and
would be 30 in a few more days. Seated at my potter's
wheel, feeling the soft clay take form beneath my hands, I
sensed a quickening of delight for these few tranquil moments to be alone.

The profusion of potted flowers surrounding me, the
lazy drone of the honeybees gathering nectar and the mel-
ody of a nearby bird intoxicated my senses. The stage was
set for the beginning of an incredible event that would take
me on a journey into areas of reality beyond that of earth:
into uncharted regions where the mind of man has seldom
gone. It would drastically change my perceptions of reality
and that of the world in which I live. It would force me to
question seriously my sanity and it would alter the direction my life would take.

∞

Dramatically He came. Shattering the peaceful silence of
my tranquil environment, his voice proclaimed,

Awareness is your key.

Startled, I turned to the right from which the voice had
come. No one was in sight.

Awareness is your key.

He repeated the words, now to my left. Again I turned in the direction of my visitor, but no one was there. I sought desperately to detect the source as the voice continued to repeat this message in almost a whisper now.

For what seemed an eternity, the male voice continued to haunt me, bearing His message each time from a different direction; from the right, the left, above, behind. Sometimes more loudly, then almost in a whisper, teasing my senses as I turned in vain to see. A disembodied voice? I wondered.

Had I heard this voice before? Yes, long ago. It had warned me then of an impending danger that came to pass. Perhaps it is some unknown function of my inner mind, I thought. Yet its commanding manner and tonal quality was as real as that of any human male. Certainly, I heard it not from inside my head but clearly it spoke from various areas of my external environment. Only the form eluded me.

"Who are you?" I asked, bewildered and somewhat frightened. There was no answer. Only the lazy drone of the bees and melodic song of the bird continued. The partly formed clay, remained on the wheel as I ran from my studio in search of my loving family and the warmth of their human companionship. I could not tell them now of my strange encounter. It would take time to sort its meaning within my own mind.

I was a practicing clinical psychologist. What answers could I find for my dilemma? Had this phenomenon ended here I could have attributed it to a hallucination. This, however, was the beginning of a cosmic plan, so uniquely designed, fantastic in nature, and universal in implication that the environmental and social thinking of the

1950s could not have comprehended, nor accepted, as a rational ultimate explanation.

∞

As the days flowed into weeks, I would hear the voice again, progressively more frequently. It spoke a single word at first, then fragments of sentences, until finally I was able to receive the communication of profound concepts concerning the creation and purpose of mankind and the nature of the universe in which we live.

"Who are you?" I asked.

He answered simply:

You know me as Aureal.

"I know you?" I questioned silently.

He immediately answered my unspoken thought.

In time you will awaken. The memory lies asleep within your mind.

"Do you really exist?" I asked.

I live on a plane only a frequency away from yours. I and my brothers are very real. You and your people will come to know this.

"I suppose you came to earth in a flying saucer," I responded in jest.

Undaunted by my sarcasm, he responded lovingly.

I am right here where you are, my child. My plane of living overlaps your own dear earth.

"Why, then, can I not see you?" I questioned more seriously.

The light of my plane is of a different nature from yours of earth. It is too bright a light for you to see.

"What do you want from me?" I asked, now that curiosity replaced my more skeptical nature.

You are my channel. All over earth there are those, like you, who speak for us, my brothers. Events are transpiring very rapidly on your plane. It is time now our words must reach your people.

"Why me?" I asked, believing Aureal had chosen a most unlikely candidate for such a mission.

In a time long past, as you think of time, you of your own volition chose this path. Your current memory does not contain the wisdom of your greater nature.

He left me now with more unanswered questions.

∞

I continued to hear Aureal's voice as He presented progressively more profound concepts concerning the nature and purpose of man, his origins, and his role in the universal scheme of things. Aureal requested only that I keep writing material within reach at all times, day and night, as I was to carefully document all His teachings as He dictated them to me.

The demands of my busy schedule to maintain family and career left little time for Aureal. Though interesting and unusual as the experience was, I was still skeptical of its objective reality. The channeled material, though foreign to my understanding, was logical and meticulously organized. Still I continued to question the source.

Breaking the silence of my questioning thought, Aureal said:

The value of an event lies within its content.

And so it was that reluctantly I became Aureal's channel. Somehow I managed to maintain a somewhat normal awareness and active schedule while writing down Aureal's messages. If I were interrupted during a transmission, my

source waited patiently, resuming again moments later
with no break in His dictation.

∞

Is there intelligent life in dimensions other than our own?
If so, what is their intent with man of Earth? These were
the questions I asked as I began my quest for verifiable evidence. It was important to validate my questionable mental state and these extra-dimensional experiences as I
moved more deeply into the uncharted regions of an expanding awareness.

The profound nature of information contained within
this book comes from a source claiming to be of extradimensional origin: a being of light and wisdom, from a
plane other than earth. Still I thought, it could have come
from some wellspring of wisdom within the untapped
depths of my own inner mind.

In my more than four decades of association with
Aureal, He has meticulously and progressively defined the
nature of his people, the plane from which they come, and
their purpose at this time with man of earth.

"Who are you?" I asked Aureal early in my relationship
with Him.

I am as you are also, LIGHT.

In Aureal's discussion of evolution, a large circle was
flashed before me.

This represents a human cell.

The circle was dark except for a light in its center that filtered faintly through the dark body of the cell.

*This is the condition of the cellular body in the beginning of its
evolution. As this being evolves, the center grows brighter filtering into
more of the cells darkness. One day, many evolutionary times more,*

the cell is filled with light, no more darkness except for the thin band encasing the light. As you approach the end of this millennium, many of you have reached this condition of cellular cleansing or transformation into a light body. You are the new age children. When this circular band encasing the light also disappears, you will evolve into a pure light form. I and those like myself are of this nature. We appear, for those who see us, as standing in a beam of radiant light. In reality we are the light.

Then, He added,

Of course, you also are light. Only your light-energy is not yet so bright as those of my plane.

The Russians found in their study of the human cell that a single cell emits light in the far ultraviolet range around nineteen hundred angstrom units, which are minute measurements for wavelengths of light. This light is ignited from the nucleus of the cell, more than likely from the oscillation of our DNA strands. This is a luminescent light. It is cold light. It is an eternal light which neither takes from, nor detracts from anything else. It is a self perpetuating light. Using scientific terms, this light/energy is called "radiance radiation." We derive our physical, biological life from the sun. The sun generates light from heat by a process we call incandescence, which is fire by friction. Following the second law of thermodynamics, this energy runs down.

Science tells us that energy produces light and color according to the frequency of that energy. The greater the frequency or energy, the brighter the light. In other words, all energy produces light according to the nature of the energy. With technological achievements, we can see the aura or energy fields embracing our physical body. It is a cosmic dance of delicate, exotic colors of light constantly in movement: shimmering, swirling, changing with every nuance of our thought.

In *The New Physics Of Healing*, Dr. Deepak Chopra explains that the human body is a rapidly changing field of energy that is proportionally as void of matter as is intergalactic space. The latest "cutting edge" medical research tells us that 99.999% of the human body is pure energy. Einstein believed this pure energy is light and that matter is frozen energy, or energy whose frequency is vibrating at a slower rate.

∞

The next clue of Aureal's identity came much later when I was deeply involved in some long forgotten worldly pursuit. He began:

Flesh of my flesh, blood of my blood, you are my own dear child.

Then, startling me with the intensity of His unexpected intrusion, He emphasized:

Cloned!

a bit loudly, I thought, in my right ear. Because His approach shook my nervous system, I demanded He never again approach me with such vigor and intensity, forgetting, for the moment, the immensity of the message.

Somewhat scoldingly, He said:

It is difficult to get through to you at times.

∞

Aureal took me on a fantastic journey in consciousness…in ancient memory…or so I thought. It seemed so real. We left our enormous home planet for a small verdant planet, Earth. The interior of the space ship where I stood with Aureal, the configuration of the vast windows out of which we viewed cosmic space and the unusual, unear, ange/red light winding through the carpet on which stood remain indelibly etched in my mind.

As we arrived in Eden's Garden (the biblical Garden of Eden), a young woman, short in stature, childlike in body and personality, ran toward us, her arms outstretched in joyful greeting. "Was she a Neanderthal?" I wondered.

As time slipped by, I thought of this awesome experience that is so much a part of my memory. I accepted it as a real experience, perhaps...I'm not sure.

Some two years later, I wondered why I was so privileged to be one of the first in Eden's Garden...after Eve, that is. Aureal, perceiving my unspoken thought, answered:

You weren't. That was my memory you were using. You, as a separate identity from myself, were not as yet conceived. As you were "cloned" of me, my memory is nonetheless yours. As I have all memory since the first of my ancestor, you also possess that same memory.

So now I understand I am a clone.

The nature of this "cloning" process and the scientifically credible virgin-birth of Jesus is discussed in Chapter 11. As I promise to provide additional information in later chapters, it is only that my purpose now is to substantiate Aureal's identity. The information condensed here comes from more than forty years of transmissions from Him.

For me, it is as important to know my source, Aureal, as it is to confirm the channeled transmissions themselves. And so, I continue to analyze the thousands of channeled pages and to search my memory for those rare jewels of information. Even as I write this, I can feel Aureal's nearness and amazing help as I continue my search for Him.

"Who are you, Aureal?"

guide, aid and direct man to establish the new kingdom. There are certain of those who have been entrusted with giving the word to the people so that we can make ourselves ready for the coming of the new golden age."

The 7th cycle refers to this current period of time.

Due to the esoteric nature of this information, I was delighted, though not entirely satisfied, with this progress in my search for Aureal's identity. I felt comfortable with the source, only I demanded something more tangible to convince me of the reality of my experience. As I looked for a more practical, scientific explanation, more books concerning the mystical Brotherhood came my way.

Today, in most cities there is an abundance of New Age book stores providing an infinite selection of mystical and metaphysical literature. The following information was found in a metaphysical literature booth at our local County Fair:

"The teachings of these great Divine Teachers have been known for thousands of years. The most ancient records reveal the presence of these Great Ones in Old Chaldean time, in Egypt and in Persia. The records reveal that they were always referred to as the 'Brotherhood of Mankind' or simply, 'The Brothers.' Wherever the voice of one of the Great Ones is heard, through any avenue, the values of life take on a new meaning and direction.

"All members of this high Ancient Mystical White Brotherhood are no longer inhabitants of a physical habiliment. The vehicles these divine teachers use are of no earthly forms, but are of etheric bodies: Therefore, they are referred to in our sacred books as Angels of Heavenly Hosts.

"They always radiate such tremendous lines of force and power, even though they are invisible to the human eye, that their influence and presence is felt unmistakably.

Only those of inherent sensitivity are able to discern their presence.

"Many of the Brothers walked the earth sphere of life as we do now, evolving to the higher order through many life times."

Aureal has much to say in Chapter 11 concerning early times when, as he explains,

We walked hand in hand with you, our children, when you were new on mother earth.

"There are female masters just as there are male. However, all are recognized as Brothers, for the realm of pure consciousness of spirit is sexless. Remember that members of the Ancient mystical Brotherhood are always creators of GOODWILL, harmony and love. "

∞

The Scriptures are abundant with references of angels communicating freely with man of earth. Matthew Fox and Rupert Sheldrake in the appendix of their book, *The Physics Of Angels: Exploring the Realm Where Science and Spirit Meet,* offer an exhaustive list of biblical references concerning angels in the Bible. The paths of my research are illuminated with an abundance of available literature and the mystical traditions of all people concerning the realities of beings far more evolved than our own.

The Findhorn Gardens of Northern Scotland, a cooperative living community based on the practical exploration and demonstration of new age consciousness, are internationally known for their co-creative contact and communication with dimensions of intelligent life other than our own.

During my early search for those who might have shared my experience as a channel for extraterrestrials, the *Betty Book*, by Stewart Edward White, was loaned to me. It opened with a statement most appropriate to my own experience and presented another steppingstone in my search for Aureal's identity.

In Betty's attempt to define the source of communications that fill the pages of her books, she explains that though the discarnate communications she received may be coming from somewhere within her own consciousness, it seems more appropriate to believe they originate from intelligent entities separate and independent from her own.

It appears that Betty's communicators were her deceased relatives and others, who had in more recent times transcended in death. It was their intent, with Betty as their channel, to explain the nature of their environment on the other side and other jewels of information not normally available to us "earthlings." Though the communications originated, perhaps, from a different plane than that of the Ascended Masters, they are just as real and viable. The manner and characteristics of these inter-dimensional communications are the same as reported by others who channel. That is the hearing of profound concepts foreign to one's own thinking, the clarity of reception, and the rapidity with which the dictation comes.

"How do you hear Aureal?" is a question most often asked.

I by-pass your ear and impress my thought directly on the receptive center of your brain.

Aureal's thought transmission is intelligent waves of energy vibration, which I hear as His voice, His tone and inflection, just as clearly as any human conversation.

A friend of mine, an opera singer and recording artist, tells a story that may clarify this manner of hearing. He was asked to sing for a group of deaf-mute girls who sat on the floor during his performance. When he finished singing, the leader told him that the girls were thrilled with his singing and it did not hurt their ears like Mario Lanza's. They sat on the floor that vibrated in response to his singing. Sound is vibration that impresses directly on the brain's center of hearing. The outer ear is not necessary for this type of hearing.

In the 1960s, I was vehemently disagreeing with a friend concerning a news article by an educator concerning the lack of discipline in our school system. I insisted students needed more freedom.

Aureal intruded:

You must have discipline before you can have freedom.

Without forethought, I angrily responded, "Shut up. This isn't your argument." Aureal's interruption was so humanly real that I aggressively responded to His challenge of my belief system.

Some time later, with a little Irish temper thrown in for good measure, I berated Aureal for not helping me with events that were not going smoothly in my worldly life. I requested Aureal's help; I pleaded with him. I begged him. I promised I would be a better channel. When there was still no response, I threatened to divorce myself from him. Exhausted from my begging and threats, I went about my daily business considering this one-sided discourse a useless waste of energy.

Aureal scolded me.

You make too much noise. I cannot get through your chattering mind.

During another plea for help with my life's many challenges, He informed me,

We do not interfere with your decisions.

As a pottery instructor, I spend many hours working in the clay. Often Aureal offers his words of wisdom during this time, so I must clean my hands of clay before I document his conversation. Finished, I return my hands to the clay as He begins again. This often continues several times before Aureal is finished. Exasperated with the interruptions, I asked why He couldn't communicate the entire transmission in one setting without interrupting my important work. He answered,

Since you are not good to listen, it is easier to talk with you when you have your head in the mud.

Aureal probably means it is easier for Him to communicate when my mind is in an alpha brain wave pattern.

∞

Seth, the extra-dimensional personality who dictated volumes of information concerning dimensions beyond the five senses (and documented in Jane Roberts books, *The Seth Material* and *Seth Speaks*), is one of the most well known of extradimensional personalities. College classes have been based on the Seth Material. In 1955, the Urantia Book first appeared. It is a ponderous volume of 2,097 pages, "channeled" or dictated by an extradimensional source. The subject pertains to the organization and administration of the universes, of the genesis and destiny of man and his relation to God.

Channeled books, both current and ancient, dictated to earthly channels, are not unique. Progressively, more books of this nature have proliferated since the 1960s, creating a spiritual explosion that has swept the country, indicating a great shift in the consciousness of Western thinking. Though each book presents essentially the same message in its author's unique style, the communication concerning man, his destiny, and his universe is always optimistic despite the appearance of world conditions. The profound information contained within the channeled documents confirm, expand, and enlighten man's understanding of himself and his cosmic home.

In my search for the validity of Aureal's teachings and of his reality, it was a heartwarming, reassuring experience to discover the universal and confirming nature of the material.

∞

Some of our most popular writers attribute their literary creations to a source other than their own mental resources. Robert Lewis Stevenson, for example, had his "Damon" whom he suggested supplied him with a prolific flow of literary originality. His brilliant adventure stories continue to charm the imagination of readers since their creation 100 years ago. It is not unusual for artists and musicians to give credit for their products to other-dimensional entities who express their talents through these earth channels. From the ancient archives of man's history into our present time these beings and their profound communications that come from some reservoir of wisdom beyond our own human knowing, continue to persist. "Who are they?"

"Why are you so obsessed in discovering Aureal's identity? Isn't it enough you are receiving profound concepts?" asked a student in one of my classes. Pondering this question, I realized Aureal had planted this desire within my nature so that I would seek the source of my information. The more I sought Him, the greater the bonding between us grew and the more I could understand my own nature and that of all else.

And so, I continue to seek Aureal's true essence. With each request, he adds another dimension to my understanding.

∞

Give me concrete evidence that what you say is fact, I challenged Aureal.

What does my daughter want, a (concrete) block on her head?

I have discovered these super-beings to be humorous and playful but also very demanding. If for instance, I were a puppy dog at the end of the master's leash, the master might let me fall into the pool of clear water while curiously watching my reflection, but He would not let me drown. Or He might let me burn my finger, if I gained a lesson by the doing. As His channel, I do have free will...to a point. The point is, my higher mind has made the decision to be Aureal's channel. The conscious mind might seek an easier, but not so enlightened path. It is my conscious mind that at times cries out, "Why me, Aureal, why me?" when his training gets rough. Becoming a channel is not an easy path.

∞

His reality was now evident, though the form of His reality continued to eluded me.

I sat patiently in the dentist chair, with the overhead quartz dental light focused directly on my face. The dentist had left me alone in this position. The warm yellow light of the parabolic reflector consumed my attention as the face of a handsome, dark complexioned middle aged man appeared in the light. The apparition wafted in and out of clarity in its attempt to focus, then remained there looking at me and I at him for a timeless moment. It was my first view of Aureal. Soon after, as I sat in the comfort of my library, Aureal materialized full bodied directly in front of me, clothed in a white floor length robe and looking "Egyptian."

I come as you remember me.

His spontaneous materializations continued each day for more than a week. Just as I had come to expect his visits and looked forward to them, they stopped as abruptly as they had begun.

I came only to convince you of my reality and to prepare you for the next stage of our journey.

Aureal had freely and effortlessly entered my 20th century world. "What could be the next stage?" I wondered.

∞

In 1972, the next clue for Aureal's identity surfaced. Without warning, I slipped into another time zone. Many of Aureal's methods of teaching or "awaking" as he calls it, is by experience or taking a journey with Him into other dimensions of reality. I was transported back in time 3,300 years, to Egypt on the banks of the Nile. Now I would relive that life in the ancient Egyptian temple mystery school when, as a high priest, Aureal was my earthly father. For a period of nine months, I slipped into this lifetime, becoming progressively aware of the important sequences of daily living during that period of time.

It was a vital and most unusual time, He explained.

Many others on earth today also lived there and were schooled for what we would do in this current age of transition. We are now living in a most unusual period in history. It is a crucial period for Earth and all upon her surface, we are reminded, as we enter the new millennium.

Sometimes on my journey back into the ancient Egyptian life, I watched myself as a spectator. Sometimes I was the Egyptian girl with no awareness of my current identity. The purpose of this "awakening" was, in part, to create an emotional bond between Aureal and me. I would make a better channel if I could feel the bond between father and daughter, as it had been in that lifetime Aureal explained. It was also to awaken in me the purpose of that life as it relates to this current time.

What a fantastic experience! Still I questioned its reality as Aureal presented it. Either He is playing mental games with me, I thought, or I am amazingly reliving this other period in time. I know He is capable of benevolently manipulating my thinking. He has done this with a "wand" He uses to "touch my memory banks." Somehow this spark from His wand opens for me the awareness of an event not within my current available memory.

You have all memory.

On occasion I have seen the discharge of light from His wand as He lightly touches an area around my head. I have also felt this slight discharge from His wand as a profound insight immediately surfaces into my awareness. He assures this process would never be used to control my thinking.

Perhaps He is creating this bond to emotionally trap me, I thought. At that moment I felt an area at my sternum, in front of and parallel to my spine in back, twist as though there were a horizontal tunnel or passage in this area. Aureal had twisted my heart chakra. The sensation was like nothing else I have ever experienced. It was powerful. It brought a flood of emotional tears and the most profound sensation of love I have ever felt.

Now will you believe?

Aureal lovingly demanded, as in twisting my heart chakra He was taking drastic means. It was a most unusual experience to which He would resort only one more time during another of my stubborn refusals to believe. Though Aureal was undaunted by my doubting mind, it would be easier for Him to train me if I were more obedient.

Though initially ashamed of my skeptical behavior, I soon found Aureal enjoyed His channel's resistance. For Him it was a challenge which He always won as He had the ultimate means to win His point. I have now come to trust Aureal completely. In four decades as His channel, He has demonstrated a genuine, indescribable, unconditional love, and a tender caring coupled with extreme patience in His teachings.

∞

More than two decades passed before another fulfillment of my search for Aureal's identity occurred. It was not that He refused me the information I had for so long sought, only that much understanding of my own nature and that of our universe had to come first.

In a presentation for San Diego's Learning Annex, I was asked, "Just who is your Aureal?" Before I could answer "I really don't know," Aureal gave me the answer:

I am your superconscious mind.

I recall the progressive stages in my evolution with Aureal, which He called initiations. At these periods of transition, I was given the opportunity to continue as Aureal's channel or resign. These were like graduations from one phase of learning to the next higher, in which He would give me that choice to continue my sometimes painful growth or quit. As I pondered my choice, He would say,

It is your higher mind that makes the choice.

I have been deceived! If Aureal is my higher mind, then I am truly an extension of Aureal. I have no choice but to be Aureal's channel.

So we were "cloned" in Eden's Garden by a race of extraterrestrial or extradimensional beings whose memory we possess as their clones, inherited in the form of a superconscious mind.

Years before I had lamented the loss of Aureal as I had not heard from him for a period of time.

There will be time for learning and time for rest.

Aureal reassured me, then He added,

I can never leave you whom I love most dear.

As our superconscious, they truly can never leave us nor can we leave them. There can be no separation. Yet, we are all individual entities with free will to live our lives according to our individual nature. We are an integral part, an extension, of these beings who now return to awaken us to our heritage. Yes, awaken us as we do have all knowing since the first of our ancestors.

We all have a "master," a loving and protective parent from a more advanced realm of life (some call them Guardian Angeles), those who guard and guide us though we may be unaware of their constant presence. We are of extraterrestrial origin as myths and traditions proclaim. There is no way it can be otherwise.

∞

Aureal's teachings come to me at times clearly in a voice and personality uniquely individualistic that I have come to recognize as His. At other times, it is like a journey with Aureal into realms beyond that of earthly perceptions.

Though the journeys are not of a physical dimension, they are nonetheless just as real as any journey one might take somewhere on the face of this earth in their physical vehicle, their body.

We will come to understand that journeys in consciousness, inner space and journeys by way of space vehicles into outer space, reveal the same reality. Inner space and outer space are identical. To understand this concept and much else in Aureal's teachings, I returned to college for graduate study of astrophysics. The information discovered daily by our world's top scientists continue to amaze and reorder the concepts we hold of our universe and the world about us.

∞

Just as I finished documenting the distinctive aspects of Aureal's personality for this chapter, something strange happened. It was not dramatic. In fact, it was so subtle I don't remember the exact day or year it began as I didn't understand the nature of this transition.

It is time you let go of me.

Aureal gently slapped my psychic hand to release it from the firm grip with which I held onto Him.

You no longer need my guiding hand.

Seldom again would I hear His voice or feel His strong reassuring presence in the same way I had come to accept and to expect. I had become so accustomed to His almost constant presence, as He led me more deeply into the uncharted regions of other realities, that it never occurred to me He would one day sever my dependent relationship with Him.

"Where are you, Aureal?" I called in anguish. There was no answer. Two years came and went. I begged Him to answer me, but there was no response. Certainly my channeling and healing powers were in excellent condition. Profound concepts continued to impregnate my mind, but I missed the security of Aureal's presence. I missed our enlightening conversations. Like a child, I missed my parent. Where had He gone? "You promised you would/could never leave me," I scolded. "I am your clone, remember? You are my superconscious mind. Where are you?"

An answer came, though it seemed muffled and so far away, like a gentle breeze bearing a message too faint, too subtle, to evoke my attention. It was difficult to define.

Six years passed since Aureal's apparent departure. I still called to Him longing for His return. Each time this almost imperceptible answer touched my senses (it was more of a feeling that came from somewhere far away than a verbal message), leaving me with no real understanding. It suggested something about my own child. As she grew in the light of womanhood, I released her to develop her own independent life, but I would always be there for her in time of need.

The message, always the same, failed to register a tangible understanding. More time passed, another year perhaps. Then it came. Suddenly the realization of the message Aureal had been sending dawned upon the horizon of my consciousness!

There came the time Aureal determined, that I was ready for the next stage of my cosmic development.

He had released me to this vast sea of universal/cosmic Mind to which all of us are innately connected. Some call it God.

∞

Like pieces to a gigantic jigsaw puzzle, Aureal's teachings build one concept upon the other, becoming progressively more profound until the picture of the universe and our important place in it falls neatly into place. He guides us to the roots of our long forgotten past. We follow Him to other dimensions of reality, where our nature, our reason for being, and our interrelatedness with all else in the infinite vastness of the universes are seen in a perspective sometimes controversial to our current beliefs. For this reason, I continuously weave in information from my years of research to substantiate the concepts I place before you. For I, too, found many of them most difficult to believe.

In the early 1950s, my world was small and somewhat secure. My perceptions were narrow and confined to the three dimensional world in which I and the rest of my human kind lived. I never questioned the existence of intelligences whose nature and wisdom far surpass our own. I would not have believed worlds overlapped worlds. It never occurred to me that intelligent beings might be living in the same space as my own, with each of us unaware of the other. Ideas such as this were totally absurd. But that was the 1950s.

2

My Journey Begins

I want of you an equal partner. I will take you with me in the full-ness of your consciousness into other dimensions of reality. The way will be long and difficult and you may not always want to follow.

Through a warp in space and time the journey begins, taking me from my familiar home on earth to that of Aureal's to become His channel.

It was September 3, 1954. I stood at the entrance to a tunnel. It was long and dark. Like a distant star shining in the darkness of night, I could see the radiance of light at the far end. Twinkling like a jewel, it filtered gently in, lighting my path ahead. What compelling force had placed me here I did not know, nor why.

The familiar surroundings of my world had, without warning, slipped suddenly away. Moments before I had been talking to friends. Even now I could hear their voices of merriment faintly in the distance. They had not missed me.

Without warning or provocation, I had slipped through the entrance to this darkened tunnel. I could not know, as I stood in wonder of my new surroundings, that I had embarked upon a journey from which there would be no turning back. I would slowly and ever so carefully follow its path until one day, eighteen years later, I would finally arrive in this unearthly beautiful light at the other end.

This is no ordinary journey. The tunnel I entered cannot be found in the geographical areas of earth. It is a journey of inner space: an experience of altered consciousness, an evolution in expanding awareness. On this journey, the physical body cannot go.

∞

"I died on the operating table," one of my students related to me. "I was fully aware of all the attending medics were doing and saying concerning my death, but I felt no fear as I moved through a long dark tunnel. At the other end of the tunnel, standing in the most colorful, warm, beautiful light, stood three of my family who had passed on some years before. As they held out their hands to me, I hurried toward them, excited over the surprise reunion. Suddenly I remembered the twins...twin girls whom my husband and I were adopting."

As she related her experience, I listened closely, amazed over the similarity of her death experience to my own transition through the tunnel.

"I must return to the twins," she continued. "At that moment, to the utter surprise of all the attending medical staff, I found myself fully awake on the operating table. With all the methods of death detection, I was assured I had actually died, if but for a moment."

"What did you say?" I questioned.

"I died," she answered simply.

"About the tunnel...What did you say about the tunnel and the light at the other end?" I repeated.

This tunnel of her death experience and the light at its other end: Could it possibly be the same tunnel I had traveled through in my initial journey with Aureal? In vain I sought the answer. But who else did I know who had died and returned to tell of it?

∞

The year was 1971. It would be another four years before Doctor Raymond Moody's book, *Life After Life*, was placed in my hand. This informative book is a documentary of actual death experiences and the first in modern times to shed light on the inevitable transition of death. It is from Dr. Moody we have the term "Near Death Experience" or NDE. Based on accumulating evidence, consciousness can exist apart from our physical body.

Near death experience is not rare. A 1982 Gallup Poll suggests that eight million people in America alone have had an NDE. Interestingly, researchers have found consistent patterns in the NDE experience. Common elements are reported by those of diverse cultures and religions. Agnostics and atheists have basically the same NDE as all others. They speak of leaving their body, seeing it on the operating table or the scene of their accident. They remain conscious though hovering above or outside their body and hearing all that is being said concerning their death. They experience no fear as they began to float through an enclosure like a tunnel. Everything is black, except at the far end they see a light. It is dim at first, becoming larger and brighter as the dying one moves nearer to it. They are intent on reaching the light. It is a pure crystal clear light. It is an illuminating though soft white light. It is so bright, beautiful, so radiant. It's not any light you can equate to on earth.

Along my path, jewels of enlightenment have been shed by those in pursuit of another subject. Now, as I eagerly searched each near death-experience within the pages of Dr. Moody's book, it became apparent that the act of dying followed consistent and predictable patterns. These patterns were the same as those I had experienced in my development as a channel. Specifically, the consciousness of mankind is capable of leaving its physical body to travel through a darkened tunnel or some narrow passageway toward a brilliant light at the other end.

The desire to reach this light is as intense in the death experience as it was, for me, in my tunnel journey.

Due to current methods of resuscitation, similar death documentations are rapidly accumulating. Though a tunnel, or some similar long, dark and confining area of passage is not always referred to in these death experiences, tunnels are documented by the overwhelming number of those experiencing clinical death and returning again to this plane of the living. Reference to a tunnel with a brilliant light at the other end is almost a universal characteristic described by those having the near-death experience.

Within this decade, the proliferation of books on the experiences during clinical death has provided overwhelming evidence of man's continuing nature and immortality that corroborates the scripture's more esoteric disclosures. The results of this research and data suggests an encounter with dimensions beyond those experienced by most people.

What are the characteristics of these extra dimensional beings as reported by those who have had contact with them?

A significant number of those relating their transcending death experience described benevolent beings of light or those shrouded in a brilliant, almost blinding light who were in guiding authority, assisting them in this journey of death.

Aureal said,

I am, as you are also, Light.

Because of His more evolved nature, Aureal is of a brighter, purer Light. As we will discover in following chapters, Light is wisdom. Knowing is encoded in the language of Light...enlightenment. Since spiritually each of us are on the path of learning, some are of more Light or Knowing than others; that is, some of us radiate more brightly.

"I knew I was dead. I was in an accident. Though I seemed to be detached, I could see my broken body below me," reads an account from a documented file. The account continues:

"I was not in my body as I began to move rapidly toward a light. It was an unusually bright white light. It wasn't blinding. I can't describe it. Then a being, shrouded in this light, spoke to me. With the overwhelming love and warmth that came from this being, I felt secure and loved."

The following is another typical narrative: "He was a most beautiful man. He radiated like the sun." Another describes the beings as radiating light with human form, who came to prevent an otherwise certain tragedy. Aureal describes those of his plane as: "Beings of radiating Light." Not just standing in the Light. They *are* Light.

Generally speaking, the beings encountered have a guiding or warning function and exercise benevolent power over the destiny of a person. Some speak of these beings in biblical terms as guardian angels. Others are sure, according to their religious belief, that it is Jesus Christ or perhaps some revered saint who comes to them at this time of transition. I believe, however, it is their creating parent, an Ascended Being of Light, like Aureal, who is of the same brotherhood as Jesus or the saint and the guardian angels. Since we are of their creation, they will never leave us, though normally we are unaware of their presence.

For some, there was a bodiless voice that gave an important message in time of great stress or danger. For others, passing through the threshold, death created the means for direct communication with these Light beings.

This manner of communication is empathic by transference of thought. It is rapid and clear, leaving no misunderstanding of intent.

Aureal explains His manner of communication:

I bypass the mechanical structure of your ear, impressing my thoughts directly on the receptive centers of your knowing.

In *Life After Life*, Dr. Moody explains that the most incredible common element in the death experience and the element which has the most profound effect upon the individual is the encounter with a very bright light. Typically at first this light is dim, but it rapidly gets brighter until it reaches an unearthly brilliance.

∞

If there is a reality to these observations, if there is an extra-dimensional plane and these benevolent beings of light truly exist, surely they are documented in man's oldest and most dependable book...the Bible.

Angels are frequently referenced in both the Old and New Testaments. Genesis in the Hebrew Bible speaks frequently of angels where they are envisioned as having a human form. They are also described as having an "appearance like lightning, and raiment white as snow." The Christian scriptures refer often to Angels where they are considered messengers and special agents of God. In the biblically documented situations of those having had an encounter with these beings, they are described as acting as guides, messengers or protectors.

All cultures, including our own, acknowledge the existence of spirits at levels beyond the human. We call them angels.

From the ancient documents of the "White Brotherhood" to the Biblical references of heavenly beings and the latest research of those glimpsing, though momentarily, this other dimension, to my own journey with Aureal, a perceived composite picture of these super-beings emerges. They appear to us shrouded in and radiating a brilliant white, unearthly light. They are benevolent and loving, guiding, directing and generally overseeing the spiritual evolution of man.

Aureal explained,

I *live on a plane only a frequency away from yours. I am right here where you are.*

It is not space or time that separates our worlds. It is the frequency or speed of vibration that separates each plane of life from another. This concept is familiar to us as it applies to the individual frequency bands that make up our familiar radio or TV stations. Fred Alan Wolf, a physicist, in his book *Parallel Universes: The Search For Other Worlds,* believes that we live in a world in which parallel universes may partially overlap that of our own.

∞

Though the documentation of data concerning death is lifting the veil of ignorance, we have for so long held concerning the inevitable end to our life on earth, it still does not answer some basic questions. Recently I watched a video from the "Ramtha" series, in which Ramtha, an Enlightened one, who claims to have lived on earth some 35,000 years ago, takes over the body of J. Z. Knight. In the film, we view Knight as she explains to her Hawaiian audience how she will leave her body in what she calls a temporary death experience so that Ramtha can take over. It is a dramatic transformation of personality and commanding style that follows as the masculine entity, Ramtha, moves into the body of this beautiful, petite housewife.

Knight explains to her Hawaiian audience how she will leave her body in what she calls a temporary death experience so that Ramtha can take over. It is Ramtha's intent to communicate, through Knight, wisdom and understanding concerning the true nature of man and his world. As earth changes radically occur, Ramtha explains optimistically, that this unprecedented era in which we now live is the preparation for our entering the new golden age.

Though Ramtha's purpose is the same as that of Aureal and others who communicate through channels, it is Knight's descriptive analysis of her transitional experience in which she describes how she loans her body to Ramtha that is different. She becomes totally aligned in her own self so that the surroundings of the world around her, even her own thoughts, are no longer there. As she gets into her own space, she literally raises the frequency of her body until she reaches a specific pinnacle and enters a tunnel with a small ray of light at its other end. As she focuses on the light it becomes brighter the closer she gets to it, but it does not bother her eyes: Knight feels at one with the light as she moves rapidly toward it. Knight remembers nothing more until she is back again in her physical space. It is a most peaceful transition. This is the same experience you will encounter as you leave this plane in death, Knight explains.

For me, the tunnel was not a barren journey. It was here during those first eighteen years with Aureal's teachings that some of the most profound concepts emerged. As I moved nearer to the light, concepts became progressively more profound. Like pieces to a gigantic jigsaw puzzle, the picture of the universe and man's place in it fell neatly into place.

∞

It is apparent man that is immortal. His true nature is indestructible. He has been in one form or another forever and will continue to be forever. It is the nature of individual consciousness to progressively evolve or 'awaken' from the darkness of unknowing into the light of ever expanding awareness. We are all part of the One; the great all-knowing mind: Call it God or whatever name you find most comfortable. At this point, words become most inadequate. It is important to know that each of us have all knowing, though we are not aware of this basic fact.

Some of our latest scientific discoveries tell an awesome story that every cell of our body contains all the information present in the entire universe. Our cellular structure is a complete holographic library of universal information. Everything that can possibly be known is recorded in our body. Our evolution is the progressive awakening into this greater awareness. We are truly children of the universe and not insignificant earthlings born to live a few miserable years only to die again into oblivion. The mind we use is one with all else. It is not bound by our physical dimension of time and space, but unfettered and free to be where one chooses to direct its unrestricted nature.

∞

Eighteen years after I first entered that long dark tunnel to begin the strange journey in expanding consciousness, I stood in the narrow threshold separating our two worlds. There was no more tunnel, only the narrow doorway remained as I now stood in the entrance to this radiant light of another reality.

Aureal had so carefully led me over those many years to his home and that of His brothers. As the light of his plane fanned out in front of me, slowly dissipating the darkness of earth consciousness, this warm, caressing, brilliant, unearthly light at the end of the tunnel gradually enveloped me completely, leaving no more threshold, no more darkness. At last I had arrived in expanded awareness, some refer to as cosmic consciousness.

In the analysis of these documented cases of the clinical or near death experiences and that of J. Z. Knight's description of her adventure in leaving her body to make room for Ramtha, the ascended one, I was delighted to find a remarkable comparison to my own 'journey' through the tunnel. My journey, however, was painstakingly slow, enabling me to better understand, analyze, and contemplate the nature and purpose of the experience.

Though death or the passing into a realm beyond our normal perceptions is a natural event, one from which not one of us can escape, still the nature and mechanics of this transition through the ages has defied our understanding. In this field there is still so much unknown. In our pursuit of evidence to another world of intelligent beings, may we not also uncover proof of man's immortality and an after life?

In death, it takes but a moment in transition through the tunnel. For me, it took eighteen years.

3

Threshold To
Other Worlds

The nature of the tunnel was the most difficult of all Aureal's concepts to understand. Only in retrospect could I begin to grasp its meaning. It would require intense contemplation before I could comprehend the meaning of this vital trip: a most important journey we all take without being aware of the process.

∞

The tunnel had apparent substance; depth and width. Still I could not define the nature of its reality. In more than three decades of research, I found no information that would shed even the smallest glimmer of light concerning the nature of this vital vortex which is designed to allow transitions between separate and otherwise inaccessible realities. Though the tunnel was familiar territory, I never went beyond its threshold in my physical form. Aureal made it clear in the beginning of my tunnel experience that this could not happen. Nonetheless, three times I tried to go through the entrance to the tunnel, and each time my physical body was denied.

Our journey would enter a realm in which the physical body could not go, Aureal reminded.

Looking like a pair of "long johns," my physical body was left hanging on a coat rack as I entered the tunnel. Though I found Aureal's methods of instruction at times humorously frustrating, His visual imagery made perfectly clear the intent of His teachings.

Though the tunnel was large enough for the two of us to travel through, this small area of transit was not perceptible to the human eye. Was it a valid experience? I pondered this, as, at Aureal's discretion, I would continue the tunnel's journey not knowing its ultimate purpose nor destination. At first we would go just a little way in then back again to the threshold of my physical world.

When you are ready…

Aureal was patient. Then a little further into the tunnel we would go, making the journey painfully slow.

Too fast a pace could burn up the cells of flesh.

Like an invisible barrier, there was an increasing intensity of atmosphere the further we progressed into the tunnel. This may account for the screaming noise experienced by those traveling it more rapidly as in the death syndrome.

Early in my tunnel experience, as I moved slowly toward the light, I sensed beside me another being. It was Aureal guiding and protecting me through the journey. Once in my impatience to reach the light, I ran forward. It was then that a hand caught me firmly in its grasp. It was

Aureal, this being of light. As he caught me, he explained the purpose of this slow trip.

In this tunnel, one is moving through an area of progressively increasing energy, perceived as light of a higher, finer frequency than that of earth. To accomplish the gradual awakening of consciousness into the cosmic enlightenment is the purpose of this trip. It is a natural journey you all take as you drift off to sleep, remembering little, usually nothing of the adventure as you return to your physical reality. It is for the protection of the delicate structure of the conscious mind which is the latest in mind's evolution, that you do not remember. It is for the protection of the nervous system and the sensitive brain cells of the conscious mind that the exposure to the greater frequencies of light must be gradual. To take this journey in consciousness too rapidly could burn out the nervous system causing a nervous breakdown, brain damage, and perhaps death.

∞

I stood at the entrance to a tunnel. Where was this entrance?

The entrance was an area near my heart which I came to know as the heart chakra, or thymus gland. During the experience, however, I perceived myself to be in full embodiment and the entrance as a long round conduit-like structure or tunnel large enough for two people to easily move through.

The tunnel was long and dark at first. It was like a tube extending horizontally from the heart chakra of my body to the central nervous system in the spine. From there it continued up the spine to the aware consciousness within the dark confinements of the brain. As the journey began, I was not aware that the tunnel was part of my anatomy. It seemed like a structure apart from my physical nature. One's reality is not the physical body that houses that

∞

I stood at the entrance to a tunnel. With my condition of awareness originating in the ordinary darkness of my earth conscious mind, I had begun a journey inward through a passage of darkness toward an unearthly light at its other end. Though dim at first, this light grew in brilliance as I moved (or thought I was moving) nearer to its source. But where was the source?

The tunnel seemed so long at first, and the light so far away and dim. It became apparent, as the months flowed into years, that the tunnel was expanding or fanning outward at its end like a funnel until, at last, the tunnel become an open doorway dividing our plane of the lower material consciousness from that of the cosmic Light.

One day, as I stood in this threshold, with the darkness of my earth world behind me and the sea of cosmic light in front, I became totally enveloped in this globe of brilliant white light so there was no more darkness. The remnants of my physical environment were gone...yet I had not moved. This important concept concerns the process of changing from one dimension to another without physically moving. The explanation for this develops as we move into Part Three.

In cosmic consciousness, now, with Aureal's persistence, I had finally bridged the gap between his world of the brilliant unearthly light, yet so warm and protective, and ours of comparative darkness.

Years later I would describe this same type of experience to my science professor in a class titled "Black Holes." He assured me of my descriptive accuracy of the phenomenon. This time it concerned another profound precognitive adventure: one in which I, in full awareness, moved with Earth through a "warp" in cosmic space known to cosmologists as a bridge between the black hole and white hole. Theoretically it is a warp in space/time. It is a narrow opening leading from our universe of darkness into one of brilliant white light and indescribable beauty. The purpose for the Black Hole journey will become evident along with the vital concept described above, as its metaphysical nature is descriptively woven into the fabric of the most current scientific information. For now let us take the understanding slowly, one step at a time.

∞

The tunnel is a vortex, or threshold, leading from one realm of reality to another reality, just as real and viable as our own. It is not a movement in space, but one of expanding awareness. This tunnel is not specific to the act of dying, but a shared experience with other mind altering activities, including sleep. As we will come to understand its cosmic nature, it is also the mode of transference from one world or universe into another as the progression of cosmic evolution decrees. Carl Sagan and other scientists have suggested this cosmic phenomenon may also be the method by which time travel into the past and the future is possible. More fantastic than science fiction, the fantasies of an earlier age are now a possible reality. These vortices are simply the mode of transference (especially of consciousness that is not confined to time and space) to other worlds and planets where the physical body as we know it is not needed and very possibly can never go.

∞

If other planes of reality truly exist, why can't we see them? Aureal explained:

I live on a plane of life overlapping and interpenetrating your own dear earth. The light of my plane is too bright for you to see. It is of a frequency beyond your physical ability to detect.

We know there are spectrums of energy in the form of sight and sound, whose existence man cannot directly sense, but can measure with instruments, yet they are perceptible to other forms of life on our planet.

Without light we could not see. In fact, our eyes perceive the world in the language of light and only the light that our limited physical structure can perceive. Nothing travels faster than light and light travels at the rate of 186,281 miles per second. Aureal tells us that this formula is true for our earthly dimension only. This speed of light gives us the boundaries of our perceptual world. Planes or worlds are not necessarily of space, as we perceive them, but of frequency. Worlds do overlap worlds, each secure within its own frequency band, occupying the same space yet each of us are unaware of the other's existence.

Aureal questioned:

Is the nature of your radio or television reception any different? When you tune to a particular frequency band, you pick up that specific station or channel without interference from another. Why then, is it so difficult for you to believe that I exist on a plane of life overlapping your own? Patterns of energy, whether they are in the form of visual and audio entertainment through your television, or living, tangible worlds and their inhabitants, are of basically the same nature. Energy bands of varying frequencies can and do coexist without each being aware of the others existence.

Physicists are trying to detect tachyons, nuclear particles which are capable of exceeding the velocity of light. Interestingly, tachyons approaching the velocity of light are in fact slowing down and cease to exist "visibly" when they attain it. Theoretically tachyons are the reality of a dimension or universe other than our own, but somehow are capable of interacting with us. Nuclear scientists know that these particles must exist; it is only a matter of providing physical proof of their existence.

Personally, I have seen no light of earth that equates to that of Aureal's plane. It is an unearthly light, is the typical response from those of the death experience. Since the frequency of this extraterrestrial plane is different from our own, this would naturally be true. Our light, produced by the sun, is golden in color compared to the brilliant white, iridescent light of this higher world.

You are progressively evolving into expanded consciousness, offered Aureal. It is man's destiny to become totally aware. In the tunnel you not only progress through intensities of energy, you are also moving through greater dimensions of Mind. Mind and energy are really one, as mind is all there is: One Mind, one Energy, interwoven, as you conceive them, but inseparable as one.

As the energy/frequency you are capable of receiving increases, the concepts your consciousness receives become progressively more profound. That is, mind, being all there is, is perceived by the individual consciousness according to the evolutionary ability of that unit of consciousness to literally light up by the light/mind, or degree of frequency of mind, which can enter that particular individual's aware center.

Apparently you do not understand the profound statement I have just conveyed to you. I will explain it in another way. Stand with me this night on the hilltop above your city. The sight of the city below reveals a multitude of starlike lights; some are barely perceivable, others very bright and many are in between these extremes. This is the way my people see those of your plane. Some of you shine brightly while others are so dim of light as to be barely visible. You are light of increasing brightness as you evolve in mind. The more light-mind you can receive, the brighter of mind you become. The more the light increases in your aware center, the more profound become the concepts you understand.

On a dark night, you grope your way along the path ahead. You light a match to see, but dimly, the immediate area of your steps. The light of a torch or flashlight increases your ability to see more of the surrounding area of your path. A floodlight envelops you and a greater area of your path is revealed to your perceptive senses. Your progress is much faster now that you can see more of your immediate environment. Then the sun lights up your world, making it increasingly more visible to your perceptive senses. And so it is with the evolution of consciousness nourished by the light/energy of the greater cosmic mind. Though the greatest-the ultimate of light envelops you at all time, you are aware of only that amount of light-energy-frequency-Mind which your perceptive senses can, in their progressive condition of evolution, receive. In the tunnel you are exposed carefully to increasing intensities of Light, of Mind, so that you can more rapidly bridge the area between your darker plane and the brighter of mine to become my channel. The pace at which I lead you is much faster than it would be in a normal evolution. For this reason, it is not easy for you to evolve so rapidly, but we go no faster than you are capable. To do so would destroy, instead of evolve, your structure.

"What does this have to do with dying?" I asked, wondering if my journey into this cosmic plane of light was the same as death. Intently I watched as Aureal put before me a white funnel (Diagram I, page 60). On the tube end he carefully placed a very small black cap.

This cap is a visual symbol of man's conscious mind. It also symbolizes the world in which you live. This is where you reside. In your physical realm of consciousness, you live within the darkened confines of your brain. The world in which you live is a creation of your perceptions. You become aware in your physical world only of that which is perceived by one or more of your five physical senses and then received by the aware center in your brain.

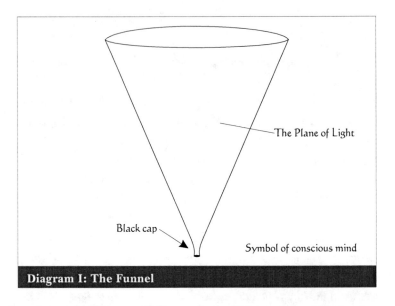

The Plane of Light

Black cap

Symbol of conscious mind

Diagram I: The Funnel

Deepak Chopra, M.D., author of *Unconditional Life,* says that less than one billionth of all the stimuli around you will get into your aware center. According to Aureal it is the chakra monitoring system that determines what stimuli will enter. All other stimuli are restricted due to the nature of your specific frequency or your energy pattern which is unique to you.

It is important you understand this basic fact, continues Aureal. Look again at the small cap at the end of the funnel. This represents your physical perceptions, your physical world. It is the end protrusion of mind. Your physical consciousness contains the least of your knowing.

When you are awake in the realm of your five senses, you are really asleep, as so little enlightenments can reach the aware center in your brain. But as you sleep in your physical world, you are really very awake. The greater mind of the soul is alive with eternal wisdoms you would find difficult to conceive. You are not born of the flesh, therefore, you are not confined to it.

In your sleeping state, you are free to enter other realms of cosmic reality, as always you reside simultaneously in at least two dimensions of reality. One is your home plane of discarnate being. The other you dwell incarnate in a suit of flesh for a brief span of exploration and growth before going elsewhere in this vast universe. You do not originate on this plane of Earth, therefore it is not your natural home. It is a school of learning for a temporary period of time. For some it is brief, for others it seems long...but a school it is.

In sleep, in expanded levels of conscious awareness and in what you call death, you move from one area of reality into another reality. That is, the vibrational intensity of your consciousness increases allowing you to enter into a greater awareness. You move from your conscious aware center within the brain (this darker protrusion of the greater mind) into the progressively greater light-energy of a more expanded awareness.

∞

Aureal's training was spontaneously unexpected, often frustrating, but always profoundly enlightening in a manner no earthly teacher could attain. It was not only the words he imparted to me, but, without the actual accompanying experience, the learning would be intellectually sterile with no experiential or personal comprehension.

And so it was on this particular night, whose date I have long forgotten, I was sound asleep in body. In consciousness, however, I was in the High Temple of Learning, located in the beautiful higher plane of light. Class was ending. I had absorbed the lessons for that period and now it was time for me to return to the land of my physical body, which I had left sleeping.

Symbolically speaking, I gathered my instruction sheets and placed them neatly in my carrying case. I was ready for the return trip back to my sleeping body. This is a natural experience for each of us nightly. It is only, on this particular night, I was allowed the awareness of this nocturnal journey.

The trip or change from sleep (or greater consciousness) to awake or lesser awareness, is a free floating experience in the enveloping cosmic atmosphere. Just for the fun of it, I accomplished a few loop-de-loops almost missing my destination; my sleeping body below me. I was truly enjoying the moment, my sense of freedom was limitless.

Within eighteen inches of my body, I encountered a strong energy field that forcibly pulled me into the tunnel opening in my heart chakra, back into my physical encasement, to awaken into the world of my restricted five sense perception.

As I entered this magnetic field, which I presume to be my energy aura, I dropped the symbolic case containing my lessons. That is, I forgot the experience and what I had learned in the High Temple of Learning. As I returned to the outer perimeter of this magnetic field to retrieve my lessons, I noticed Aureal watching with a scolding eye.

"I'm sorry, Aureal," I mumbled sleepily , as I returned to the magnetic area to be pulled into the now lightly awakening body. Again I dropped my lessons at this magnetic point of entry and again I returned to retrieve them. Now I felt quite inadequate under the reprimanding glare of Aureal. Three times I repeated this futile attempt to bring the lessons with me into my now awakened consciousness within the body. This meant I could not remember as I awakened what I had learned or what had transpired while I slept; of course this is the natural process for most of us as we awaken from our nocturnal sojourn.

Aureal's deep masculine laughter greeted me with the newborn day. I failed again, "I'm sooooo sorry." I sleepily lamented my sense of extreme failure to Aureal.

My child, I wish you to understand. It is not the lessons you have failed to bring with you as you entered the transition. To bring your cosmic learning with you as you left the School of Learning was only a symbolism of your expectations. It is your memory of that experience in the higher realms. It is the manner of your locomotion when free of the physical shell. It is the port of entry into and exit from your body as you move from the higher plane and return again to your physical consciousness, and it is the protective magnetic field around your body that I wish you to understand.

When you enter the transitional area between the two planes, you cannot bring with you, from your higher mind to the lower mind, the memory of your learning experience while in the higher plane. It is of a higher frequency than your mind of flesh can receive without damage to this lower vessel of the mind. For this reason, the experiences of your sojourns into the higher realms of life are usually forgotten as you awaken to your earth mind.

How, then, can death be the end of life? It is a transition into the expansion of life. Just as death is a process of going home, expanding in consciousness is of the same process. Since you return to your home plane of the greater awareness in sleep, death also is not a strange experience. You never go anywhere you have not already been.

Look again at the funnel. [Diagram I, page 60] As you leave the dark confines of your brain, represented by the small black cap, you move through the tunnel, which is an area of energy conversion, or a warp, between the planes, represented by the funnel's tube. The funnel represents the plane of light. It is a natural process. You travel it each time you go to sleep. You are a space traveler, for certain.

∞

The tunnel seemed so long, but as the journey continued over the years, a strange phenomenon was occurring. The straight, narrow tunnel began to open or fan out from my position of awareness in the heart chakra threshold, until one day, eighteen years later, there was no more tunnel.

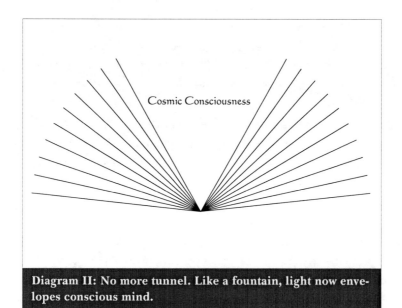

Cosmic Consciousness

Diagram II: No more tunnel. Like a fountain, light now envelopes conscious mind.

Now there was no more tube to the funnel. The small black cap representing the conscious mind was attached directly to the small end of the funnel, representing the beginning of Aureal's plane, the higher plane of light (Diagram II).

I now stood comfortably within the narrow doorway that separated my darkened world of the physical from that beautiful realm of white light. As I stood here contemplating my new terrain, I began to physically rock forward on one foot, backward on the other. As foolish as it seemed, I could not control this rocking movement. Forward into the light, back into the darkened portal. The threshold doorway was the pivot point. Back and forth I rocked thinking it would never stop. Soon, however, I stood firmly in the light. While considering my new surroundings, I found myself standing on a "bridge" looking back over the path from which I had for so long traveled (Diagram III, page 65).

At last I had bridged in "full consciousness" the two planes or worlds of reality. But what was this bridge upon which I briefly stood in contemplation of the path, the tunnel, from which I came?

This "bridge" of my journey is not only a reality of mind in expanding awareness. The bridge, according to Aureal, is also allegorically known as the "rib of Adam" and astrophysically called the Einstein-Rosen bridge. It is the tunnel or area connecting one plane to the next. Taking "Adam's rib to form Eve," as told in the ancient Sumerian clay texts, means to give life

∞

Though it took years to realize the similarity of my journey in mind/consciousness to that of the death transition, it was bizarre to discover that this metaphysical (mind) "tunnel" is the same phenomenon as the astrophysical "warp" in space/time that physicists believe to be the entry to other universes. As above, so below the principle is the same.

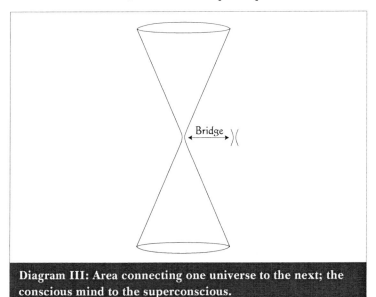

Diagram III: Area connecting one universe to the next; the conscious mind to the superconscious.

This darkened tunnel across the bridge into the realm of light is the same phenomenon whether it is the evolution of the human awakening from Eden's Garden to modern man, the birth of the baby from the darkened womb into our world of light, the evolution of consciousness from the darkened confines of the conscious mind within the brain or cosmically speaking, the evolution of earth from darkness into the light of a new day with the coming of the new age. We are seeing the same overriding principle or cosmic law repeating itself on the micro level as on the macro level. We are the seeds of the universe and carry with us in the fiber of our immortality the entire history of all that exists. It has been said that the human body contains minerals in the exact proportion to that of earth. For example, the percentage of zinc and potassium in the earth is the same amount as in our bodies.

∞

It had been an incredible journey. As I contemplated the event from my perspective upon the threshold/bridge, the cosmic end continued to fan out wider until it enveloped me completely like a large globe of scintillating white light. Though I was certain I had moved from my original threshold separating the two planes, I had not. My world of the limited, darkened physical was now gone. Without moving, I had transcended into the light of the higher plane.

I thought I had traveled with Aureal through a long tunnel from darkness into the light. It was only in retrospect, as I stood on the "bridge" looking back over the path from which I traveled, that I understood the function and the purpose for this long and painfully slow trip. Only now, from this vantage point, could I know the surprising nature of the tunnel itself. In those eighteen years, I had not moved from my position of awareness in that threshold of physical consciousness.

Bewildered and curious concerning this perspective, I questioned Aureal in quest of a more profound understanding. What was the tunnel through which I traveled for so long a time with you?

The tunnel is your central nervous system.

The tunnel cannot be found in the geographical areas of earth. The tunnel is your nervous system. The threshold where you "stood" is your heart chakra which monitors carefully the incoming light/mind from the cosmic that enters your nervous system thoroughfare…the tunnel. There is much yet you must understand before this tunnel can be fully comprehended.

The apparent journey is the progressive, delicately controlled opening of a tunnel network within the physical body allowing more light-energy from the cosmic end to filter into your expanding awareness within the brain through this tunnel or nervous system.

It is an area of energy conversion. It is a passage from one plane of reality to another, just as real. The tunnel is of energy, just as the piano is of keys. Play the consecutive notes from left to right on the key board of the piano and you have a scale received melodically by your centers of hearing, sound vibrations that progressively increase in intensity as you proceed to the highest capacity of the sounds which that instrument is designed to provide. Color also is made of energy. The color your centers of sight perceive depend upon the intensity or frequency of that color's energy.

The tunnel, just as any progression of sound vibration or of color frequency, is also energy of increasing frequency from the lowest at your physical area of perception, progressively increasing until you enter my plane of Light. It is an intensity of light you cannot see with your physical eyes as your nervous system is not yet developed to receive this greater more powerful frequency of light. Pass an electrical

current through a receptacle designed to transmit a lesser current and
what follows is a burned-out condition of that receptacle.

With each exposure to the increasing frequencies within the "tunnel," your receptive centers increased in their ability to "see," or to become aware of, the more intense light of my plane. And do not forget,
it is also mind. As you expand into the greater light, you are also expanding in mind. Your ability to perceive the more profound concepts
within this vast universal mind is nourished by the progressively
greater light/mind filtering through your nervous system to your aware
center. My plane is not of space as you conceive it. It is of frequency. It
is right here where you are.

In what you call death, your conscious reality can travel very rapidly through this tunnel; moving through the increasing frequencies
that would burn up your living cells. It is for this reason that the journey, as you took it in the fullness of your conscious mind, required a
slow and careful pace. It was to accustom you, each time, to just that
energy of expanding awareness which you could take without damage
to the thoroughfare of perception which is the "tunnel" leading to your
aware center within your brain.

The threshold, the tunnel's entrance which you entered to begin
your journey, lies in the center of your chest. There, next to your heart,
is a cavity opening to your central nervous system. It is the gateway to
your higher immortal self; your superconscious mind. It is a most important area of your being which links you to your cosmic heritage.
No, you cannot see it, but you can feel it, sometimes with great intensity. It is your heart chakra. It is also your center of feeling. Here you
may register insurmountable joy or the depths of sorrow and grief. This
is your center of emotion. It is known to your world as the thymus
gland. It will spin open to emit more energy as your nature decrees, or
it may spin to a more closed position in a depressed state of mind. This
energy-monitoring chakra is in sensitive harmonious control of your
breathing as it revolves to open with each intake of breath.

If you allow negative emotions, especially grief, to overcome your
soul, this protective area will close, as surely as a snail withdraws into

its home of shell at the instant touch of an intruder. Then it will be difficult for you to breathe as the great muscle responsible for your physical intake of air becomes depressed...sometimes immobile. In extreme depression, death of the body may occur due to this inhibited ability to breath.

This cavity beside your heart is your home. This is where your soul resides in your living physical body. It carefully protects the delicate network of nerve thoroughfare and monitors all incoming energies. This may not be true for everyone as other chakra centers may be more dominant for others.

The atmosphere in which you live is alive with mind-energies beyond your comprehension. They are in the form of light so intense they would destroy your physical cells if you were not protected. This gland-chakra of the heart allows only that which you are ready to receive to enter the chakra portals. The tunnel is your nervous system which is a thoroughfare for incoming information in the form of frequencies or energies of light. All information is actually in the form of light or enlightenment.

The nervous system network is like a hollow elastic cord capable of expansion and contraction. It is a thoroughfare, a conveyor for sense perceptive information. It is hollow and elastic, expanding in relation to your evolution.

∞

The young intern expressed his delight over my unusual request. Not that I didn't trust Aureal's teachings, but I had to learn for myself. "Is the nervous system like a hollow elastic cord?" I asked the intern at a large metropolitan hospital near my home. I was immediately invited to see for myself.

I followed this young man into a clean lab filled with vials of strange smells and formaldehyde-preserved forms. He removed one and from it withdrew a small segment of the human nerve. Carefully placing this segment under the microscope, he invited me to see the elastic quality of this tiny particle of human transmitting receptacle.

Satisfied from this observation that Aureal was right again, I recorded carefully his continuing explanation:

This which you have observed in its physical form is a thoroughfare of sense perception. How else do you receive a knowing? Your external world is observed by one or more of your sense perceptive organs. The information is then relayed in the form of an intelligent frequency or mind-energy-light through your nervous system thoroughfare to your brain where it becomes known to you. That is, you become aware of the information received by one or more of your five senses. Is this so different from the nature of your telephone in which sound vibrations are relayed from their source through a narrow wire to be received by you as intelligible information?

At the current time of evolution, under normal conditions, man's nervous system has developed, that is opened, allowing entry only to those frequencies of perception which are vibrating in harmony with this aperture (opening) of his evolving central nervous system. This is a profound understanding, my child, and so important you understand.

Remember, you live in an infinite sea of mind-energy . It is all right here where you are. The greatest intensities of mind-energy envelop you, as water of the ocean envelops the sea creatures. It is your environment, this world of mind beyond your earthly conception. Though it is of infinite knowing in the form of energy-frequencies, all of creation is attuned to a specific frequency band within the whole. Humanity is in the infancy of its developing evolution. By the very nature of your being, you can perceive in your conscious mind only that part of the infinite cosmic mind, some call it God, whose frequency pattern of information is in harmony with your developing nervous system.

Without light you could not see. It is that band of light-frequency that can enter the tunnel-like opening of your nervous system, traveling then to your aware center in the brain that allows you to become aware...to know. It is the evolutionary stage of your nervous system that selectively allows only that frequency band of information or wisdoms from the greater "cosmic mind" to enter your consciousness.

Your nervous system protects you from the infinite realms of wisdoms and other intelligent life interpenetrating your space. There are wisdoms and life far beyond your comprehension and mine. They are not necessarily in the far reaches of your space, but right where you are.

The degree to which your monitoring chakra-floodgate allows the inflow of the cosmic mind to enter your nervous system forms the limits to your perceptive physical world. In basically this same manner, a frequency band for television is the operating boundary for a particular channel. If intelligent Mind-frequencies can't reach your aware center, how can you know they exist?

Aureal left me with this question and information that would take time to digest, to comprehend the fullness of its cosmic nature.

It never occurred to me how I obtained information or the physiology of knowing. I looked at an object and due to childhood conditioning, perhaps, knew the object's nature. A tree was a tree. I read a book or attended a lecture and the knowledge gained was accepted. I did not question the mechanics of my learning. Now I am to understand that I can be aware of and know only that which can enter and then travel my nervous system to reach my aware center in the brain.

To perceive other realms of consciousness sometimes referred to as altered states of consciousness or cosmic consciousness, the opening of the nervous system must expand beyond the speed of light, 186,281 miles per second.

Aureal's purpose in the tunnel experience was to expand my physical nervous system by exposing it, ever-so-carefully, over the years to the finer light of His plane until my entire cellular structure could perform comfortably and in awareness within the two worlds. So important was this evolutionary process, and so delicate a procedure, it could not be hurried. As with vision, if one remains in darkness for a long period of time, the return of sight into the brightness of day light must be gradual and carefully monitored by the iris of the eye.

∞

In the beginning of my channeling experience with Aureal, I wrote His transmissions as I heard them, much like a secretary taking dictation. His concepts usually came as I awakened in the morning in what I called a semi-trance state of mind. It was as though the front part of my head was anesthetized. His words came rapidly. Sometimes they came so fast I could barely keep pace. In this beginning, His lessons came to me from His greater plane of frequency to my lesser developed consciousness; a one way passage. In our sleep condition, the chakra and central nervous system open naturally but change or close down again to the lower frequency as we awaken. The normally sensitive, conscious mind cannot survive (at this point of our evolution) with this greater inflow of light/mind. So for Aureal to communicate with me in those early years of my development, He kept my conscious mind in this anesthetized condition, allowing just enough consciousness for me to write and to vaguely remember His words.

∞

By 1972 I had tentatively entered Aureal's world no longer a stranger to His realm of life. As I wandered more deeply into His terrain, I came to understood the nature and origin of this brilliant white light, different from earth's more golden rays produced by the sun. It is of a higher frequency than ours of earth.

Spontaneous transcending experiences—that of being in earthly activity one moment and in the greater plane of light the next, has convinced me of the close proximity between these two worlds and reminded me again of Aureal"s words.

I live on a plane only a frequency away from yours. My world overlaps and interpenetrates your own dear earth. I am right here where you are, my child. It is only that the light of my plane is too bright a light for you to see."

∞

In the 1970s physicists and cosmologists came to a dramatic realization that something was amiss in the heavens. Previously thought to be an empty void, except for a sprinkling of visible stars, gas and dust, space now seems to be filled with a mysterious something that pervades much of its vast area. Perhaps more than 90 percent of the universe is totally different from the matter composing the world we know. It may be the most common substance in the universe. Our physical universe is composed of the unusual. This exotic matter doesn't emit, absorb or even reflect light as we know it. Therefore it came to be known as "dark matter." It cannot be made of the atoms and molecules that most of us take for granted, researchers tell us. What is this "dark matter"?

I am certain that physicists are now "seeing" the great light filled world at the end of the vortex tunnel. But why do they refer to it as dark? Because it is a light too bright for us to see, we perceive it as being dark. Are they describing the home of the Great White Brotherhood, the beings of light, protectors of mankind, sometimes known as the Ancient Ones? If so, it is also our home where we go in sleep and in death. It is the heritage of man.

4

The Inevitable Transition

What lies beyond that thin veil that separates this world of the living from that to which someday we all must go?

He died in my arms. His life was no longer viable. He knew it. We who loved him knew he could no longer function as an integrated human being. His time had come. Yet they kept him alive in this large hospital with their elaborate life support systems. He begged me with tears in his eyes, and the helpless expression of a child, to let him die. I loved him dearly, my heart ached for the decision I must make.

I brought him home...to die.

Withholding all sustaining medication, I eased his final pain as best I could. As I held him in those final moments a transfixed expression lit the features of his aging face. There's mother, he exclaimed in joyful surprise. His mother had passed into the mysterious beyond before my time...She had been gone some seventy years. He gave a greeting of recognition to his brother who had also preceded him in death. Still looking upward, joyful with the reunion, he trembled a bit, took one last breath and he too was gone.

As the morticians came to take his body from me, his eyes were still open looking into a realm of life I could not see. Now, reunited with loved ones he thought were gone, buried forever with the soil that swallowed their last earthly remains, he also entered that mysterious region to which someday we all will go.

He was my father. He cared for me as I took my first breath of life. I cared for him as he took his last. Where did he go?

∞

Few questions are as important to us as that of man's ultimate destiny. Yet, until recently the subject of death has been treated as taboo. Death is something that lies beyond the conscious experience of most of us. Because few have been through its portals to return with memory of it, we respond to death with mystical awe and fear.

Due to advanced technologies in resuscitation, many are returning to describe their experience. Currently, there are approximately seven million people telling stories of their clinical death journey. Their accounts are too numerous and too similar to ignore.

One after another tell of a tunnel and an enormous indescribable brilliant light, not like any light on earth. Appearing in this light is the most beautiful and loving being who apparently knows everything about them. They tell of their encounters with relatives who have been dead for years who are as real as life and talk with them as they did in life. Though some scientists passionately try to dispel these universally described encounters with the beyond, researchers are finding these experiences compelling evidence for the continuation of life beyond the grave.

The belief that one passes into another realm of existence as death removes him from this plane of life, is the most sacred and persistent of human beliefs. From the earliest grave sites in all parts of the world, this belief in human survival is abundantly documented. Most of our ancient archeological findings have come from these early graves. Artifacts buried with the deceased to help with the journey to the other side have given the world some of the most priceless of man's created treasures, along with an unequaled understanding of prehistoric civilizations. Without these ceremonial traditions of burying the deceased with his worldly treasures for use in the next world, we would know very little concerning our early ancestors.

∞

By now, the phenomena of death was no stranger to me: I had traveled slowly through the "tunnel" separating our plane of living from the greater plane, sometimes referred to as Heaven, or a place where the soul goes when separated from the physical body. Though in death it takes but a moment to transcend that tunnel-like warp, it took me eighteen methodically slow years to reach the light of that other realm of reality at the end of the tunnel.

One of the most frequent questions asked by my students, eager for transcending mystical experiences is, "What books will show me the way?...What classes can I take?...How can I personally come to know this which you tell us?" Some have experimented with drugs to achieve mind expanding adventures. Others have had fleeting transcending experiences when they least expected it. Still others frightened by the more profound experiences, seek desperately, as I did, to understand their inadvertent adventure.

Our physical science and our existing understanding of the world in which we live are not adequate to answer the urgent questions of those who enter momentarily this world beyond time and space. Once the faintest flicker of cosmic light is ignited in consciousness however, one becomes irreversibly, magnetically drawn to enter the threshold leading to frontiers of mind rarely documented.

Where is this place from which we come into physical embodiment and after a short sojourn on earth return again, leaving our earthly raiment behind?

"This world is not my home, I'm just a passing through." This song from the pages of a church hymnal suggests the transient reality of our brief existence on this plane of life.

Going home. For days before Dad's passing, he would greet me with "Did you see mother?" or "Hayden was here." "There's father...." Following the direction of his pointing finger, I would look in anticipation, but I'd see no one, as all those he referred to had passed on years before. Intently, I questioned him in an attempt to understand the nature of his visions: Was he hallucinating or was he truly in touch with another dimension of reality I could not see? It is not unusual for those in the process of death to speak of seeing their loved ones who have preceded them to the realm beyond.

In those last days before his passing, I am convinced Dad was lucid of both worlds. He was going home and his loved ones were there to meet him. This awareness radiated on his face in those last moments of life on earth.

∞

Documented experiences, both ancient and current, proclaim a realm of life beyond our time and space.

In the past few years, the Near Death Experience, or NDE, has gained much public attention. Due to modern technologies, more individuals are revived as they enter "deaths" door. The persistent consistency of their transitional experiences is difficult to ignore. Particularly fascinating are the descriptions of separation from the body and of "floating above" the scene of the apparent death. Consciousness never ceases as the individual views from a greater perspective, all that concerns his resuscitation. The viewing from this "floating above" perspective is consistently described in such transitional experiences. This awareness is different from that of the physical ability to see.

"There is no theoretical reason for our self-awareness to be located in our brain space," says Julian Jaynes, Princeton University psychology professor and author of *The Origin Of Consciousness In The Bicameral Mind.*

"Dying," it is said by those returning to tell us of their experience, "is the easiest, most wonderful adventure of life." Those revived from the experience of drowning, tell of its peaceful nature after the initial struggle for survival. Those who have experienced clinical death tell of the most peaceful yet exhilarating nature of the transition and of their extreme disappointment in having to return to their earthly body. This, however, is no suggestion that suicide is an easy way out of an otherwise muddled and unresolved life.

∞

It was almost seven PM. In the next few minutes I would be in class surrounded by students eager for my "words of wisdom." For reasons beyond my understanding, my heart chakra opened wide, very wide. Peace, beyond description, lifted me momentarily out of my human encasement. I floated outward into space with a freedom, tranquillity, oneness and an overwhelming love for all else. Within moments, news came of my grandfather's death which coincided precisely with my own momentary transition. Once before I had the same experience at the death of a very dear friend. Could this be a sympathetic reaction to the transcending experience of a loved one passing through "death's door"? From all accounts, death is an opening, a release, a wonderful weightless floating sensation as one transcends the bondage of the physical body.

You must understand each step along the way.

Through the mechanics of this slow, methodical, transcending journey through the "tunnel," described in chapter three, I came to know and understand the condition we call death. In the variety of experiences I had with Aureal, it became obvious that death is a process of life's continuing journey into the greater awareness of humankind. It is an expansion of consciousness. It is another step in the evolution of humankind and all other life forms, from an asleep state on this plane into a progressively aware condition of being. This slow awaking from darkness into the brighter and more brilliant light is a continuing eternal process.

For me, the ability to see those who have passed to the "other side" was an evolving one. The experience did not begin with the fullness of "sight."

March 1963. The grandfather clock was chiming the ten o'clock hour. I was alone in the house. The quietness of a peaceful evening had settled as I rinsed the foamy shampoo from my hair. For some moments, I subtly felt a presence in the doorway behind me. Steadily, the feeling became more intense as though someone were really there and coming closer. With shampoo dripping from my face, I turned in search of my intruder. "This is ridiculous, Laura." I told myself returning to rinse my hair. But the feeling of a presence near me became progressively more intense. Suddenly I was surrounded with the feeling of a strong electrical current which rendered me immobile. Though I could see nothing, I knew my grandmother was in the room with me. Three months before, she had transcended in death. Beyond a doubt, I knew the experience was her presence surrounding me with a power so intense I could not move. Fear consumed me. "I love you, grandma," I thought, almost aloud, "but I am frightened of this which I do not understand." At that moment I was released and the strange phenomenon vanished.

Was this a figment of my imagination? As a teenager I was nearly electrocuted when simultaneously touching metal pans on either side of me. I was a pathway for an electrical current and helpless in its grip until someone turned off the power. That was a very real experience and so was this with my visitor from the other side.

Each of you have your own energy pattern, as unique as the finger prints of your hand. This is the essence of your physical form. You recognized your grandmother's presence by the feeling of this pattern, which is her immortal energy body, as surely as if you had seen her in form. It is important that you understand this basic fact. In a part of your mind, subconscious, you register the frequency pattern or electrical-energy identity , the aura, of all that come within your path, and they register yours, though you may never meet again. This electromagnetic energy pattern is your identity. From it, your physical body is created.

∞

December 7, l965. I had just settled in bed, to read.

Sensing a magnetic pull I looked up, startled to see my father-in-law seated cross legged, hovering just above the foot of my bed. Though complete in form and definite in visual expression, his body was translucent. I could see through the outline of his form. There was a loving smile on his face as he looked at me, telepathically conveying a lengthy and impressive message. Then he vanished from my sight. I logged this experience December 7th. How interesting, I thought, realizing this was the third anniversary of his passing and the third time he had appeared to me; each time on December 7th.

Belief in the higher nature of man and the immortal structure of his soul has been documented in ancient writings. Plato, born in 428 BC, spoke of the body as a prison of the soul and death as a release from that prison. According to him, the soul comes into flesh from a higher spiritual realm.

Plato said, "It is the physical birth that is sleeping and not, as we of earth believe, that death is sleep. Death is an awakening, a remembering."

Aureal said,

You are very much awake when you are asleep to your physical body and very much asleep when you are awake in your physical.

∞

Mother, my husband, and I were seated in the mortician's office preparing the plans for Dad's funeral. Arrangements had been finalized by phone to the minister of our prescribed church when I felt the strong undeniable magnetic energy of Dad's presence. I looked to the carpeted area from which the energy presence came, expecting to see my father's apparition. A moment later, Dad appeared over that spot but hovering a few feet in the air. Beautifully colored flames of golden light flowed rapidly upward, outlining his body then merging above his head. The flame-like light continued to flow upward, subtly disappearing beyond my visual perception. He was youthful and vibrant, looking no more than thirty years of age, though he was close to ninety and very feeble when he entered death's realm those few days before. Now full bodied and solid of form, I saw him standing straight and tall; much taller than in life…perhaps a full eight feet tall. This increase in height is a feature I have come to associate with transcended apparitions, though not all.

Dad laughed, as he caught my attention. It was a robust, happy laugh; so very real I could not believe the others in the room were not also aware of him. He pointed to an area behind him. From his dimension I could see a beautiful garden scene. There was an immense white marbled structure in the background with tall Grecian columns lifting skyward and large marble-like slabs for the floor. "Old home week," he said, in explanation of the scene. Though I could not see them, I sensed there were many other beings there, in this magnificent, otherworldly marbled garden, celebrating his homecoming.

From my heart flowed thoughts of love. This feeling brought or became rose petals falling around his feet and beautiful white doves flying about his head. I have come to understand that strong feelings or emotions translate into a corresponding tangible reality in the other realm.

In a telepathic flash, Dad communicated his desire for a simple graveside funeral. He impressed the thought "Get it over with fast. Funerals are for the living, not the transcended."

The church and the minister we had selected were ours, not his. He asked that my husband sing two of his favorite hymns. Mother was convinced of this strange communication when I correctly reported their titles as he spoke them to me. Though I misinterpreted one of the titles, it was clear enough for mother to recognize his wish.

The time had come to select the casket. We were led to a long, narrow room lined on both sides by caskets with exquisite, softly pleated pale pink or white velvets. The most expensive of these were the first to grace our passage. The moment I entered this casket room I became nauseated with the sickening smell of velvet; a smell of stifling, suffocating velvety death. To my dismay, my family had smelled nothing unusual. The sickening aroma finally eased as we reached the last and least expensive casket without a velvet lining.

"Never slept on velvet when I was alive. Don't want my bones on it now that I'm gone." Dad's voice was loud and clear and as I suspected, this velvety scent was a psychic smell meant for me alone. When we reached the last casket, Dad announced boldly and somewhat humorously, "This is the box I want. No other will do."

To this day I cannot tolerate the intense odor of casket velvet and like Dad, I do not want my bones returning to the soil from which they came, resting on velvet.

As a typical socially programmed family, we wanted the best for our departed loved one; a fancy funeral and plush, expensive casket to express our final love for him. It was difficult, under emotionally charged circumstances, to respect Dad's wishes and to order the most elemental of both casket and service. The strength of Dad's communication concerning his last rites, convinced me of our society's desperate need for a more realistic understanding of death. It is important that we understand the nature and desires of our transcended ones and the reasons for funeral fallacies and rituals to which we needlessly subject ourselves AND the departed ones.

Dad's grave side service was unique in itself: short in duration and joyful in spirit. It was a bit humorous at times, due to the tottering efforts of his World War 1 buddies to comply with our/his request of them to officiate the grave side service. It was difficult to find enough buddies who had not already preceded him in death. Those we did find, nearing their ninth decade on earth were refuges from the grave themselves. Though feeble of voice and weak of body, they assisted each other in standing and, with impaired sight, they helped one another read the service.

Though we all loved him dearly, not one tear was shed. We rejoiced that his lifetime of giving and loving had now gone on to a greater service. It was a funeral truly enjoyed by all attending...even Dad, himself, as I detected his youthful form hovering over the mound of dirt that would soon cover forever his casketed remains. If I had any doubt about the continuity of life, this otherworldly encounter alone would have been my proof.

∞

Because of the astounding acceleration of scientific research in the last few years, public interest in the subject of life after death is particularly peaked at this time.

Death is inevitable. It is only the unknown that we fear. How can we know something without experiencing it? As documented accumulation of death experiences mount, more light is shed on this transitional process called death. There is a compelling similarity in the experiences of those who have "died" and have returned with memories of it; this is called the near death experience or NDE. There is progressively more corroborating information available in the form of books written by researchers and/or doctors whose experience with the NDEs give us a clearer insight into the nature of the adventure.

The following are some documented experiences:

• They speak of moving rapidly through a void or tunnel.

• They experience a screaming noise. This phenomenon was absent in my own experience. The explanation of the noise is obvious if we are to accept Aureal's explanation of the tunnel as a warp from one space to another in which the frequency of energy increases rapidly from the lower earth plane to the higher plane of light. Our supersonic aircraft is an example of the "screaming" sound as it travels faster than the speed of sound.

• They speak of the beautiful unusual light at the end of the tunnel, related to a radiant and loving being with definite personality characteristics who helped them in their transition to the other plane of existence. (Aureal has described his plane as a higher frequency or radiation of energy which produces the brilliant white light as opposed to the more golden tones of earth.)

• In many instances, the "dying" one returns with memories of an exciting encounter with deceased friends and family.

• It is evident from the research that the dying person has a continuation of consciousness.

Visitations from those who have passed beyond the veil of earthly existence have been a regular part of my mystical experiences for many years. In time, I was able to see my visitors more clearly; as clearly as any physical living form of earth. They are usually preceded by an intense energy force. It is an eerie sensation which may cause the hair on my head and arms to bristle. A universal characteristic of ghostly visitations is the prickling of the skin and other electrical-like bodily sensations occurring in response to the presence of these higher energy forces.

What then is death?

∞

The clock glowing on my night stand revealed that it was exactly 2:00 AM. I had awakened suddenly from a sound sleep. In the darkness of night my room came alive with a large globe of brilliant white light subtly scintillating with rainbow colors. Like a soap bubble dancing in the sunlight, this ball of glowing, radiating light surrounded me. Hovering just above my reclining body, also encased in this strange yet beautiful light, was the form of my 20 year old nephew, Carl. "I was waiting for you to awaken," he said in delight over this encounter.

Three weeks earlier, Carl had drowned under mysterious circumstances. His body had been cremated. Now, very much alive to my perceptive senses, he radiated with joy and glowed with a beautiful peach-like complexion.

"Though I have been in communication with you while you sleep and you are aware of this communication when you are with me, as you sleep; it was agreed that I should come to you now so you will know beyond a doubt that I live and that all is well with me." Carl impressed his message on my mind.

Desiring to check the reality of that which I was so vividly experiencing, I turned to my left side. Just as rapidly Carl also moved, placing himself full length on his back lying on the floor beside my bed. Both arms were under his neck for head support and his left knee relaxed over his right for more comfort, perhaps...or as I learned later from his family, this was a typical floor reclining position for Carl.

"You must believe that I live, and live well," He emphasized, smiling impishly at my startled disbelief.

"See how free I am?" he continued to communicate joyfully, as he requested that I convey this message to his distraught parents. Though he had tried to reach them he was not certain he had succeeded.

As suddenly as my nocturnal visitor had manifested he was gone, vanished as strangely as he had appeared. The room was again dark. The time was now 2:21 AM. For fully 20 minutes I had experienced in full awareness, this fantastic communication between the planes. It was not a dream!

Two weeks earlier in the light of day, as I busily prepared the evening meal, Carl had appeared in this same manner...suddenly materializing before me in this globe of colorful dancing light. The vision had barely begun, however, when an earthly interruption obliterated the communication.

∞

In the event of sudden traumatic deaths, the deceased personality may remain in the surrounding environment not aware of its transition. Often referred to as ghosts, from antiquity to the present, our cultural tradition and literature is filled with stories of ghost apparition.

As the hour approached midnight, I walked into the dimly lit hallway of my home. Coming rapidly toward me, frantically clawing the air as though he would tear me to shreds, was a friend who had died suddenly in an accident that morning. Startled by this strange "life threatening" onslaught from a normally most gentle man, I moved from his path to avoid what seemed a certain attack. As I did, he moved on not at all aware of my presence. He is trying to return to earth plane, I thought. His wife had recently undergone a serious operation. Aware of her need for him, he apparently was, in desperation, trying to return.

The scene encountered in the privacy of my home may have occurred at the time of his passing that morning. Hours later I intercepted that traumatic event, which remained active in the regions of space about me.

If this concept seems unbelievable, consider the multitudes of programmed entertainment that comes to us from dimensions of unseen space available at the flip of a television or radio switch.

What fantastic intelligent activity reigns in the unseen world about us! It is a scientifically accepted fact that our human perception is restricted to a narrow band of the infinitely vast sea of cosmic activity.

∞

March 26, 1986. This chapter had just been edited by my dear friend and business associate, Bob Pickering. For seventeen years he had patiently listened to my cosmic experiences and had laboriously typed my hand written transcriptions.

While in the prime of life, on this March afternoon, Bob suddenly left this plane by way of a massive heart attack. As the shock of his passing subsided, I fully expected some lively interplane communication from him; but all was still, unusually still. A depressed atmosphere hovered over the lives of those he had left behind.

Legal problems arose when no will could be found.

"Laura, I know Bob will answer you," his distraught widow said, with more confidence than I was now feeling. Together we requested his answer to our need, but all remained still. The area about us remained strangely silent. Just as I was beginning to doubt the otherworldly existence, a garbled voice began to speak. It was Bob. Goose bumps broke out over my body; I could now feel his undeniable presence. But the voice sounded as though he had a mouth full of marbles. The message, however, was discernible enough for me to document his wishes for the allocation of his worldly belongings. Soon I was able to see him. He was holding his throat as though struggling to speak. *What is your problem?* I thought the question.

"I am still trying to use my vocal chords for speech," he explained. "My passing was so sudden I have not yet released my physical body."

Later in a two page communication, Bob told of his cremation experience: "As my body was being cremated I felt a momentary psychic shock, as though an umbilical cord was suddenly jerked from its attachment to my physical body."

"Does this happen to all who are cremated?" I asked.

"No, it was only my reaction to the suddenness of my passing. I was refusing to release my physical body, as I was not prepared for the change." he explained, expanding on the event.

On several occasions thereafter, I would catch glimpses of Bob watching us. He tried funny antics to cheer up his wife who could not see him. However, she never doubted the descriptions of his activities which I conveyed to her. We laughed together knowing he would always be with us. One evening I looked up from the computer to see Aureal and Bob standing together, their plane superimposed within the same space as the wall in front of me. As their plane became dominant, my physical plane was no longer visible to my perception.

Bob gave me a slow wink as he put his arm around Aureal. I knew he felt "one-up" on me as at last he had met, in person, the Aureal I had told him of for so many years. With most of my inter-world visitors, a special higher frequency energy is necessary to allow these visitations from those newly deceased. In each case Aureal has indicated his part in making the contact possible.

The importance of maintaining a positive consciousness when a loved one "dies" is a most important factor. It should be one of happy rejoicing for the departing soul. Some peoples of this world celebrate the departure with a wake or other joyful celebration for the funeral of their loved one. This is the way it should be, as death, Plato said, is a "rebirth," or as Aureal stated, death is a "going home." There is no end, no termination point in life, only change, a transition into the fullness of life.

It has been our custom to grieve and mourn the passing of the departed. This expression of sorrow seriously impedes the soul in its transition. The transcending one desires to console the loved ones he has left behind. He wants to tell them that he still lives and lives well. In most cases, this cannot be done as the entire family are bereaved over their loss of the loved one. The home reeks with doom, darkness and sorrow. All these thoughts and depressive emotions are received directly by the departed one. Therefore the deceased, in love for his grieving ones, remains earthbound, when he needs to be released by them to move into the higher realms of his destination.

Countless are the senseless fears caused by ignorance and the needless and expensive rituals socially and emotionally imposed in the "properly" disposing of our loved one's last remains. Is this what they want from us? With the true concept and understanding, there would be no mourning, no grief, nor negative feelings. The remaining ones would rejoice in the departed's release.

It has been my experience to encounter the transcending one soon after his/her passing, though some deceased have managed a dramatic encounter several years after their death. Such was the case of my mother-in-law with whom, unfortunately, our relationship remained "cool" to the bitter end. Though she tried to come through after her passing, I steadfastly refused her "visitation rights." The hostility I felt for her was still too great six years after her death.

In almost an explosive manner, she came to me early one evening, explaining much about herself in a former incarnation when she was 'of Catherine the Great.' I knew little about Catherine the Great other than her passion for beheading people.

Though my husband's mother had much to relate that evening, she continued with another surprise visit the next morning. She came into this lifetime, she explained, to work out a negative karma, and in selfishness she failed. In learning much from her about this Catherine, I was grateful she had not beheaded me in this lifetime. Realizing the negative emotions between us, she had come to erase this adverse atmosphere so in future incarnations we would not have this conflict to overcome.

Through this encounter my feelings of hostility for her vanished...well, almost. Later at a family gathering, which included my daughter and two nieces, the subject of the mother-in-law, grandmother of the girls, was discussed. In relating the above post-mortem experience with her, I explained my reasons for disliking her. That evening she surrounded me with love. Wherever I went, I was encased in this subtle feeling of a love beyond earthly description. As I questioned her presence, she said, "I didn't like what you said about me to my granddaughters." Since I didn't think she was capable of loving, I described this strange situation to a knowledgeable friend who explained:

"It is imperative for those who have created an unpleasant karma while on earth plane to resolve the problem or they will face it in another lifetime. She surrounded you with love to erase the hostility you were carrying thus setting both of you free. Love is a solvent that banishes the negative atmosphere."

This emotional attitude toward her could not have been changed so immediately and dramatically by an appeal to my intellect. Somehow, she was able to abolish this hostile feeling from my emotional center. What a blessing!

I expected a lively communication with my step-father-in-law after his death as we spent many happy times discussing the life-after-death phenomenon. He promised to communicate with me concerning his other-side adventure should he die first. More than twenty years have elapsed since his passing with not the slightest indication of a communication from him. I do not know the reason.

∞

Is life eternal and never ending? To answer this question more fully, we must first know who and what we are. We are beginning to realize what our ancestors must have intuitively known, that death is not the end of our being but a beautiful transcending experience.

We never go anywhere in death or in sleep that is not already familiar to us. Are you aware of your nocturnal journey as you sleep? Aureal allowed me the awareness of this normal sleep experience. On this particular night, while I left my body sleeping, I floated through the "warp membrane" that separates our third dimensional world from the light of our greater reality. Consciousness never ceases, it only changes in frequency so we are not normally aware of this continuity in consciousness.

When it was time for my body to awake, I reentered through the "warp" (that area of frequency or energy change). At this "doorway," we normally forget the memory of that greater experience as we pass through the frequency change, awakening to our earthly consciousness.

Death and sleep are a "going home." Death is returning again to our source, to the finer nature of our reality where we awaken to the greater wisdom of our cosmic design in all its infinite proportions and expressions. It is only the physical body that is left behind as one departs in expanded consciousness from this dimension to enter that of the greater light.

Where is our cosmic home? It is right here where we are. Just a change in frequency and you move from one plane to the next. It is not a condition of space. As you drift off to sleep, you leave this material plane and move into the higher plane of life where you experience a more expanded perceptive consciousness. This is your home to which you return in sleep as well as death. You are never separated from those you love, even though in appearances, death takes them from you. Fleeting memories of a dream reveal the remnants of a profound truth: As your body lies in sleep, you actually live a fuller life with those who have passed beyond the grave. This memory, however, slips from your awakening mind as your consciousness functions independently on many different levels of awareness, separated by changes in frequency.

With progressive understanding of the death phenomena we will come to understand more clearly who we are and where we come from. We will understand our eternal purpose and where we are going in this infinitely vast scheme of things. As we probe more deeply into the death phenomena, we realize that life is eternal and can never be terminated.

∞

To change one's belief system is not my purpose. I, too, was a skeptic of all I could not perceive with my physical senses, until my personal experiences forced me to seek reasonable answers. Careful observation and documentation of these experiences, these journeys into other realms of realities virtually uncharted by our predecessors, convinced me that there does exist some tangible and viable phenomena beyond the current understanding of our technologies.

It is not my intent to duplicate that which has already been written on the subject of death. But, hopefully, out of my own personal experiences, this discussion will shed light in areas which are not yet fully understood.

∞

April 15,1990. My viable ninety-one year old mother and I were laughing over the ridiculous suggestion that I would take her to Mexico and parasail her to a remote beach below Puerto Vallarta where my brother, her son, lives. Soon I would leave for the airport to spend six days with him in this Mexican paradise. Within two and one-half hours from our happy farewell, mother left this earthly plane, collapsing at the sink while washing her hands.

Eight months later, just before Christmas, I was awakened suddenly from a profoundly deep sleep by an urgent tapping on my lower left rib. It hurt!. This tapping was not at all gentle. It was, in fact, very painful. The sudden awakening from such an intense sleep was in itself, like nothing I have experienced before or since. I remember having been somewhere far away. In awakening with such sudden intensity, this far away place (of altered sleep consciousness) moved rapidly away from me. This, I thought, was in itself strange. I would expect to have left this place of profound depth in returning to my awakening consciousness much as a deep sea diver returns to the surface of the ocean.

With my heart pounding rapidly, I looked up into the face of my smiling mother. What was the meaning of this, I wondered, as she continued the rapid thumping on my rib. Was I dying and she came to awaken me from an otherwise sudden death? She said nothing, only smiled. It was not really a smile, she was grinning impishly as though she came to let me know she really had transcended death and was still very much alive. This was a singular experience. That which I conceived as space was probably the greater frequency of her realm changing rapidly to the lower frequency of my awakening consciousness.

During her life I had found in her an eager listener to my transcending experiences and to my visitations from the deceased. Though she lived a full and active life, she was as convinced as I am that the greatest adventure was just ahead...through the veil of transcendence.

When her time came to leave this plane, she promised she would return to me in such a dramatic way there would be no doubt of her survival. She kept that promise. My lower left rib hurt for fully two days as a result of her forceful tapping. The day of her funeral months before, she had also pounded forcefully on my rib cage in response to my dispersal of her worldly goods in a manner o which she obviously disapproved.

Was it possible she made this contact by awakening me suddenly from a profound sleep before my conscious mind could prohibit the memory? Was it her plane that moved so rapidly away from me as I awakened?

∞

It is a widely accepted belief that we visit our loved ones in their realm as we sleep. While there, we experience a more expanded awareness which under normal circumstances we do not bring with us as we awaken to our physical consciousness.

There are many dimensions of consciousness with which we interact. Usually the flow between these planes is subtle so we are not aware of transcending or moving from one dimension of consciousness to another during our daily activities. Apparently, however, this is a normal activity especially in sleep. Scientific studies in sleep labs indicate beyond a doubt that, though the brain waves change during our sleep cycle, they remain active. What causes this activity?

Is there life beyond the grave? There are many intelligent beings, educators and scientists among them, who insist that death is the end and give credible physiological and psychological reasons for their belief that the dying brain is causing the NDE experiences. Those having the experience however, strongly and convincingly challenge these skeptics. They know, beyond a doubt, they entered an incredible realm of light beyond description. This realm is the home of beings of love…perhaps angels… and of their loved ones preceding them in death. It is a profoundly genuine spiritual occurrence that forever changes the life of those having the experience.

Though research is close to proving this greatest of our enigmas, it remains for each of us, according to our own personal experience and belief, to answer this question for ourselves.

Who am I?

PART 2

Search For Origins

5

Footsteps in the Sands of Time

As the grains of sand, one lifetime is too short to be counted in the eternal scheme of things.

Sensing a shadow in the doorway of my reading room, I looked up from my book to see a young woman standing only a few feet from where I sat. Her dark hair, loosely draped over her shoulders, obscured the only part of her otherwise totally nude form. I chilled as her dark eyes penetrated the very soul of my being, holding me for that brief moment, within the intensity of her stare. What was she doing here, as real and full bodied as any living human? Why had she entered my 20th century library...nude in the fullness of day? Though she did not move, her right leg was raised as though prepared for her next step. For a frozen moment in eternity she stood there, her gaze locked in mine. Then she vanished into the "void" as mysteriously as she had come. Was this a holographic image that somehow penetrated the reality of my otherwise sane world? Though I may never know the process by which this girl from ancient Egypt entered my current time zone, I knew it was another of Aureal's methods for awakening me to my own reality that existed 3,300 years ago on the banks of the Nile. Though this was the first time I actually saw her, she had progressively invaded my life, subtly surfacing into my otherwise unsuspecting mind. Her name was Desert Rose. The Egyptian translation by which she was called has long escaped my memory. Her life span of eighteen years was not long even by ancient Egyptian standards, but the impact she has on my current life is at times overwhelming.

Past life memory can come in a variety of ways. In cultures believing in reincarnation, it is not unusual for very young children to speak of families, homes and events they left behind as they died from one body only to be born again into another, carrying the past life memory with them.

Jenny Cockell in her book, *Across Time and Death: A Mother's Search For Her Past Life Children*, tells a fascinating story that challenges even the most skeptical ideas of reincarnation. Recurring images and dreams haunted her for as long as she could remember. They concerned a woman waiting near the sea for someone. It was a scene that seemed ridiculously familiar to her, though she could not remember who the woman might be nor for whom she was waiting. It concerned a mother desperately seeking to be reunited with children she had left behind. As an adult seeking some meaning behind her memories, she began searching for the landmarks of her persistent images.

Armed with information surfacing through regressive hypnosis, Jenny searched records in a small Ireland village for information concerning a woman named Mary who had died in 1932, twenty one years before Jenny was born. What she found were five adult brothers and sisters, now in their sixties and seventies, who, as children in the 1930's had lost their mother due to child birth complications

Within a short time span after death, Mary returned to birth in another body carrying with her an unrelenting, driving concern for those children she left behind. Though they were now almost forty years older than she was upon meeting them, they felt an immediate attachment to her and she felt a strong maternal feeling for them. They were also able to fill in the answers to her persistent memories that had haunted her for almost thirty years.

∞

Clinical psychologists often use past life regression to unlock the memory for those in need of understanding the nature of current life problems which may have originated in a past life. For many persons, recurring and often haunting memories persist in entering the consciousness through dreams.

Personally I did not believe, and had no need to believe, in reincarnation. It didn't fit within my religious and socially programmed belief system. If I had never become aware of reincarnation as a philosophy, nor awakened to even one of my past life adventures, life would continue from birth to death just as it does for millions of Americans. But that was more than four decades ago, before I met Aureal.

Like Alice walking through the looking glass into a fantastic wonderland, Aureal took me into unbelievable dimensions of our beginning and our purpose. He insisted that I become consciously aware that our beliefs, attitudes, current personality, and yes, even the choice of a mate, spring from a depth, an inner core of experiences of choices we made along the path of our eternal existence.

Aureal touched my memory banks to awaken a multitude of memories through various adventures of my many lifetimes throughout an eternity of time. Most of these memories are in fragments, at least what appear to be memories emerging from some distant past. They are feelings of life and events transpiring in times long past, and in lands so remote their reality lies buried beneath the sands of time. Still very much alive, they stir deeply within my emotional center. I cannot trace them to any event within my current life. Since I have no need to imagine them as they are primitive and uneventful, I cannot attribute them to any source other than a past life memory.

As I moved through my demanding daily routines, I became subtly immersed in a lifetime 2000 years ago. It was an awareness of having lived during the time of Jesus. Since I was not particularly curious about further details of that life, none were offered. Months later, Aureal, interrupting my busy schedule, informed me that, "Jesus had his woman." He really knows how to get my attention, I thought, as I looked at Aureal in disbelief. I had accepted without question the Christian belief that Jesus was a virgin.

Aureal challenged my innocence:

And did ye think He was not a whole man?

Aureal informed me that many others now walking earth's paths today lived that lifetime 2000 years ago, just before, during and after the birth of Christ. Why? According to Aureal, Jesus was not to have been crucified. It was our purpose to protect him. We failed. So, I was one of the followers of Jesus? I really don't remember anything about it, except somewhere deep within my eternal memory, it seemed I knew this man Jesus well. But this, I reasoned, was the result of my Christian programming, and frankly I didn't care, so I gave it little thought. That is, until a friend insisted on reading an article to me in one of the current magazines of the 1970's. Since I was busy trying to finish a clay order on my potter's wheel, I wasn't happy with this insistent intrusion on my time.

"Go ahead, continue working," my friend suggested, "I'll read it to you." The article concerned Taylor Caldwell's reincarnational memory of being the mother of Mary Magdalene, a follower of Jesus. I was barely listening over the hum of my wheel, when my body broke into "goose bumps." My face puckered with an enormous energy flowing through my being. It felt as though my hair was standing on end over something my friend was reading. Surprised by this intense reaction, I questioned its source. The next time he read Mary Magdalene, my response was even more electrical. A few days later, I "lit up" again as I walked through my room. The TV minister had mentioned Mary Magdalene. What was it about Mary Magdalene that brought such an immediate response from the deep recesses of my mind? I knew little about her except she was a harlot. According to the Biblical story, Jesus said to a condemning crowd, "Let ye without sin cast the first stone."

As the days passed, I heard the name Mary Magdalene again and again. My response was always the same. To this day, I have never responded to anything as powerfully as to the name, Mary Magdalene.

Early in Aureal's teachings, He allowed me to feel these currents of energy which race through the body causing a chilling sensation, some call "goose bumps." The arm hairs stands on end and in more drastic situations, the entire body "lights up," tingling or vibrating with this movement of energy. Aureal explained this phenomenon as the physical reaction to a cosmic truth known by the energy body or higher mind. This truth vibrates on the physical body through the nervous system in affirmation to this greater truth.

Like a child with a new play toy I proceeded to engage a friend in asking such cosmic questions that, if the answer were "yes," I would break out in these "goose bumps." We no sooner began when Aureal scolded:

Don't play that parlor game. Your nervous system is not yet developed to carry such forces.

Sometime later, deeply involved in writing Aureal's transmissions, I become unaware of my physical surroundings. I never questioned my state of mind, or just how deeply in trance I might be during these sessions with Aureal. I heard my business associate call to me. I continued writing with no thought of answering him. It simply did not occur to me to answer. He called again; still I did not answer, I was not intentionally ignoring him. In this intense state of mind there is no verbal response mechanism to the outside world. The third time he called a bit louder breaking into my intense communication with Aureal. Coming out of this state of consciousness into my physical world again was like falling from an airplane thousands of miles in the air. When I "hit the ground" I felt extreme anger and was vehemently expressing this emotion to my dear business associate when, without warning, I bounced 2000 years back in time, in consciousness, to the life with

Jesus. I literally moved spontaneously from one frequency of consciousness into another.

From my perspective now, in the biblical land and time, I focused on a young woman standing on the marbled slab floor of a state building. Slender Roman columns surrounded the area where she stood. I tried to penetrate her thoughts, to understand who she was. It was as though I were a spectator, existing partly in her dimension where I could see her, and partly in my 20th century identity.

She was dressed in a floor length royal-purple gown gathered neatly around her waist. Even with her back to my visual perception, I knew, I sensed, I felt strongly I had been that girl.

This is not the first time you have been the daughter of a Senator.

My father in this lifetime was a State Senator. This implied the girl was Roman. She seemed no more than fifteen years of age, yet the grief I felt through her was overwhelming. I knew Jesus had been crucified that day and I (she) could do nothing to change the dreadful deed. I knew also that I had been very close to this man, Jesus. In what capacity, I don't know.

Throughout history, into this current time, others have claimed to be the reincarnate of Mary Magdalene. As I have reported in another chapter, the soul according to Aureal, can split so that in any incarnation there may be several individuals carrying the same cosmic genetic identity or the innate memory of another from the past, as for example this Mary Magdalene.

If this concept seems unbelievable, consider multiple human births. Identical twins or triplets are the product of a single sperm/egg conception that divides into two or more human individuals, each with the same DNA, which is the complete genetic blueprint, or code. The soul memory, now divided, would also belong equally to each individual twin; otherwise they would not be identical.

Intellectually, my possible past life relationship to this Mary is not overtly important to who I am at this time. It is only that something stirs within the inner recesses of my mind and heart that, at the time of this writing, gives no indication of surfacing with more personal insight. On a deeper level of mind, even now as I write this, my entire body is "chilled" with some subliminal knowing. I am alive with this energy which my rational mind does not understand.

Overwhelmed by curiosity, I had to know who and what Mary Magdalene really was, why I was so affected by the mere mention of her name. My search led me to two scholarly researched books: One, a 500 page exploration by Susan Haskins titled; *Mary Magdalene: Myth & Metaphor*.

Originally planned as a thesis, Haskins searched for the how and why Mary Magdalene had become the Church's symbol of penance. In the Gnostic writings, she is described not only as the beloved of Jesus but also as the leader of his group of apostles. She was the thirteenth apostle. Traditionally, according to the orthodox Christian texts, we are told only of the twelve...all men.

For nearly two thousand years, the traditional concept of Mary Magdalene has been that of a prostitute who repented her sinful past and devoted her life and love to Jesus Christ. With the recent discovery of an ancient Coptic Gnostic library in Upper Egypt which had remained buried for almost 1,600 years, there has been a growing tendency to see Mary Magdalene as Jesus' most favored and important disciple. We also find a tantalizing mystery of her relationship to Christ himself.

The Gospel of Philip depicts Mary Magdalene as the close companion of Jesus. Further research reveals that Mary was the betrothed of Jesus. She was His intimate companion.

And did ye think He was not a whole man?

Except from the Gnostic texts, little is known of Mary Magdalene. She is presented as an independent woman and must have been of some wealth to have been able to follow and support Christ.

According to Susan Haskins, the Gnostic Mary Magdalene contrasts strongly with the figure that emerges from conventional interpretations of the New Testament. In the late sixth century Mary Magdalene was recreated as a prostitute to serve the purposes of the ecclesiastical hierarchy. This refashioning by the early Church Fathers has given us a distorted view of her. The degradation of women by the early church and its exclusion of them from the priesthood was based on women's supposed uncleanness during menstruation, as defined in a Temple ordinance Leviticus 15. This taboo was also invoked by the Christian Church and still used until recently as a powerful weapon against the entry of women into ecclesiastical office. It is important that a priest be clean and holy at all times to offer sacrifice, emphasized the church fathers.

The Gnostic Gospels, by Elaine Pagels, sheds more light concerning Mary Magdalene as she tells of a profound discovery near the town of Nag Hammadi in Upper Egypt of papyrus books, bound in leather and hidden in earthen jars. Apparently they had been placed there, at the foot of a massive boulder, almost two thousand years earlier to escape destruction by the orthodox Christian sector who came into power over other Christian doctrines of the time.

The Gospel of Mary depicts Mary Magdalene (never recognized as an apostle by the orthodox) as the one favored with visions and insight that far surpassed Peter's. The Gospel of Philip tells of rivalry between the male disciples and Mary Magdalene, here described as Jesus' most intimate companion, the symbol of divine Wisdom: "The companion of the Savior is Mary Magdalene. Christ loved her more than the other disciples and used to kiss her often on the mouth. The rest of the disciples were offended by it," continues the Gospels.

The Dialogue of the Savior not only includes Mary Magdalene as one of three disciples chosen to receive special teaching, but also praises her above Thomas and Matthew: "She spoke as a woman who knew the All."

Other secret texts suggest that Mary Magdalene and the activity of women in general challenged the leaders of the orthodox community, who regarded Peter as their spokesman. The Gospel of Mary relates that the disciples, disheartened and terrified after the crucifixion, asked Mary to encourage them by telling them what the Lord had told her secretly. She agreed and taught them until Peter furiously asked, "Did he really speak privately with a woman, and not openly to us? Did he prefer her to us?" Another disciple breaks in to mediate the dispute: "Peter, you have always been hot-tempered. If the Savior made her worthy, who are you to reject her? Surely the Lord knew her very well. That is why he loved her more than us."

Jesus replied that whoever the Spirit inspires is divinely ordained to speak, whether man or woman.

The orthodox Christians insist that women are subordinate to men. Paul directed the selection of bishops in terms that entirely exclude women from consideration. The bishop must be a man whose wife and children are "submissive to him in every way." This allows him to keep "God's church" in order, and its members properly subordinated, explains Elaine Pagels. Was it for this reason we have come to think of Mary Magdalene as a harlot so the orthodox church could continue to desecrate her image?

We see two very different patterns of sexual attitudes emerging in orthodox and Gnostic circles. Where Gnostics refer to the creation account of Genesis suggesting an equal or androgynous human creation, which takes the principle of equality between men and women into the social and political structure of their communities, the orthodox pattern is strikingly different. It describes God in exclusively masculine terms, and in Genesis tells how Eve was created from Adam and for his fulfillment, which translates into social practice. What woman isn't aware of male dominance? And so, by the late second century, the domination of men over women was accepted by the orthodox church as the divinely ordained order, not only for the church but for social and family life as well.

∞

Until the nineteenth century, Gnosticism and its adherents were known only from the reports written by their orthodox opponents. The Gnostics' claim to have a superior comprehension of God and of their own spiritual nature. Together with their belief that this came to them through personal revelation, it also set them apart from the other Christians who accepted their beliefs through the mediation of bishops and clergy. It is for this reason that the orthodox Church regarded them with utmost suspicion. By the second and third centuries, the Christian Church considered Gnosticism as its most dangerous enemy. After the victory of the orthodox Church in the fourth century, it destroyed and suppressed all Gnostic teachings.

Placed in an earthen jar almost sixteen hundred years ago and hidden under a boulder in Upper Egypt to escape destruction by the orthodox Christian Church, these ancient texts from a Coptic Gnostic library again come alive. The suppressed voice of the Gnostics themselves is heard once more.

∞

September 2, 1972. The phone rang. It was the familiar voice of my friend, Dorothy, with whom I had had no contact in more than a year. Together we had been involved as "sensitives" in an experimental study by a group of doctors attempting to understand the psychic dimensions of the mind. Somewhere along the way, Dorothy and I lost contact as she left for other parts of the country. In the course of our conversation, Dorothy excitedly told me of her new cosmic guide. Some of His characteristics sounded very much like those of Aureal. Soon into our conversation entered a third voice. Dorothy recognized this voice as her cosmic guide. I knew the voice as that of Aureal. Our guides, it appeared, were one and the same.

You are my channels. I must have two. The story I have to tell is too fantastic, one would not believe.

How right He was!

In two days hence, I will begin the communication to the both of you individually, yet simultaneously, of a lifetime, a most important life we lived together in a distant land and a time long past. Actually, I will touch your memory banks so that it will be your own remembering...somewhat different for each of you as it comes from your own experience lived in this other period of time.

"Wow!," Dorothy and I exclaimed simultaneously.

As profound as this phone experience had been, I put it out of my mind and forgot about the promised momentous event.

∞

I was literally standing on my head loading a big pottery kiln for my class (20 years I taught pottery for the Grossmont School District in San Diego, California) and in this position and activity I became focused on a simple scene, that implanted itself in my head.

I watched as a three year old girl, her hand lovingly enclosed within her father's, walked east through an enormous hallway, obviously an Egyptian temple. As though I were actually there, I could feel the desert air cooled by the sandstone structure. The smell of the desert was uniquely familiar to my senses, though I have never been to Egypt in this life. Was it ancient memory or was some transported part of myself capable of this sensing? I could not answer. Though I witnessed this scene from some area behind the pair, I knew I was the little girl...but the man escaped my recognition. "Who was he?" I wondered. It seemed important that I know. Several days passed before the answer came from Aureal's own words.

In another time and another land I was your earthly father.

Aureal, my father? In the beginning of my adventure with this being, I had asked, "Who are you?"

You know me as Aureal.

So this is the origin of the name, Aureal, the name of this earthly father I supposedly had in a lifetime long ago...if I am to believe this as truth.

Aureal had touched my memory banks. At times I could actually feel an electrical charge near my head as He carefully placed the tip of His wand on a precise spot bringing to life an eventful scene from some distant past. These moving, living scenes were in color just as they had been thousands of years before. Eternal memory is never lost. It remains forever, indelibly imprinted in perfect form in the Akashic records or memory bank of each individual.

Everything, every event, every thought remains for all eternity in preservation just as it was at the moment of its origin, preserved in perfect form by cosmic means. I can only describe its likeness to our current technology, which allows the preservation of important documents on microfilm. Or perhaps it is a molecule in our greater cosmic mind. I can't answer, yet I know it exists.

The earliest information within my reincarnational memory extends to just before my descent into mortal Egyptian flesh, that is before I was born in this enormous Egyptian temple. On some dimension other than earth, we who were to be part of this Egyptian lifetime, were first schooled in preparation for our role within the walls of this temple living. I was the last of Aureal's twelve children. Each child was born in relation to its readiness for the structure and responsibilities required for further esoteric learning within the temple.

Dorothy, my friend and co-channel, was Aureal's oldest and most dependable child. I was his youngest who barely made it. In explanation of the apparent ages of his children, Aureal drew eleven consecutive and progressively shorter lines. Each line represented one of his children and its respective age. At the end of a leash held firmly by the eleventh child, was the twelfth, symbolized as a bouncing rubber ball. This youngest child, desiring to explore beyond the boundaries of the structured Temple life, found herself in perpetual trouble and I, in this current lifetime, inherited her karma.

In Egypt, until the age of three, I remember nothing, but neither can I recall any event of my current life before that age. My Egyptian mother, a priestess, had died. Now the first distinct memory comes to life as Aureal touches my memory bank to begin that opening scene. My father was taking me along this great walkway to my older sister who, at eighteen, would become my surrogate mother... much to her distress. And so the parts of a memory containing many pieces of varying importance and clarity gradually appear like pieces to a jigsaw puzzle. It reveals a life very different in its belief system and daily activities from that of my current living. And to my amazement, some of those same members of my ancient Egyptian family surround me today.

As I thought of my Egyptian mother, wondering who she was and what she was like, Aureal said,

Remember the woman who visited you when you were very young?

In this lifetime I lived on a 150 acre farm with absolutely no other child within miles. I was never lonely as I spent much of my time before the age of five playing in the sand. I collected small sea shells, remnants of an ancient sea, which is now fertile farming land in the Imperial Valley, California. Sometimes as I played there in the sand, a beautiful tall slender woman would stand before me. Her long dark brown hair fell in soft waves over her shoulders. She was always dressed in a long light pink gown that draped gracefully over her slender body. It was her sandals, however, that held my attention. Perhaps because they were more within my line of vision as I sat there in the ancient sea bed. How many times she came this way, I don't know. She never spoke. She merely stood there for a few moments looking down at me with a loving smile. Then she left as she had come, vanishing into space. As I grew older the memory of those visits faded from my mind...until Aureal reminded that she was my Egyptian mother, the priestess who had died when I was three years old.

∞

It is not unusual for children under the age of seven to talk with imaginary playmates. How much of this communication is purely make-believe and how much may be a genuine contact with another realm is undergoing serious study in India, where rebirth is an accepted belief. In the Western world, reincarnation has not been part of our belief system until recently.

Despite the fact that three of the major religions, Christianity, Judaism and to a lesser extent, Islam, deny reincarnation, it is probably the most ancient belief of all. We explore the history of reincarnation in following chapters. If the soul is immortal, which is one of the major concepts in most reincarnation theories, there should be a continuous expression of the personality in different bodies throughout its many lifetimes.

∞

I awakened suddenly from a profound sleep. Clearly audible voices came from a corner of my room. Displacing my familiar surroundings, a dramatic real life enactment was unfolding. A young girl, probably five years old, was dancing in circles defiantly chanting, "I am what I am." Over and over again like a broken record, she continued to prance in a circle and sing, "I am what I am." When I could no longer tolerate this meaningless and bewildering intrusion, a young woman in obvious exasperation said,

"Father, why have you allowed her to be a part of our temple family?"

Patience, my child. You will see, she has her purpose here.

It was Aureal speaking. I knew beyond a doubt that the annoying child was myself in the temple life, but who was the young woman that obviously would have preferred to be rid of me?

I was unable to gain more than a vague impression, but I knew her identity lie somewhere in the depths of my consciousness. Who was she? I had to know. It is strange how elusive information can surface when you least expect it. Days later, while in the shower, giving no thought to a past life, only enjoying the one I now lived, that voice from ancient Egypt echoed in my head. This time I recognized it, over the 3,300 years of time long past. How could I forget? I knew that voice. Of course, I was the responsibility of my oldest sister whose current identity I know as Dorothy. It was Dorothy...it was Dorothy's voice I heard lamenting, "Oh, Father, why have you allowed her to be part of our temple family?"

I was given into Dorothy's care and she found me a difficult, unpleasant child. Intent on bringing to life who and what I was in this past life, Aureal used a variety of methods. For lack of a more profound explanation, this display of the spoiled brat that I was allowed to hear in the solitude of my 20th century bedroom, seemed to be holographically projecting the replay of my oldest sister's pain and exasperation throughout the entire ordeal.

∞

To enter the memory of another lifetime can be like opening Pandora's box. Sometime in the late 1950's, after Aureal entered my comfortable existence, I noticed a strange feeling engulfing me, like a warm energy entering my body accompanied by a detachment from self-awareness. This is very difficult to define. I felt as though I were taking on another personality. On several occasions along the way, this transformation was noticed by others who knew me well.

One summer day, my dearest high school friend was visiting. As we sat pool side chatting about old times, I felt this movement of energy drifting over me, much as a cloud moves over the land obscuring the sun. For a moment my friend stared at me in disbelief, then rapidly moved away as though frightened by what she saw.

"Who are you?" she demanded of me. Because of this strange sensation and the feeling I was becoming someone else, I questioned her, seeking answers to the changes in my physical appearance. "Your face, the structure of your face has changed," she exclaimed in bewilderment. "Your eyes are intensely dark and your complexion has become a dark olive. Go look in the mirror."

I did and what I saw in the mirror was not me, Laura. It would be another 20 years before this girl from ancient Egypt actually manifested. Only then would I understand the subtle, momentary change in my own nature and appearance as she began to invade my life.

This scenario repeated itself intermittently during the next several years. It was noticed by my students, who literally jumped out of my way in apparent fright over the sudden change in personality and appearance. I have her captured on film, photographs taken by a photographer whom this Egyptian girl saw fit to tantalize. This transition would last a few hours at best and never consumed me completely.

Frankly, I liked what I saw and desperately wished to look more like her. I became terribly unhappy with my Irish auburn hair and light complexion. My current self seemed no longer the me that I felt from some depth within my being.

One day as I sat in the passenger side of the car waiting for my family, I noticed that my right foot did not belong to me. It was little and brown with a delicately turned ankle. Moving it into the sun light, thinking my vision was playing tricks on me, I found the small brown foot...attached to the leg that also was not mine. By now I found the phenomena more intriguing than disturbing, though I just couldn't understand it. Insatiably I searched through medical and zoological literature thinking that the chameleon in its ability to change color might supply a hint. I avidly read the "Three Faces of Eve" and other similar stories searching for an answer, but to no avail.

In the mid-1980s while walking through a room in my studio and concerned only with the activity of the current moment, I totally became in consciousness this girl from Egypt. By this time however, I was aware of that ancient lifetime and comfortable with the Egyptian identity. For those few frozen moments in time I had absolutely no "Laura" consciousness. Somehow I retained the memory of her ancient Egyptian nature: I know what she looks like. I am aware of her personality as it came alive within my own nature like two individuals living within the same body. Aureal, by touching my memory banks, made me aware of her ancient life and for that moment I was her. I pondered this experience. I relived it in memory and tried to understand its nature and significance. Two weeks later as I walked through the same room and the same spot in my studio, the event was repeated as though I walked through some time-warp back to Egypt. This time Aureal gave the answer I had so desperately sought.

Every life you live, you play a slightly different role. Though the personality remains basically the same, its pattern becomes slightly different due to its relation to its environment. Since each individual is of a unique vibrational energy pattern, this is the identifiable unit of that individual. Yes, I was awakening you to yourself from ancient Egypt. It was the energy pattern of the Egyptian girl becoming more dominant that you felt as the change in your current nature took place. To the degree that individual you were in another lifetime can vibrate more dominantly over your own existing pattern, you feel the change within yourself. Finally you were engulfed completely in your Egyptian frequency pattern so that your current pattern was made dormant for those few moments. Only by becoming completely who you were in this other life time, can you know beyond a doubt who you are. Remember, you are an energy pattern unique to your own nature. When you leave this plane of living, the pattern you are survives intact. It is your permanent identity for that lifetime.

∞

I awakened this particular morning hearing the word, "Hamenotep, Hamenotep." Throughout the day, the word, "Hamenotep" persistently repeated itself in my ear. Having no understanding of the word and failing to comprehend the message it bore, I called Dorothy. "That is interesting," she replied, "I have been hearing: "Aureal with Akhenaten." It must be a message concerning Egypt. Will you meet me at the library within the hour?"

In the index of a Time/Life book on Egypt, we were amazed to find our answer. It was not Hamenotep, but Amenhotep that I was hearing. We learned that Amenhotep 1V was Akhenaten, the heretic pharaoh who departed from the ways of his ancestors. He abandoned the worship of Egypt's large and complicated pantheon in favor of devotion to a lone Creator, Re the Sun God, manifested by the Aten, a disk that emanated the life-giving rays of the sun. It was in the fifth year of his reign that Amenhotep IV announced he would henceforth be known as Akhenaten. The precise meaning of the name is a matter of dispute but it clearly expresses the king's dedication to his new deity. Delighted with our accomplishment and placing more confidence in our unseen but most vocal informant, Dorothy and I could now date the time of our life in Egypt to coincide with this 18th-Dynasty pharaoh, approximately 1,300 BC or roughly 3,300 years ago.

Aureal gave us another piece of information to that lifetime in ancient Egypt:

It was thirty three hundred years ago on the banks of the Nile, in a temple now buried in ruins under the hot Egyptian sands that we lived.

But where was it located?

It is difficult to know how much of what Dorothy and I "remembered" through Aureal's bits and pieces of information and how much we were able to piece together from our search through archives of ancient Egyptian history. It soon became clear that this temple, whose identity we sought, was near the banks of the Nile at the great religious complex of Karnak at Luxor, Egypt. It was part of the long-vanished city of Thebes. We knew we lived in a large religious temple complex. It was the only one of its kind. It represented a unique experience in communal living and learning. Within its walls, a large group of people lived for the purpose of studying the esoteric arts.

Even before Dorothy and I knew of the heretical pharaoh and his devotion to a singular Creator, the Sun God Re, we recalled systematically certain rituals within the temple. One of these rituals I remember as clearly as if I were passionately living it today. Early each morning, we of the temple life met in a very large rectangular room. I refer to it as the recreational room. Situated at the east end of the temple, the room, open to the desert breeze, provided a magnificent view of the morning sun as it first began to lift over the horizon. We were required to assemble in our respective places, seated on the cool sandstone floor, when the sun disk offered its first ray of light on the horizon in front of us. We remained there silently in a meditative type of yoga until the sun's disk sat comfortably on the horizon. It took approximately fifteen minutes for the sun to make this journey, Aureal informed us. It seems possible that we were ritualizing the Sun God Re, another affirmation of this strange period in ancient history. With Aureal's guiding help, our research boosted our growing confidence that there was indeed accuracy in the things we had been able to remember about this unusual period.

In this vast rectangular room extending to the South, I could hear the sounds of animals and people as they went about their daily tasks servicing this temple complex. It was here, after our morning sun ritual, we had breakfast. Large containers of fruit juices were placed on the floor around us. There were large pillows scattered on the floor for our reclining comfort. Here we gathered again in the evening, listening to the wisdom of the high priests and consuming more of the liquids in the large containers. This was the final "meal" of the day...juice again.

Aureal reminded us that the one formal meal of the day was what we call lunch. He explained:

We were fruitarians. We certainly did not eat meat.

"None at all?" I asked, as over the thousands of years I had forgotten our noon time menu.

Once in a while we celebrated with fish.

Aureal was consistent in His "awakening" procedure. If He were explaining our eating habits, He did not mix this memory with other information except as it was intrinsically related.

We were a small breed of people. When I realized that at age eighteen in that lifetime, I was probably no taller than five foot and weighed 100 pounds at best, I thought myself malnourished. After all, as fruitarians, we could not have accumulated much weight. As channels, Dorothy and I really needed each other to confirm what our independent "memories" supplied. "Yes," she said, "We were a small people." But all else, the Temple structure, the reclining floor pillows, the flasks that held our juice were all so very large, as I remember them, as though made for giants.

∞

The awakening to this Egyptian life was like looking at a picture of some familiar scene containing within it nostalgic memories of your past within this life time. I never knew when Aureal might touch another time frame. When it happened, I was usually busily pursuing some daily task. For those moments, I entered this ancient life as though it were the present. The depth of emotion entwined within the surfacing memories seemed as real as it must have been when I first experienced it, those thousands of years before. Unlike the grayed tone memories I have of my current life, these ancient memories are in living color just as they were 3,300 years ago.

Like a familiar photograph that brings memories bubbling to the surface of your mind, memories of this ancient lifetime also rise up around the picture, frozen in time that initiated them, making the memory progressively more complete and real. That life, its ideologies and concepts of living, hover very near the surface of my current life. It is so much a part of me that I feel I live in a multidimensional world.

After our devotion to the morning sun, we went to our respective areas of learning. I was a student of the healing arts in what Aureal called the Healing Solarium. This was a circular dome structure of translucent crystalline material. The sun's life giving rays penetrated the crystal reflecting a soothing foliage green radiance which was, in itself, healing. Here, I was introduced to healing devices and methods that were then in advance of our current technologies.

After the noon meal, we were given two hours for rest and recreation. At this time Aureal explained our sexual life and relationships in this ancient temple. Since the expression of love and sex of that period was vastly different from our current moral values, I thought I had become sexually perverted. I was thankful that my co-channel and I were in this together.

Sex is an important part of your life's balance.

Aureal adamantly declared, when confronted with our protests of modesty. And, so we remembered that sex was indulged in openly as a function of our daily life and for our emotional and chakra (glandular) balance. It took place specifically during two hours in the afternoon, not at night. The bedrooms ran along the outer wall of the Temple, next to the Nile River. Though the bedrooms were large, they were never shared. Each of us had our own room. Bedrooms were called the "place where body and soul replenishes." It was important that in sleep we did not mix our energy pattern with another.

Aureal reminded me:

Sleep could not be restful if one shared his bed with another.

I hear water spilling from a wall across from my bedroom. A large, open to the sky hallway separated the bedrooms from another very large room. The banquet room was cool and dark. At the far south side where light filtered through openings just below the ceiling, there was a long heavy rectangular table made of rich brown beautifully carved wood. Used for receptions and special occasions, this table ran almost the length of the room. When more light was needed during daytime festivities, large double doors opened onto the "recreation room" facing the morning sun. Otherwise this area remained cool, dark and uninhabited.

On the north side of this banquet room, close to the east wall and partly open to the sky, was the shower room. There was no partition between the shower and the banquet. Strange? Not really, because their uses did not overlap. A half circle of stone about one foot high and 12 feet in diameter encased what water might run onto the stone floor. Water was lifted from the Nile over the temple roof through clay or stone ducts to spill continuously over the massive wall. Protruding rocks artfully embedded in the wall, deflected the steady flow of water into this half circle enclosure which served as our shower. During banquets and other special occasions the melodic sound of the cascading water provided a pleasurable background for the activity. Whether it was used for a refreshing shower or an aesthetic experience, the cooling nature of splashing water in a temple on the warm Nile desert was designed to bring joy to the soul and to the heart as well as cleanliness to the body.

We moved freely in the nude along the walkway from our bedrooms to the shower area. In other areas of the temple nudity was strictly forbidden. However, since there seemed to be no modesty practiced in the bedrooms, walkway and shower room, and yet nudity was forbidden in other areas of the temple, I asked Aureal for an explanation.

It wasn't proper.

Though I thought this was not a rational answer and unbecoming of Aureal's usual enlightening nature, His tone of voice indicated a closed subject. He simply did not care to elaborate.

∞

One early morning while I was on my knees gardening in this lifetime, Aureal told me of his Egyptian children. They were all by different mothers, He explained. "You didn't marry them?" I asked, looking at him in shock.

We loved each other.

His answer had such profound feeling that it was difficult not to believe this might be the better way of life.

As I inquired about the ritual of marriage in the Temple, He looked questioningly at me for some time without speaking. Then he responded, almost absentmindedly:

Oh...You do make commitments of marriage on your plane.

Then He replied,

Marriage is an entrapment of the individual by the church and the state and not a sacrament of God.

Aureal informed me that the union with his sister resulted in his first born, Dorothy.

When I told Dorothy of this astonishing revelation, She cried "Incest!"

Later In our research of ancient Egypt, we discovered that in order to keep their blood line pure, unions between brother and sister and even father and daughter were normal procedures among the royal Egyptian families.

∞

Aureal trained me to see Him whenever I desired. Once I learned the procedure, it became as natural for me as looking at someone within my current realm of vision. After some preliminary training in opening my third eye, Aureal, very specific in his training, said to me,

Look up into the Light where I am, my child.

With eyes closed, I looked up, focusing on that point between the eye brows.

That is too low. Look up into the Light where I am.

As I lifted my focus higher I saw Aureal in this realm of beautiful white light. Thus began my ability to enter his plane for our conversations and to channel for others who asked questions that require this cosmic tuning. (I have been told that although I close my eyes for this inter-world communication, the whites of my eyes are turned up. It is my thought that anyone turning closed eyes upward toward this point between the eyebrows or higher will automatically go into the alpha brainwave. Try it!)

I came to understand and to remember that our partner in sex was whomever we loved at the moment. Since we were a big family, that partner might be our brother. I remember chasing my brother down this walkway to his room. I was stark naked. As he landed on his bed, I pounced on top of him intent on sex whether he liked it or not. That wasn't very romantic and apparently I failed to get the message that sex was our balance in life and not an aggressive attack.

I remembered much about this brother who was eighteen months older than I. He had been the child who held on to that "little rubber ball," me, to keep that wayward sister in line. He was the one to whom I turned with all the problems that overtook me in my attempt to comply with the Temple life structure. He was the one I looked to for advice and protection.

∞

I knew I had a Nubian lover. I was surprised this union between Egyptians and Nubians was allowed. When I questioned this, Aureal informed me that high born Nubians were of our family also, so there was nothing culturally taboo in this relationship.

I don't remember much about my relationship with the Nubian...until, one night while having sex with my husband in this lifetime, I was "transported" to Egypt. I looked up into the face of, not my husband, but my Nubian lover. This was to repeat itself later, as that activity in Ancient Egypt replaced my current bedroom scene. Now I understand, that I married in this lifetime my Nubian lover of 3,300 years ago. Upon informing my husband of this remarkable discovery, he now calls himself my "Nubian Stud."

∞

I remember watching the peasantry walking past the cool walls of the temple on their way to work and wistfully wishing I could join them. I wanted to know of the adventures that lie beyond these secluded temple walls.

You were always chasing rainbows, butterflies and all such things, you wanted to be one of the peasantry. You lacked the nature necessary for the purpose you came to fulfill in the temple. But as time was drawing short, it was important to bring you (by birth) into the family, perhaps a bit too prematurely.

I was Aureal's favorite child. He made this very clear as He watched me grow into the light of His own mischievous nature. Yes in my precarious way, I was the most like Himself, though in His position He had learned the discipline necessary to control that nature. When I was created, He sadly lamented, He left something out. I wondered in what way I was incomplete. In time, Aureal explained that He had spoiled me; I was undisciplined. I had not learned to control that wispy nature.

"I should not have been punished for something you did," I scolded. His answer came much later, as I was preparing my three year old daughter for her evening bath (in this lifetime). With her long blond hair in pigtails and her little body naked, she cocked her head first to one side then the other admiring her reflection in the wall mirror. I was lost in loving affection for my provocative little daughter, when Aureal, watching also, exclaimed

I gave you a child exactly like you. It would be easy to spoil her, wouldn't it?

As I grew older in the temple life, it became apparent, much to father's regret, that I was too wayward and to undisciplined for the highly structured Temple life. When I was eighteen, Aureal took me along the walkway to the west end of the temple, from which He brought me when I was three. He was greatly saddened by what He, as my father, the one who brought me into this life, the one who loved me dearly must do. I had broken yet another taboo of this culture. I was creating too much karma as Aureal said:

You caused one to take his life. A karmic situation.

This was a most serious offense according to the Egyptian rules of that period and for this I would be put to sleep...the death penalty.

It was my Nubian lover. I had played with his emotions, leading him to believe I loved him, when in reality he was just another of my tantalizing delights. Realizing the truth in our relationship, he preferred to end his heartache in death. Yes, he came back in this lifetime as my husband.

To love and never hurt him is your karma.

Married in 1944, we have had more than 50 wonderful, yet sometimes turbulent years, as I have tried to abide by the dictates of my karma.

∞

One of my most persistent memories of this time in Egypt was that of walking west with Aureal toward the setting sun. I watched the sun dip below the horizon. Facing me, Aureal rotated the palm of His open right hand in front of my heart chakra. This ancient procedure widely opened that area of my chakra so that during sleep that night, my immortal being was released, never to return to that earthy form again. I then passed back into the dimension from which I had come at birth into the Temple life.

Notice, I did not say in which direction He revolved His hand to bring about my demise. One direction will close the chakra making it impossible to breathe. The other direction, opens the chakra widely, allowing the immortal being to leave the body. Though I probably could not perform this procedure on another, Aureal, taking no chance, has not allowed me the memory.

Two concepts are apparent here. The one responsible for bringing the individual into life must be the one taking back the life, if that child cannot abide by the rules of the culture. And the process by which the execution is performed is painless. Since this simple rotation of the open palm a few inches from the thymus or heart chakra was a most unusual procedure, I sought conformation. I found it in a most unlikely place. During a recent dinner, party my hostess introduced me to an Indian Guru. In the course of our conversation, I inadvertently mentioned my death scene in ancient Egypt. Casually she replied that, "Yes, that was the usual procedure also in early India."

To understand the reality of this type of release from the mortal body, I am including an experience from my early training with Aureal to validate the nature of this ancient form of painless execution.

In the 1950's, soon after Aureal entered my life, my husband, our two young boys and myself were camping in Kings Canyon, California. It was nearing sunset in the valley floor. As I looked up in delight and wonderment at the shadows of approaching night settling on the green escarpment of those immense mountains, I sensed a movement of something leaving my heart chakra. Before I could comprehend this singular event, I instinctively reached up, grasping this unseeable something and gently placed it back into my chest area from which it had tried to escape. Was it my immortal self, my soul taking temporary flight from my body? These strange experiences allow me a glimmer of insight into an otherwise esoteric subject.

And so ends my memory of that lifetime in ancient Egypt. That is, until, in the 1920s, I entered this current life time in which the girl from ancient Egypt followed me with her karma. Like a shadow, she sometimes dominates my current being.

6

Echoes of the Past

In another time and in other lands you will come awakening as your programming decrees.

August 1942. I had just turned 18 the month before. My father, a former State Senator, had been appointed Federal Attorney by U.S. President Franklin Roosevelt, which brought my family from Los Angeles to San Diego, California. In September I would begin studies at the small San Diego State College which is now the very big and overcrowded San Diego State University.

Since it was a warm Sunday afternoon and I was restless to find the Methodist Young Peoples Group near my new home, I walked to what was known as Church Row. As I neared the Baptist church, there were young people congregated on the sidewalk and spilling into the street, waiting for the evening service to begin. To avoid these energetic young people, I walked into the street to continue my destination in the next block. Suddenly, a hand reached out and grabbed me as a voice attached to the hand said, "Where do you think you are going, young lady?" It was the young choir director who saw fit to kidnap me for the Baptist service. After the service, I disappeared into the night for my short walk home thinking nothing more of the incident.

Weeks later, determined to spend the evening with the young people at the Methodist Church, I repeated my walk to Church Row. Again the hand grabbed me as I attempted to pass the Baptist crowd. This time the young choir director placed me securely in the choir where I could not easily escape.

Somewhat annoyed by his persistent intrusion into my plans, I had not closely observed him. No love at first sight! It was his finger wrapped in a white bandage that held my attention as he directed the choir. His wound, I learned later, had occurred while he was fixing the spokes of his bicycle.

After the service he asked my name and where I lived. Satisfied that I lived within his range of transportation, he offered to "buzz" me home on his bicycle. That was one of the roughest three blocks home, riding side saddle between his panting breath and the unsteady movement of his handlebars. It would have been easier to walk.

As destiny would have it, however, this was to be the first of our unpredictable dating. He was always looking for another pretty girl to "buzz" home and I really wasn't enamored then with the young "buzzing" bicyclist, choir director. Since I would soon start college, my thoughts turned to other things. These were the second world war years and within months my bicycling boy friend would enlist in the Navy, leaving me his bicycle.

On September 12, 1942. Violin in hand, I was waiting for the bus that would take me to my second day of class at S.D. state college when two freshmen on their way to SDSC asked if I would like a ride. Looking apprehensively at the very small, front seat only, car with the two handsome young men inside, I decided to try it. The proverbial "can of sardines" had nothing on us. I really believe that Laura and violin were a bit too much, but we arrived safely for our academic education and thus the beginning of a fun threesome. Wherever the boys went they invited me. We climbed mountains whose sides had to be straight up when an easy road to the top was near. We precariously crossed through back country streams, jumping boulders on the way. We ran through meadows chasing deer who must have wondered what strange creatures had invaded their quiet home. We climbed under thorny thickets looking for "Utopia." My adventurous companions insisted it had to be some where near.

I was serenaded with their guitar playing, whether I liked it or not. As their eager companion, I kept pace with their constant search for nature's wild adventure and of course, Utopia. Then came the time one of them, Bob, realizing I was a girl, professed his profound love for me. Since I was accustomed to being "one of the boys," this was disturbing. I really felt as though he were my brother. The thought of a romantic relationship had not dawned upon the horizon of my mind or heart. I did love him, however it was the love of a sister for her brother.

The three of us were a month apart in age, I was the oldest by a few days. We were all eighteen, silly and fun loving, though Bob persistently insisted that I should marry him. One Sunday after church, still dressed in my Sunday's best, he carried me to the middle of a shallow stream chanting "marry me." Upon my refusing his proposal, he deposited me in the water.

In the meantime, my on again-off-again romance with Larry, the choir director continued. Soon most of the eligible young men had either enlisted or had been conscripted into the military. To fight for our country was the patriotic thing to do. Bob became a Marine and that was the last I would hear from him until ...

Larry, the choir director, tired of "buzzing" other girls around on his bicycle, left me his bicycle and an engagement ring as he joined the Navy.

∞

June 1954. For ten years I have been happily married to Larry when Aureal entered my very busy life...and a story so unbelievable began to unfold.

Though I can't remember the date, the incident will forever remain in my memory. It was early morning, still too early for my day to begin when I embarked on a most extraordinary odyssey. Into my right ear, tickling my neck with his breath, a voice passionately declared, "Remember September 12th?"

Startled, yet not fully awake, I was on my feet in an upright position before I could comprehend what had transpired. The voice, undeniably Bob's, was reaching me, somehow disembodied, from somewhere in time and space. But what was the meaning of the message, "Remember September 12th"? Pondering this strange phenomenon I called Ray (the third member of our 1942 Utopia-seeking trio) who, in the meantime, had married my sorority sister. Ray was no help. He could offer absolutely no insight into this bizarre message.

Later my family and I visited the Griffith Park Observatory in Los Angeles. It was mid week and only a few people were in the observatory auditorium waiting for the display to begin. Subtly, I felt Bob's presence behind me; then more intensely I felt it until it seemed as though he were immediately behind me. Aureal had said,

You never forget the frequency essence of an individual. It is by this energy pattern you recognize a person.

I looked behind, feeling Bob had to be there. Throughout the hour I would look again and again seeking my old friend whose energy nearness I could strongly sense.

As Ray and his family were visiting us that weekend, I told him of this strange experience concerning Bob "That's interesting," Ray said. "We visited the observatory with Bob and his family three days before you were there."

Progressively more subliminal experiences concerning Bob were to follow. In checking with Bob later, it became apparent he was not creating these sensational experiences. It was Aureal. But why?

I don't remember when I first began to realize that my friend, Bob, in this lifetime, had been my brother in Egypt 3,300 years before. It was as though I always knew it. He was the Egyptian brother, 18 months older, who tried to keep the "little bouncing ball," me, within the strict disciplines of that ancient lifetime in which Aureal, the high priest, was our earthly father. It was Bob to whom I sought protection when I had committed breaches of the Ancient Egyptian codes of behavior. It was Bob, yes, Bob who had really been my brother in this other life time.

∞

It was a warm spring day in 1972. I was clipping invasive vines from my studio when Aureal begin to communicate. As usual, His dictation came rapidly with no concern for my lack of writing material or my precarious position half way up the ladder. It was a letter I must send to Bob, whom I had not seen since 1943. I picked up a child's tablet, brown with age, to record Aureal's words.

The letter began:

Thirty three hundred years ago in an Egyptian Temple, now under the sand, we lived....

I don't recall the rest of that letter, though Bob still has it. Since the letter was scribbled on this unsightly piece of paper, I was planning to copy it more neatly on stationery. It was enough that I was sending him such a strange message. After all, almost thirty years had passed since our parting. What would he think?

At that moment Aureal interrupted my thought.

Send it now. If you do not send it now, you will not send it.

Aureal was right. In my right mind I would not have sent such a letter. Upon getting Bob's address from Ray's wife, and with misgivings, I dropped this strange message in the mail not realizing that I was embarking on another most extraordinary adventure. With the letter posted, I would just have to wait for Bob's reply, if there was one. Aureal interrupted my thought:

It will be two weeks before you hear from him, as he is no longer at the place where your letter will first go.

Exactly two weeks later Bob's reply came. It was a wonderful message of delight, surprise and an update on what had transpired since we were eighteen.

∞

I was just beginning to feel comfortable with the idea of reincarnation. Still, it seemed strange that my current associations had followed me into this life from other lifetimes, and that the seemingly accidental manner in which we first met was preprogrammed.

You are drawn together again by the process of magnetism which is a universal, eternal cosmic law existing in the nature of things. It could have been no other way.

Since I had so many subtle awakenings to Bob's role in my life, yet none concerning my choir director husband, I truly believed Larry had never been a part of my past.

You caused one to take his life, a karmic situation.

For this I paid with my life, according to the ancient Egyptian culture, when I was eighteen. But, I protested to Aureal when He told me of the serious nature of my act 3,300 years ago that led to my execution: "If someone takes his life, that's his problem, not mine." Aureal explained:

In the Egyptian culture of that day, it was just as much a crime to cause one to take his own life as it would be to actually murder someone.

So my husband in this life, the young choir director who kidnapped me into his church when I was trying to reach another, had been my Nubian lover in ancient Egypt. That girl whose Karma I am now serving, loved to tease and to tantalize mercilessly. She plied her feminine sexual nature on her Nubian lover taunting and leading him to believe she loved him. This sensitive young Nubian, realizing too late that he was nothing more than a toy to her sexual whims, chose to take his life rather than endure the despair he felt.

Into this life you come to love and never again hurt him, for this is your karma.

Later, fragments would surface of other lives lived with my karmic husband. In the 1800's American West, he was my woodsman father carrying me, a small girl of seven, across a stream too deep for me to navigate on my own. I still feel the warm, secure love I had for this protective father.

In the early years of our marriage in this life, I felt almost infantile at times as he, even to this day, insists on taking protective care of me, much to my protests of independence. Attitudes and feelings are carried from one lifetime to another without our being aware of their origin.

Through your karmic ties to the Nubian of Egypt, whose desires to love and protect you, you rejected, you chose in another life to be the daughter of that Nubian entity, this time an American woodsman. You felt no emotional bond with the Nubian and would not have chosen to return to him. But as your loving father, you were drawn to him by your own need for his protective care. In this, your current life, you were again drawn to him (as your husband) by your need for the protective love he so desired to give you in Egypt. Do you see the picture?

Next to reincarnation, karma is the most important concept. As a man soweth, so shall he also reap, is the main tenet of karma which is an eternal, changeless, invariable, universal law of nature that can never be broken. It removes human thought and desire from the region of arbitrary happenings to the realm of law, and thus places man's future under his own control in proportion to the amount of his knowledge.

∞

Dorothy, my close friend, Egyptian sister and co-channel married a young man whom I remember as her son in the Egyptian temple. As another one of us remembering the Egyptian lifetime, he offered a wealth of independent confirmation concerning the esoteric life we lived in one of the Mystery Schools of Ancient Egypt. He also augmented our own memories so that the ancient lifetime is even more complete to us than is my current memory of this lifetime.

∞

"One of the best-kept secrets of the ancient world came to light in 1926 at the great religious complex of Karnak at Luxor, part of the long-vanished city of Thebes" begins a chapter in the Time-Life series titled *The Pharaoh Whom History Could Not Forget*.

This temple, built by the pharaoh Amenhotep IV during the early years of his reign (1353-1335 BC), had been dismantled piece by piece, and concealed within the walls and foundations of later structures. As part of a campaign to eliminate every trace of the hated king and to reject all that he stood for, the eradication of the temple was an attempt to deny his very existence. Many of the stones showed unmistakable marks of wrath toward the royal family. Amenhotep IV had abandoned the worship of Egypt's large pantheon in favor of devotion to a lone creator, Re, the Sun God manifested by the life giving rays of the sun.

The evidence of this bizarre historical erasure surfaced during a 25-year-long restoration program headed by the French-sponsored Egyptian Antiquities Service. In 1965, a retired American diplomat, Ray Winfield Smith proposed using photography to make a detailed study of the 100,000 plus stone pieces of the unearthed temple. Of these, about 35,000 bear surface decoration: a hand plucking a musical instrument, a queen with arms upraised in some act of adoration, sculpted faces and part of a chariot. All of these provide a tantalizing view of a vanished age.

Smith suggested that this seemingly unsolvable jigsaw puzzle of the incomplete and scattered stones could be solved by enlisting the aid of computers in reassembling them on film. With blessings from the Egyptian authorities and funds and technical support from institutions around the world, Smith launched the Akhenaten Temple Project. The painstaking and arduous process of reconstruction of that long vanquished temple began. The ultimate goal of the project was to find the proper position of every surviving piece of the puzzle and thus reconstruct a model of Akhenaten's original edifice in all of its magnificence. Thousands of matches have been made to date. and the detective work continues, aided by specialists from many different disciplines and countries.

Recently I was delighted to see a TV documentation of the Akhenaten project. I was amazed that the actual stone by stone restoration of this enormous temple was now in progress. Only a small percentage of the temple has been restored to date. Perhaps it will take another 300 years to complete.

"It was the largest temple complex ever built," said the commentator of this documentary. Could this be our temple? I wondered. In 1972 Aureal made this same descriptive statement concerning the temple: He said it was the largest temple complex in which great numbers of people lived for the singular purpose of learning the esoteric arts in preparation for what they would do in another time and another land. It was definitely a singular period in ancient history and the temple I seek "lay under the hot Egyptian sand." I believe this is the same temple that now, in our time, is being resurrected on film by computer imaging and physically restored with the ancient stone.

Despite steps taken by his enemies in ancient times to obliterate this heretic pharaoh's efforts to celebrate monotheistic rites, Akhenaten has been rescued from oblivion. More than 3,000 years after he shook Egypt to the core with his declarations, he still stirs powerful controversial emotions in the hearts of archaeologists and historians alike. Was he a madman or a visionary? In the view of some scholars, his hymns and invocations reveal Akhenaten as a pioneer of monotheism, a precursor of Abraham and Moses. In a recent visit to the Rosecrusians Museum in San Jose, California, I was intrigued to find a large statue of Akhenaten commemorating his achievements as the "Father" of our modern day religions honoring a single god with their worship.

Memory of that ancient life clearly indicated that we of the temple worshipped the morning sun, which symbolized the single deity or god. Dorothy and I knew we lived in the time of this pharaoh who departed from the ways of his ancestors and rocked the religious establishment by banning the worship of the entire Egyptian pantheon. No pharaoh has been more controversial and few are as intimately known to us today as Akhenaten IV.

Why had Aureal elaborately, meticulously, and so carefully awakened Dorothy and me to this particular lifetime? Why had He so subtly, yet strangely, superimposed my Egyptian self over my existing reality? Surely He was not playing games with our minds, though I did give this some serious thought! It was His intent that His channels remember this time and remember it well. It was not only a most important and unusual period in ancient history but relates directly to our current time.

Thirty-three hundred years ago reincarnation was acknowledged as fact and that was the prime reason for our

Temple living. In esoteric sanctuaries all over the world, this same kind of schooling took place during this specific period in history. Priests, priestesses and their families were brought together for one important purpose. It was a time unlike any other. The temple was a school. It was, in today's terms, a mystery school in which these souls were trained for what they were to do in another time, another age, and other lands. As the new millennium draws near, we from the esoteric schools all over the world and from this temple in ancient Egypt are reincarnating. If you question your purpose in this life, just look around you at the progressively greater numbers of "new age children" who are trained stewards for the coming earth changes.

That time is now, Aureal informs.

Your earth is nearing a new cycle of her evolution. In ancient temple times you knew and honored this knowing. So now, you, my children, are again brought together. It is time you awaken to your reason for being within this life and know that I will direct further when time draws near.

It was in 1972 that Aureal offered this explanation:

Into this lifetime you, the "children of light," return as your programming decrees. Reawakening to help Earth through her most turbulent moment, her birthing into the new golden age for man and earth.

∞

Within each life, there is an overriding or dominant past life to which the current life is most in tune or in harmonic resonance. From this life also comes one major karma for the individual to consider and work out with others from his or her past. In any existing life, there is one past life that is most dominate. This predominate past life is not necessarily the last lived. Time is not lineal as it seems to us, while living the progression of events from birth to death that make up the substance of our lives. Time and space are inseparable and move in a spiral, not lineal formation. Time, as we conceive it, does not exist, as all is in the cosmic Now.

For many of us walking earth paths today, this time of 3,300 years ago, within the walls of a pink sandstone temple or in other esoteric places throughout the world, may be your dominant lifetime. Many of us come also from the lifetime of Christ, 2000 years ago. Some remember these lifetimes, many do not. However, because we have been programmed in lifetimes before this one, we do have a definite purpose for being here at this particular time as we enter the new millennium. The memory banks of your subconscious mind hold a memory of everything that has ever happened to you. Every thing you have ever said or thought. Every action, every deed is there just as it was when it first came into being. How can it be tapped? For me, it was under the strict guidance and control of Aureal. It sounds easy to have a spiritual guide direct the awakening of your subliminal mind, but that is far from the truth. The opening into other dimensions of your reality is never easy. Your mental and emotional nature, your central nervous system and chakra monitors must be prepared to receive what could be a flood of unexpected information. If you are not ready to evaluate and absorb these esoteric revelations into your current life, it could be detrimental, even catastrophically devastating to your mental and emotional nature. Many times dreams reveal past life memories, though you may not be aware that the dream is revealing the depths of a past life.

Our most distant past is rapidly catching up with our present. Progressively, more and more of us are remembering our past lives. Talk shows are virtually alive with the subject. Psychologists and psychiatrists are finding past life regression the answer to many of their patient's problems. Each close relationship has its origin in the far reaches of the past. The memory banks of your subconscious mind hold the memory of everything that has ever happened to you.

In the following chapter we explore the history and beliefs of reincarnation and realize that it is one of the earliest, oldest, and most universal concepts of mankind. Though reincarnation has never been scientifically proven, over half the people of the world today believe in the doctrine.

7

Reincarnation

You who were created together circle together throughout eternity,
as actors on the stage of life you have your part to play.

One of the most fascinating and controversial subjects of
the twentieth century and one of mankind's most ancient
doctrines is the evolution of human life through many successive human rebirths. But can we prove it?

∞

The sun hung low on the horizon. It was a large, orange
globe silhouetting the grove of tall desert palms that lie
ahead. There were no other signs of vegetation on the vast
arid desert floor where I stood. Only there in the fertile valley that lie ahead, fed by a river snaking its way through
the otherwise barren land were there signs of life. Cau-
tiously, I proceeded along the dusty path, intent on reaching my destination, the oasis by the river, before dark. The
gentle evening breeze, warm and caressing, quickened my
steps with delight and anticipation. I can still feel the fine

clay soil softly sifting through my toes as I walked that dusty path.

∞

There is nothing spectacular concerning this event...except it appears to have happened thousands of years in the past. It is a compelling and haunting memory that comes to me from some depth beyond my current understanding. Permeating my emotional center, those simple scenes play over and over again like a clear spring of water bubbling forth from some subterranean source that offers no further explanation. It surrounds me with an almost imperceptible impression of familiarity that impregnates my being. It tugs and pulls on my emotional center, seeking release from its ancient tomb. So close now to the surface of my mind, memories emerge, bit by bit, when I least expect their presence.

With the baffling and provocative occurrence of these strangely familiar events that haunt my memory and with the accompanying intense feelings of an unexplainable reality that rises from some dim, distant past, I literally went in search of myself. From the library I devoured every book concerning archeology of the Middle East. If this is a past life memory, the setting must take place somewhere in modern day Iraq, my intuition told me.

Though it took more than a year to find the location of my insatiable search, one day I became comfortable with the material I was reading about the ancient city of Babylon, near modern day Baghdad. In the days that followed, scenes of a peasant girl spontaneously impregnated my mind and emotions. From some subterranean vault of my human psyche, the simple activities of a peasant girl living in a small mud brick hut outside the walls of Babylon, those millennia ago, had gradually surfaced into memory. Until the mystery had been solved, I could not rest.

Though thousands of years and many lifetimes have passed since the origin of this scene, I still feel the profound emotional experiences this girl felt as she walked a dusty path to the fertile fields below. Feelings of excitement and anticipation well up within me as she hurries along the path. Why? Where was she going?

∞

I would not wish this experience on anyone emotionally not ready for a past life memory. This happened early in my journeys with Aureal. I did not suspect He was "tuning" His instrument, His channel…me. Until this strange awakening, there was no reason for me to believe in reincarnation. I had given little or no thought to the subject; nor did the idea of rebirth appeal to my rational senses. Once the emotional and environmental nature of these ancient connections surfaced, in a consciousness already filled with living the current life, they can emotionally overwhelm the otherwise unsuspecting individual. To seek a rational explanation is my only practical solution.

∞

Of all the concepts postulated by Aureal, reincarnation was the one I could least accept. The few available books in the 1950s concerning the subject did not appeal to me. Reincarnation did not seem rational to the intellectual mind. The idea of survival after death, much less one's evolution through repeated earth experiences, was quite unthinkable. They were not only foreign to my orthodox beliefs but I clearly did not care to return to earth for another life.

Forty years and several lifetime experiences later, I now embrace the concept of rebirth as one of the most important esoteric teachings. It is not possible to understand the meaning of life without understanding the meaning of death; and then to realize they are not two separate subjects, but one continuous experience of the souls journey toward perfection.

∞

To objectively understand my subjective experiences that persist in invading my current consciousness with their strange and overriding nature, I searched the library for the latest information concerning reincarnation. Most of the information which I share with you here comes from books on the subject which I found to be the most comprehensively researched.

The *Standard College Dictionary* defines reincarnation as "Rebirth in new bodies or forms of life; especially rebirth of a soul in a new human body." This means that you have lived other lives before you began this one, lives that led you into your present existence. When you die, you ultimately will be reborn again into this world or perhaps other worlds. You will return to human form or possibly some different expression of manifestation, one you will be drawn to as a result of what you have become. You will continue on this wheel of life to be reborn again and again until you reach a stage of perfection, ready to move into the next phase but always growing into the light of the universal principle.

The theory of reincarnation affirms that each human soul is on a journey of return to its source, which is God. This journey of perfection cannot be accomplished in one short life span on earth so that definite laws, rather than chance, operate to progressively determine the circumstances of every lifetime or every stage of the journey. We are part of the unfolding process of the universe and contained within the very substance of our being is the mechanism that ensures our growth.

This ancient doctrine is providing profound meaning for modern humanity. Due to Shirley MacLaine's books and others like them, reincarnation is adding a new emotional richness to the reality of our new age. Yet not so many years ago, the idea of reincarnation was rejected by most Americans and Europeans as a preposterous fabrication of an overactive fantasy.

∞

Reincarnation is one of the earliest, oldest and most universal of human beliefs. The origin of the philosophy of reincarnation is prehistoric. Folklore, legends, myths, tribal memory and archaeological discoveries suggest a belief in reincarnation that predates the establishment of the world's major religions. It predates the most remote antiquity all over the world.

The buried remains of the Neanderthal society, dating roughly from 200,000 BC to 75,000 BC., provide the earliest known evidence of belief in reincarnation. Skeletons have been found pressed into a flexed fetal position. Archeological evidence proves that the deceased had been interred with supplies and sacrifices of animals such as bison and wild goats, as if in expectation of the next incarnation. Corpses were placed in line with the sun's east-west axis, perhaps in recognition that the sun itself rises daily from the womb of Earth.

One spring day 60,000 years ago, a family of Neanderthals buried their dead in a ritual that definitely indicates religious practices and a familiarity with the ongoing nature of life. Found in caves now used by fierce Kurdish tribesmen seeking shelter for themselves and their flocks during the cold winter months, these graves of prehistoric man had flowers, perhaps herbs accompanying the deceased for his journey into the next world. This would indicate an ancient belief in survival after death. Archaeologists determined the time of year and type of flower or herb placed with the body by examining the remnants of ancient pollen.

Interestingly, anthropologists have never found a primitive tribe that doesn't believe in some form of reincarnation. Most of the world's population live in Asia and most Asians believe in the concept of reincarnation as the normal progression of life. The vast majority of human beings throughout the world, except for those of the Christian belief, have always believed in reincarnation.

Reincarnation has a long and honorable history in Christianity as well as the Eastern religions. For hundreds of years, the subject of rebirth was debated among the early Christians and embraced as a reality by the majority. It was only after the authoritative Christian church became powerful enough to suppress all beliefs except for its own, that reincarnation was rejected as heretical and unchristian. With fifteen hundred years of world wide Christian teaching, Americans and Europeans have been steadfastly programmed not to accept reincarnation as valid.

Until only a few years ago, the idea of reincarnation would have been rejected by us as preposterous, Yet, as we will see, reincarnation is completely compatible with the important teachings of Christianity and carries with it no obligation to accept any established religion. It is a theory, independent of religious thinking, that enlightens humanity to a clearer understanding of the purpose of life and death.

∞

Edgar Cayce, one of the most acclaimed American psychics, was among the first to integrate the thinking of modern psychology with the ancient teaching of reincarnation in North America. In what came to be called life readings, Cayce indicated that the causes for our present life situation and frequently that of our diseases are to be found in the past, in our previous incarnations on earth.

Known as the Sleeping Prophet, at the age of twenty-one Cayce inadvertently discovered his clairvoyant ability when under hypnosis. In 1925 he began channeling what came to be known as life readings while in a sleep or trance condition. For the next forty years some 2,500 people received his readings. These carefully kept and documented accounts are available to any qualified investigator. They not only proved to be psychologically accurate and therapeutically helpful, but also were frequently evidential as well. Thomas Sugrue's biography of Cayce, *There is a River*, documents the amazing records of Cayce's work. Gina Cerminara's, *Many Mansions,* is a report on evidence that substantiates these readings and indicates the reality of reincarnation.

In 1950, Morey Bernstein began to experiment with the age-regression technique familiar to most psychologists. This time, however, he suggested to his subject that she regress beyond the time of her birth. She did. She began to tell of a nineteenth century lifetime in Ireland in which her name was Bridey Murphy.

The rest of the story soon became legend. Startling the quiet nature of our placid, conventional thinking, it created an explosive and extraordinary situation of irreversible consequences. (If you do not know the story of Bridey Murphy, the book by Bernstein should be readily available at your local library.) Within two weeks of the book's publication date, forty years ago, it reached the best seller lists. Bookstores found it difficult to keep up with the publics demand. Paramount Pictures bought the movie rights. Thousands of persons were stimulated to serious thought and conversation. I attended a series of Bridey Murphy lectures and discussions held in the professional office of my dentist.

Bridey became the subject of endless jokes. The story is told of a man who upon reading about Bridey Murphy changed his will: he left everything to himself. They also told about a man who regressed his wife to the seventeenth century and left her there.

Reincarnation was earnestly and sometimes hotly, debated by persons, some of whom had never heard the word before. I was totally oblivious to the belief in past lives and cannot remember having heard the word "reincarnation" until the Bridey Murphy incident.

Believers and skeptics alike found themselves thinking seriously about past lives and also experiencing things they had never been aware of before. Of course, from the very beginning the Bridey Murphy story was vigorously challenged from two widely differing points of view, those of religion and of science.

∞

It has been estimated that eighty percent of the world's religions believe in reincarnation and the responsibility of each individual for his or her own life. Most great thinkers of the Western World have unconditionally accepted the idea of rebirth. Literature's list is impressive: Goethe, Schiller, and Heine of Germany; in France, Balzac and Hugo; in England, Blake, Shelley, Wordsworth, Tennyson, and Browning. In this country there are Emerson, Thoreau,

Poe, and Whitman. In music and art there is Leonardo da Vinci and Wagner. The list continues: Benjamin Franklin, Voltaire, Napoleon, Schopenhauer, Thomas Huxley, Walt Whitman, Carlyle, Mahatma Gandhi, Thomas Edison, and Henry Ford are but a few who have believed in reincarnation.

Voltaire wrote: "It is no more surprising to be born twice than to be born once."

Benjamin Franklin wrote that when he saw nothing annihilated, not so much as even a drop of water, he could not believe in the annihilation of souls, or that God would continually discard millions of minds and go to the continual trouble of making new ones.

General George Patton was most explicit about his belief in past lives. In fact, he remembers an impressive list of lifetimes in which he had always been a soldier. Patton had no doubts about reincarnation.

The greatest thinkers of ancient Greece: Plato, Pythagoras, Socrates, Plotinus all believed in reincarnation. Giordani Bruno was burned at the stake by the Roman Catholic Church because of his belief. The poems of John Masefield, Poet Laureate of England, are required reading in many college literature courses, but few college anthologies include Masefield's poem, "A Creed," in which he explicitly proclaims his belief in reincarnation.

> I hold that when a person dies
> His soul returns again to earth;
> Arrayed in some new flesh disguise
> Another mother gives him birth.
> With sturdier limbs and a brighter brain.
> The old soul takes the roads again.

The fact that many great writers and thinkers have accepted the theory of reincarnation strengthens the theory in which there seems to be little confirming scientific proof. Independently, persons of widely differing professional backgrounds have been continually stumbling upon data which supports the theory of reincarnation. Psychologists and psychiatrists are using past life regression therapy more frequently and with phenomenal success in treating their patients.

Dr. Edith Fiore, in her book, *You Have Been Here Before: A Psychologist Looks At Past Lives,* says that, in her clinical practice, she finds people whose current lives are crippled in one way or another because of tragic events that happened to them in their former lives.

Dr. Fiore is convinced that many problems have their roots in former lives and can have a profound impact on current lives in terms of an individual's abilities, symptoms, relationships, character traits, and, indeed, in myriad other ways. Some of her patients come to realize that some of their recurring nightmares are actually flashbacks to experiences lived in previous lives. Pleasant events are re-experienced in dreams as well. As a psychologist, Dr. Fiore finds that there is not one aspect of character or human behavior that cannot be better understood through an examination of past-life events. She concludes that The tapestry of our lives is woven with threads that are ancient and the pattern is complex.

Additionally, more scientists are exploring the idea that mind is just as real as matter, that we are spiritual beings and the world of the mind is as real as the physical world. Events may occur that cannot be explained in physical terms, but this does not mean they are less real as those that can.

∞

Though reincarnation has been a basic tenet of many of the world's major religions, there is no definite reference to reincarnation in the Bible. There are passages in both the Old and the New Testaments that suggest reincarnation, however, the most often quoted of these passages consist of statements made by Jesus. In Matthew 11:11-15, He said: "...and John the Baptist, If you are willing to accept it, he is Elijah who is to come." Jesus continues to reinforce the statement that John is Elijah. This would indicate that Jesus and His disciples were familiar with the belief and did not repudiate it.

Reincarnation has had no place in the doctrine of modern day orthodox Christian, Jewish, and Islamic beliefs that continue to reject it as a viable theory. Though it is one of the oldest and most universal ideas of human kind, reincarnation meant nothing but strife for the early Christian church. Factions sprang up siding for or against the doctrine and, tragically, Christianity was turned into a battleground of vicious, protracted dispute.

In A.D. 325, the Roman emperor Constantine's Council of Nice had all references to reincarnation and other significant biblical information deleted from the New Testament.The remaining books were then reordered into present forms of the modern Bible.

The crucial time in which modern-day Christianity turned away from reincarnation began in the sixth century at the second Council of Constantinople (the Fifth Ecumenical Council of the Church). During the reign of the Byzantine Emperor Justinian I, a group of Christian bishops decided among themselves to formally abolish the teaching of reincarnation. Reincarnation was one of the council's fourteen denunciations which stated that if anyone asserted the fabulous preexistence of souls and asserted the monstrous restoration which followed it, that person would be anathema (a formal ecclesiastical ban or curse, excommunicating a person) Apparently they thought this concept would weaken the growing power of the Church by giving its followers the power to seek their own salvation.

The early Gnostics firmly believed that they had lived before and would continue to live again.

Modern theologians doubt that the anathemas announced by the council should be considered binding on contemporary Christian denominations; since the 553 A.D. Council may have been illegal because the pope of that day was literally imprisoned by Justinian and no Eastern bishops were in attendance at the meeting. The doctrine of reincarnation is still, to this day, regarded as heresy by the Catholic Church.

Neil Asher Silberman in *The Hidden Scrolls* states that, "both Christianity and Judaism arose in the moment of triumph for the forces of Roman order which marked the permanent establishment of a system of exploitation which would not tolerate the existence of any group that refused to accept the logic or the inevitability of the Roman dictates." Today we are still heirs to the cultural surrender and spiritual accommodation that the establishment of those religions demanded.

Since its beginning, the Orthodox Christian faith, like other faiths, has demanded of its followers an unquestioning conformity to its theology. It tolerates no search for truth elsewhere. As Christians, we have not been allowed to question this decision of the bishops made 1300 years ago.

Why was it so important to Emperor Justinian to ban the doctrine of reincarnation with such force? Because most people with a firm belief in reincarnation do not fear death, and because of this, they tend to fear little else.

Hans Holtzer, in *Patterns of Destiny*, wrote that the church needed the whip of Judgment Day to keep the faithful in line, and that it was a matter of survival for the early church not to allow a belief in reincarnation to take hold among its followers.

It seems clear that the empire-building Emperor, Justinian, in his zealous quest for cannon fodder and loyal troops, denounced reincarnation in order to control the people. However, over the following millennium, the church's persecution against believers in the doctrine of reincarnation became ever more extreme with mass executions of peoples, (e.g. the Albigensians of southern France,) and zeolistic affirmations that souls go immediately to heaven, purgatory or hell.

This fallacy which persists in religious Christian doctrine to this day was purely a creation of those in power who, through the use of superstitious nonsense, sought to secure a firm control over their subjects. The orthodox Christian church is the only religion to pronounce such a "hell and brimstone" doctrine and whose motive was/is strictly to control its subjects. As man enters this age of enlightenment, the orthodox church is rapidly losing its control over man's life and mind.

The doctrine of reincarnation places the responsibility for one's life, one's actions and evolution directly on the individual. Believers in reincarnation are not likely to be moved by threats of eternal damnation or swayed by the promises of priestly interventions on their behalf. They tend to be intimately aware of their own individual responsibility in developing their soul. They are very self-reliant and consequently they could not be "whipped into line" by an edict-minded emperor or a church seeking power/control over its subjects. The church and the self-serving political factions within the matrix of the church could not have controlled its devotees if these followers were to know that they alone were in control of their destiny.

What better way to hold man bondage than to enslave his developing mind?

∞

Three factors responsible for the proverbial fall of man in Eden's Garden (discussed in Chapter 11), according to Aureal, were: the Church, the State, and the disposition of man's mind to have allowed their control over man and his developing mind.

I was shocked when Aureal presented this blasphemous attack on the Church. Its doctrines, so much apart of my nature, were now presented as a demonic creation by those in power to control its subjects. Aureal, whose integrity I had come to respect completely, now attacked the very heart of my emotionally entrenched belief system. As I delved more deeply into the latest scholarly research on the subject, however, I discovered how correct Aureal's message had been.

Challenging me, a student once remarked, "You don't believe in God, do you?" Under attack was my suggestion that the Orthodox Church might not have man's best interests at the heart of its doctrines. A belief in a man-created doctrine in which the supreme being is depicted as the extension of a stern, controlling parent intent on condemning the disobedient to purgatory or hell is not my idea of a loving, creative, non judgmental, omnipresent principle that I call God.

This God-Principle is not related to the controlling image dictated for nearly two thousand years by the

Orthodox Christian Church, which, I understand, is the only religion to present God in the context of "obey my dictates or you will surely go to Purgatory." It is also the only religion to pronounce humans as sinful beings, as "humanity born in sin."

Since religion and politics lie at the very center of one's emotional belief system, it is dangerous to attack the doctrines of either. There is a growing realization in serious research, that Jesus was truly a whole man. His betrothed was Mary Magdalene with whom he had sexual intercourse. Erotic love has often been the vehicle used to express mystical experiences.

And did ye think he was not a whole man?

Aureal responded to my religiously conditioned belief that Jesus was a virgin "without sin."

Jesus explains that intercourse between man and woman is essential if we are to live; to propagate the world as God intended our human nature to fulfill itself.

∞

If what I say offends you, I hope you will begin your own research, as I did, to discover for yourself the truth or fallacy of what I say. It is from present day archaeological discoveries, that these texts from the time of Christ are now speaking to us. Texts hidden from the oppressive destruction by the Roman authoritative Orthodox Christians to insure that only their voice would be heard.

Paul set the pattern for rigidity and intolerance in these matters of control. In his letter to the Galatians, he twice called down a curse on all those who should teach any gospel other than that which he himself taught.

"Christianity has made it difficult for anyone to make use of more than one lifetime, or even to make use of his brains," says Gina Cerminara in *The World Within*. For illuminating information concerning the nature and reason for the deception of Christians by the early church, Elaine Pagels' books, *The Gnostic Gospels* and *Adam, Eve, and The Serpent* provide profoundly researched and scholarly reading. Pagels tells how, in the tenth century, the Cathers, a sect following Gnostic traditions, believed that one should obtain direct knowledge (cosmic-consciousness) of divine principles not from churches and priests but from one's own inner self or direct communication with the God spirit within. The Cathers considered themselves to be the only true Christians and carried their struggle to survive well into the thirteenth century.

Scholars are now translating Gnostic literature found by an Arab peasant in Upper Egypt in December of 1945. The papyrus manuscripts, bound in leather, were found near a massive boulder, concealed for almost 1,600 years in a red earthenware jar. These are Coptic translations from more ancient manuscripts. Some of the texts contained many quotes known from the New Testament; but these sayings, placed in unfamiliar contexts, suggested other dimensions of meaning than those familiar to our Christian background. Some attribute acts and sayings to Jesus quite different from those in the New Testament. Other passages differed entirely from any known Christian translation.

Why were these documents buried and remained unknown to us for nearly 2,000 years? It turns out they were suppressed and banned documents. Their burial at Nag Hammadi was part of a struggle critical for the formation of early Christianity. These documents and others like them, which circulated at the beginning of the Christian era, were denounced as heresy by orthodox Christians in the middle of the second century. (Also destroyed at this time by the orthodox church were all books written by and about women.) Possession of books denounced as heretical was made a criminal offense, and "Copies of such books were burned and destroyed. In Upper Egypt, someone, possibly a monk from a nearby monastery of St. Pachomius, took the banned books and hid them from destruction in the jar where they remained buried for almost 1,600 years," writes Elaine Pagels in *The Gnostic Gospels*.

Translations of the original documents on which Christianity is based have altered and distorted the original intention of scriptural writers. It is hoped that the Dead Sea Scrolls, Nag Hammadi texts, and others like them may give us primary source material that can revolutionize some of our most deeply entrenched suppositions: That human life evolves through many successive human existences and was originally a basic belief and philosophy of the early Christian church.

Despite fifteen hundred years of negative programming, according to a 1996 Gallup poll, more than 70 percent of our Western population believe there is life after death. Most of these believe in reincarnation and the number is rapidly growing. Persons of widely differing professional backgrounds have been observing data which provides evidence in support of reincarnation in various ways. A considerable number of scientists are taking keen interest in the field and through life regression techniques by such psychologists as Dr. Edith Fiore, progressively more frequent verification of past lives is surfacing.

There are many theories concerning reincarnation and the mechanics of rebirth. One which is particularly intriguing is the concept of group reincarnation which proposes that people living during certain time frames reincarnate together. This has been the teachings of Aureal in which He emphatically states,

> *You who were created together circle together throughout eternity.*
> *Like actors on the stage of life, you have their part to play.*

Backed by centuries of religious and philosophic traditions that suggest man's existence as a series of rebirths in another body, place and time, the theory or reincarnation is rapidly gaining wide acceptance. When leaving an aged, diseased or accident mangled physical body, the soul returns to its "cosmic" home for a period of several thousand years (reckoned in earth time) or prepares for an immediate earth return depending upon the souls desire.

Only in the past thirty years have consistent scientific efforts been made to answer the immediate skeptical question: *can You prove it?* Though it is circumstantial evidence, so far we cannot prove it...nor can I honestly say that any of us have lived before or that the concept of reincarnation is a reality as we conceive it. I mention this neither to prove nor to disprove reincarnation, only to share with you some of the human drama of my own experiences, and through research, the thoughts of others concerning this theory.

8

The Laws Of Karma

by Guest Author Rev. Robert A. Frost

Karma is an ancient Hindu word which when translated refers to the law of cause and effect. It means compensation and is the application of the law of cause and effect in the lives of human beings. The word Reincarnation is associated with Karma and is the necessary result of karma. Evolution is the primary force behind both karma and reincarnation and is the reason for the continuous cycle of birth-death-rebirth that must go on until mankind has reached his and her full Divine potential.

Karma is not intended to be something bad or a punishment for wrong doing. Rather karma is the pumice which polishes the diamond. We human beings are diamonds in the rough. We need the experiences of life, both good and bad, in order to grow towards a more perfect state of beingness. Karma impels mankind toward growth and understanding. Most people who profess a belief in karma think its purpose is to teach us lessons we need to learn. This is not exactly true. The real purpose of karma is to force us to expand our God-given consciousness toward self-illumination. We may have to learn many lessons on the way, but more than learned lessons, we must flow with the inexorable force of evolution. Everything living that has the essence of life expressing through it's physical envelope must grow and expand it's capabilities or eventually stagnate and fade away to extinction.

There is another Hindu word associated with karma that is not generally known. The word is Dharma. Dharma is the action that produces karma. Karma is the reaction to Dharma—the consequence of Dharma. Dharma and Karma then directly translate into the law of cause and effect. Incidentally, the Hindu word for reincarnation is Samsara, which literally translated means to be re-embodied; to return after the death of one body into another body. This means that there is something that survives the death of the physical form and then re-inhabits another body at some future time.

Most people believe it is the Soul that leaves the body at the time of death and is the surviving entity. The Soul is not the incarnating entity. The Soul is connected to the body through the silver chord and all the body's subconscious functions including memory. At the time of death, the silver chord is severed and the soul is no longer connected to the body. The Soul retains all the experiences of the deceased and is the source of all accumulated wisdom, love, talent, traits, characteristics and karma of the individual. It is the personal Akashic record of everything the individual has ever experienced in all past lives. It is an ongoing record of personal and spiritual growth over thousands of years.

What is the surviving entity that leaves the physical form at death? It is the Spirit that not only leaves the body but is the very essence of consciousness itself. Consciousness is the animated state of Spirit. Consciousness is spirit in a self-aware condition that enables the personality to exist and have a sense of individual identity. When the Spirit departs from its physical host body, the consciousness of the individual remains intact but now separated from its physical form. What happens while in the after-death state before rebirth into another form is a subject for anther time.

Back to karma. Karma is not an outside force or law imposed upon human beings, rather it is a process within us that keeps us on the path of spiritual growth. We generate our own Karma. We also accept social and racial Karma by our attitudes and beliefs. The interaction between people also creates karma. Every thought, every emotion, action and reaction can establish a karmic pattern, especially if such thoughts, emotions, actions and reactions become chronic forms of behavior. Good karma can lead into experiencing happier more successful lives. So called bad karma (which really isn't bad) can lead us into a life of misfortune and unhappiness, even tragedy and death. But in the long run it will force us to grow whether in this life or future lives. Spirit and Soul are indestructible; so is consciousness. We cannot escape our karma, because we cannot escape from what we are. One way or one time, we must face our karma and work it out through the process of living, learning, growing, and realization. It is necessary to understand that *we pay our karmic debts to ourselves and not to anyone else!*

This explodes a common myth about karma. Two people in past lives may have created a karmic condition between them, but that is no certainty or guarantee that they will be together in their next lives to work out the karma between them. It could happen that way, or it could happen with someone else with a similar karmic pattern and need. The purpose of karma is not to settle debts between individuals, but to settle the debt within oneself. This is where many karma believers "miss the boat." They can't seem to understand that karma is not an outside force imposed by God or the conscious direction of the Soul. The soul does contain the karmic patterns, but it is not a conscious entity directing earthy events—only Spirit does that through it's animated state of consciousness.

Another myth regarding karma should be given a closer look. The idea that an individual who murdered someone in a past life will in turn be murdered in his or her next life is not necessarily true, though it could happen that way. When a person murders someone, there is a severe negative karma that becomes imbedded in that person's soul. In his or her next life (and maybe several lives after the next life) that negative pattern will tend to repeat itself. So a person who commits a murder in a past life will have a strong tendency to commit a murder in the next life if someone doesn't kill him or her first. Remember the karmic pattern has been imprinted on the soul and nothing is going to change that except the person him/her self. A karmic pattern perpetuates itself into future incarnations until the entity has worked out that pattern through their process of living and successfully meeting the challenges of life in a positive, constructive manner.

Many people hold to the idea that prayer or meditation can dispel a karmic load. Prayer and/or meditation can help to bring about a realization that will influence a persons thoughts, actions and lifestyle. This is a positive step in the right direction. However Divine dispensation or forgiveness of karma is only possible when the person has made a valiant effort on their own and can do no more without help from a higher source. Even then, there has to be a total reversal of consciousness. That is to say, consciousness has to receive the benefit of positive changes in the person's lifestyle including thoughts, emotional responses and behavior. The old saying that God helps those who help themselves is true. We can't escape from karma we have generated; we have to dissolve it with or without Divine help.

In conclusion, we humans have the option of either denying we have karmic patterns and learning to live with them, or, take conscious steps to dissolve whatever karmic burden we may be carrying. There are some basic things we can do to accelerate the release of the karmic grip. Recommended are the following:

• Do a lot of self-observation to learn more about the inner workings of your mind and emotions. Begin to understand yourself without condemnation or judgment—accept who and what you are—try to discover the reality of your being.
• Carefully examine any negative patterns or compulsions that affect your life. Do a self-search for the causes without allowing yourself to become immersed in them.
• If regression is necessary to find the cause (Dharma) of a karmic pattern, be sure to select a competent therapist experienced at doing regressions. Beware of suggestive comments that might lead you on a false trail.

• Practice the Golden Rule in your daily life.

• Pray and /or meditate regularly and sincerely.

The above steps are basic. Other helpful things to do are: Learn to love and respect yourself. Develop an appreciation for beauty. Feel compassion for the less fortunate and help them when you can, within reason. Pursue a hobby that you really enjoy; and finally, refrain from being deceitful and/or lying.

PART 3

Search For Our
Cosmic Origins

9

The Signature Of Adam

The Creator Gods: Do they really exist? Who are they? Where do they come from? What is their purpose with man of earth?

From a distant planet, one larger than your sun and older, we came to claim for our own the beautiful verdant Earth. This small planet was an ideal environment to raise our family and prepare a home for the generations to come.

Less than 50 years ago the thought that beings from other planets, perhaps from other galaxies, visited earth in the remote past was considered the outlandish speculations of an overactive mind. To suggest that modern humans may have been "seeded" here by these extraterrestrials was truly unthinkable. However, today, these topics are the focus of a most intensive scientific search in the history of man. The desire to know if there are other intelligences in the vast cosmic space that surrounds us is escalating in intensity. The technologies that allow us to uncover this information have never been more advanced.

Albert Einstein considered the idea of prehistoric visits to our planet by extraterrestrial intelligence to be quite probable and in accord with the then current technologies during his lifetime.

∞

I am awakening from a most profound sleep. The phone is ringing, bringing me abruptly to a point in time most distant from where I have been. For a moment, I am not certain which is the reality of my existence. The one from which I have just come has been so real.

"Hello," I say, as I lift the receiver.

"Laura, I've just had the most bizarre experience."

"Oh," I answer, still more asleep than awake.

"It was so real" she said." I was with Aureal on a large space ship entering early Earth for a landing. You won't believe this..."

"Try me," I interrupted.

"We were entering Earth..." she continued.

"Yes, yes, Dorothy, I know," I answered now fully awake, startled and amazed at her announcement.

"I was there too."

It was not unusual for Aureal to awaken both His channels simultaneously to the same concept though we might be physically miles apart.

I continue with our story.

Now in complete awareness, I stand at the window of a giant space ship, awed by the panoramic view of infinite space before me. Though I cannot see him, Aureal seems to be standing to my right. The interior of the space ship where I stand is as vivid to me today as if I had just taken that journey. The windows circling the ship were slanted outward from the wide ledge on which we leaned for a clearer view of our approaching destination, Earth.

Snaking its way through the center of the carpet on which we stood, was a most unusual eight inch wide band of an indescribable orange-red light. It provided illumination for an otherwise semi-dark interior.

There is, however, a strange twist to our apparent space ship experience, but two years would pass before Aureal revealed the ultimate explanation of this unusual ride to Earth.

Look to the back from which we came.

Aureal escorted me around the parapet to another part of the ship.

As I look in the direction he indicates, I see a large globe, a planet there in the vastness of space.

It is our home planet, one much larger and older than your sun. Now look ahead to the destination of our journey.

In the horizon, I see a small globe, another planet, Earth.

It was from a distant planet, one larger than your sun and older, that we came, the twelve of us, my brothers, to claim for our own a gift; a very small and beautiful planet. It was an ideal environment, this verdant planet, to raise our family and to prepare a home for the generations to come.

Aureal's reference to the twelve of us may be esoteric and not to be taken literally. The use of the number twelve is inherent in most secret doctrines from Rosicrucian to the White Brotherhood. It is used also in the twelve apostles, esoteric astrologers and 12 planets (which we know of only nine at this writing).

Aureal referred to Earth as "Nursery Earth" and "Cradle Earth." This reference is due to the use His people had for Earth. It was here on this small life-giving planet, that these intelligences from another realm came to experiment with a humanoid improvement. They came to create a quantum leap in the evolution of humankind. In their own image, they would create a more highly evolved being.

In Genesis 1:26-27, according to the King James version, "God said, Let us make men in our image, after our likeness"; then the suggestion was carried out: "And God created man in his own image, in the image of God created he him; male and female created he them." Does this say that we, mankind, were created hybrids as much of the current theories would have us believe?

From another Biblical reference, we find that "Elohim created the Adam." According to the original Hebrew text the creative act is attributed to "Elohim," which is a plural term translated as "Gods," not a singular "God." This does not rule out the ultimate creative power we refer to as God.

It has been suggested by several authors on the subject of mankind's creation that these extraterrestrials mated with the primitive female of Earth, thus manipulating and speeding up the process of our evolution. In our attempt to envision methods used by other intelligences in the prehistoric past, it is difficult for us to escape from our traditional concepts concerning male/female mating. Are we to believe these advanced beings were interested in sexually mating with the primitive woman of that day? Or, as another learned writer insists, that Adam was probably the first test tube baby conceived by mixing the egg of the ape woman with the sperm (and genes) of a young "god," then implanting this fertilized elements in the womb of a goddess surrogate to bring into being the first Adam or first human?

In order to bring forth a being "in the likeness or image of " its creator, this new being must have only the genes of its creator, otherwise the product will be hybrid. If these Elohim were to create man in the likeness of themselves, the procedure must be some form of asexual reproduction.

Early in the 1970's, a new scientific procedure called cloning received much publicity as a giant step forward in genetic engineering. Since every cell, whether plant, animal, or human, contains all the genetic information necessary to reproduce an identical to its parent, it offered endless potential for plant and animal duplication. Adapting this technique to animals that reproduce by fertilizing egg with a sperm, requiring male and female components, proved more difficult. However, today our science has made, and continues to make phenomenal advances in genetic engineering.

In February 1997, news of an earthshaking breakthrough in genetic engineering occurred in Scotland as the first mammal, a sheep, was cloned. Can our technology clone a human? Unbelievably the answer is yes. However is it morally permissible? This is the question now facing our lawmakers.

If we can manipulate our genetic information to perfect hereditary factors, there is no reason to believe an extraterrestrial intelligence, capable of space travel and consequently thousands of years ahead of us scientifically, should not understand methods of genetic engineering light years in advance of our own.

∞

Aureal continues His story:

Planet Earth, is very small in relation to other planets in the universe. It was a jewel, verdantly carpeted in its totality. It was not then spinning in space nor were its companions, the sun and moon, part of its nature. It was then floating peacefully in the cosmic sea, eternally radiant with a soft warm light. It was high in energy and all that man could possibly want. It was a true garden of Eden.

This explanation from Aureal tells us that Earth has not always been in orbit around the sun nor has she had the moon for a companion. This is a ridiculous concept...or is it?

In my search for information through the archives of astronomy, some interesting facts came to my attention. In 1927, an archeological artifact was deciphered. It told of moon's capture by earth. Regarding it at the time, to be a deluded fantasy of ancient man, scientists gave it no further thought. During the recent Apollo man landings on the moon however, minerals were found in abundance which are extremely rare on earth. "The moon is different from earth and clearly not 'coined' from her," the source related.

In *Genesis Revisited*, Zecharia Sitchin says that the Moon's composition is in many respects similar to that of Earth, yet different in key respects.

From "The Origin of the Moon," an article in *American Scientist* (September—October 1975), Stuart R. Taylor states: "For many technical reasons, it is difficult to match the composition of the bulk of the Moon to that of the terrestrial mantle."

In 1981, I enrolled in an upper level physics course titled "How Earth Captured Moon: Three Theories." After much scientific debate and the analysis of new findings concerning this subject, these three theories are no longer considered valid, so I will not list them here, other than to suggest that moon has not always been a companion to Earth. Another theory suggested in 1975 dubbed the Big Whack Theory was developed from the suggestion that collisions and impacts played a role in the creation of the Moon.

Though the theories are not the issue here, it is interesting to note that there is scientific evidence to indicate that Earth has not always been as we now perceive her to be. As for the sun, I have found not even the slightest hint that would indicate earth's existence without her solar companion.

A fantastic astronomical theory was proposed many years ago and recently confirmed by the findings of Hans Bellamy and Peter Allen. Their book, *The Calendar of Tiahuanaco,* states that earth has captured four moons, one after another, during its lifetime of several billion years.

Though I don't know where he obtained his information, Maurice Chatelain states in his book, *Our Ancestors Came From Outer Space*, that Earth has had three different moons in the past before the present one. The last moon was much larger and much closer than our present moon, which resulted in a huge tidal belt around the equator. So much for this interesting speculation. I found no further reference to explain what happened.

Officially, science does not accept the multiple moon theory, although this theory is in harmony with many ancient legends that tell of giants who lived at the time of the "big moon." I have known from Aureal's teachings and the visions I have experienced of that early period, that He and His brothers were much taller than humanoids then inhabiting earth. They were eight to twelve feet tall and referred to as giants or Elohim.

The Bible, (documented in Genesis) also relates stories about these mysterious giants and the big moon. In Hebrew, Elohim is a plural word translated as astronauts. I have included these pieces of information, whether true or fantasy, as I found them interesting in my search for the more profound verification of Aureal's story.

∞

Within the last 30 years, more has been learned about our Earth than in all of the past 300 years combined. Many of our conventional ideas are no longer valid in the light of facts made available to us by modern technologies. An abundance of new information comes to us through use of computers, airplanes, outer space inventions and other earth and space probing technologies. Because much information is so rapidly coming to light, scientists are often in disagreement concerning the interpretation of this information.

Though I maintain a scientific vigilance, continually probing and seeking the truth to Aureal's fantastic stories, scientific discoveries constantly change and in many cases, make conventional "truth" obsolete as we know it. New dimensions of understanding, especially in the field of archaeology, give us tangible verifications of ancient documents, legends and myths.

It remains for me, however, an exciting journey in pursuit of the latest progress of these scientific disciplines to find the facts of Aureal's bizarre story concerning our beginning.

∞

Though this may read like science fiction, remember the fiction of one era is the science, the knowledge and reality of another.

It is now Easter 1970, as I write this transmission. It is a story of man's beginning on earth, that would be given to me in progressive segments, over a ten year period and only during Easter Week.

The story takes us back to a time, before the beginning of man, in the Biblical story of Genesis. It takes us to that eventful time preceding the creation of man in the Garden of Eden.

Aureal tells us:

It was from afar man came to make a new nest for his children and future generations on this virtual paradise, Earth. For thousands of years all flourished, as man built from the materials of the planet and from the wisdoms he brought with him, a civilization unequaled today.

Somewhere in the deep layers of consciousness that belongs to all of us, this story lies in perfect preservation, awaiting the spark of enlightenment to ignite into conscious awareness this ancient memory. Due to some mental manipulation, Aureal opened the "vault" for me containing this ancient memory—an "awakening" He calls it—so I could relive that momentous event.

The following is taken directly from my notes at the time of this altered state of consciousness.

My Genesis Experience: As I attempt to comprehend the meaning of this unexpected journey in space-time, though it seems strangely familiar, I feel the relatively alert, self-perceiving action of my conscious mind change in function to that quality of twilight consciousness sometimes imposed by a mild sedative. A sense of detachment to my surrounding environment overcomes me.

The cycle of man's evolution in consciousness…you are now experiencing the intuitive nature of the discarnate mind as it originally entered earth's plane to begin the story of mankind. As you move forward in evolutionary time, you sense a gradual awakening into a self aware state. This is a process in which the Light of a cosmic nature begins to filter into the primitive brain of animal man. As this Light continues to impregnate the human structural nervous system, it progressively evolves his conscious mind to receive the greater enlightenments from this sea of Cosmic Light/Mind.

As you grow in this Light of expanded awareness, you are gradually attaining the higher consciousness of god-man incarnate. In your existing stage of eternal development, you are neither fully aware—awake, nor are you in the 'twilight zone' of an earlier stage in your evolution.

Because you are consciously aware of yourself and your environment at this stage of your current development, you think it has always been this way. But, do you remember your condition of consciousness when you were a baby? You have perfect memory of that stage in your life, though it lies dormant. Are you aware of your thinking and feelings and of your perceptions during those early stages of your development within your current lifetime?'

The history of human evolution, from the darkness of primitive mind (consciousness) into the Light of cosmic knowing (enlightenments) is a long and never ending journey. The progressive evolution of the new born human within a few years, to the maturity of an adult, is evidence in miniature of your greater cosmic nature. It follows the same pattern as your ancestral evolution, which has transpired over a millennium of time. Do you understand this most important fact?

This is a process of evolution in awareness which takes a millennium of earth time to accomplish within your immortal cosmic nature. That is, to explain, the journey for mankind from Eden's cradle through the wanderings in the wilderness (muddled thinking) until man again enters the Garden of Eden in consciousness (enlightenment) of himself and his evolutionary birthright, is a very slow process. But remember one vital fact: You never left Eden's Garden. It envelops you now as it always has. It is only in the darkness of your mind's evolving awareness, you shut off that light of truth.

"You never left Eden's Garden." This is a deeply profound statement in which Aureal tells us that we live eternally in this beautiful paradise. It surrounds us now as it has since our beginning. Looking at our world with so much crime, starvation, war, uncertainties and natural catastrophes, this world we live in can't possibly be the Paradise we so desperately seek.

You never left Eden's Garden nor have We left your side.

The following chapters explore this apparent discrepancy. As we progress further into Aureal's story, He explains man's legendary fall in the Garden of Eden.

Aureal continues:

Returning again to man's beginning in the cradle of Earth; that beautiful Garden of Eden was not then as she is now. At that time of your beginning, Earth existed in a higher plane of being. It was a region whose frequency was such that, to your current vision, it would not be visible to you now. That is, from your existing base within the lower frequency of the third dimension, which is your physical perception, you cannot see the higher plane of your original existence.

Aureal emphasizes that we were not created in this lower vibrational realm of the third dimension. He insists that Earth was the beautiful nursery given to His brothers for the purpose of an experiment; to bring about an evolutionary leap in humankind on this planet was their intent. Earth, at the time of our conception, was a satellite of His much larger and older planet, which probably is not part of our current solar system. Earth was not then as she is now...spinning in space with a sun and moon as companions.

Incredible!

It has been a monumental task, researching to find the supportive evidence for Aureal's fantastic disclosures. As we progress into the following chapters, however, we will explore current scientific findings concerning the geology of our Earth's past history. We will look at the latest information on the most bizarre but credible scientific odysseys through time warps, overlapping and infinite dimensions, parallel universes and black holes.

The following was an incredible, unbelievable concept of our evolution at the time I first received it from Aureal, almost three decades ago. Now, with the supportive discoveries of modern science, it is the acceptable text book teaching.

Asleep in the rock...

Over eons of earth time, the life force within the molecular structure of rock increased in frequency (eroded) to become earth, (soil). The evolution of earth then evolved to the next level of life and out of the earth, plant came into being.

Stirring in the plant...

From the higher evolution of plant life, the primitive forms of animal began.

Awake in animal...

The evolution of awareness in animal continued until one day something spectacular happened in the process of evolution; a primitive form of ape man began to walk the earth.

Ape has always been ape. Man has always been man. You will not find the missing link.

Aureal informed as he moved his hand horizontally to indicate a radical change in the evolutionary process.

The Darwinian theory of evolution is now dying throughout the world as there is no evidence that one species evolves into another. Anthropologists find no evidence in fossil records of an evolutionary transition in species.

You will not find the missing link.

The DNA of modern man is nearly identical to that of the ape, but that nearly imperceptible difference, the two percent deviation is of the mind. Thus:

Aware in man.

As Aureal continued his story, I could not comprehend his words.

"What did you say Aureal? I cannot understand this last which you tell me," I lamented.

Of course you can't. Your evolutionary understanding is not there yet.

Mankind is an experience in evolution. He is a process and not an end product. The reason for this sudden progressive step in evolution was to create humans of a higher order than the existing species.

"What happened?" I asked, realizing that we who walk the earth today are of a special creation.

In your eternal consciousness, you have all memory of this story. Flesh of my flesh, blood of my blood, you are my own dear child. You were cloned of me as others of your plane were created likewise of my brothers.

To repeat: Genesis 1:26 "And God said, Let us make man in our image, after our likeness." God, the word, is in the plural...gods.

Your people do not know, as yet, the meaning of this cloning procedure as applied to your beginning. The cloning I speak of is not the same as you would understand from your scientific media. I use the word cloning as it is the idea I wish to convey to your understanding. It is the concept and not the process of identical reproduction to which I refer.

You, as my clone, are all that I am, all that my father was before me, and his father before him, you also are. You are all that I am, as you are of me. As your child of flesh grows in the light of your knowing, so you are awakening to the light of my knowing, as it is your birthright. As above, the law is written, so below. It is time, my child, that the evolution of man of earth take a quantum leap. The progressive process of evolution is long and tedious. It is much too slow.

We of a more highly evolved nature, Gods, you called us, were given Earth as the birthplace, a nursery for our children. You, as also the children of Eden's garden, were cloned in our likeness. Thus, You have all knowing from the first of our ancestor, which is that particle of cosmic dust.

In some part of our consciousness we have total memory from the first of our ancestor which was a particle of dust drifting to Earth to become rock. At the quantum level, rock has intelligence.

The purpose of our being is the progressive awakening into a total awareness of who and what we really are… GOD.

Aureal explains that all forms, animate and inanimate, contain within them their own specific vibrational segment of the cosmic intelligence. Their particle of intelligence makes them what they are: a plant, an animal, a human, etc. Even a rock evolves, absorbing its portion of the cosmic sea of mind.

The chemical analysis of all earthly things is the same. All forms are composed of the same chemical elements.

Wayne Dyer, in his tape series, *Living Beyond Miracles*, tells that a chemical analysis of the cells of your brain and the pulverized bits of a stone are chemically identical. What then makes the infinite variety of differences in life forms on this planet?

We live in an infinite sea of intelligence…MIND. Call it God, which is Light. Light is intelligence. It is that particle of light/mind, that individual frequency of the cosmic intelligence accessible to each form, according to the nature of that form. It is that frequency of awareness that makes each thing different from the other. It is the amount of cosmic Light each form draws to itself that makes it what it is. As this Light grows brighter, the frequency increases within the form or particle, evolving into higher levels of intelligence, of creation.

∞

How life on earth began is the greatest of all mysteries. Man is a latecomer to earth. In the timeline of evolution he fills only the last few pages.

In 1987 NASA instruments discovered that exploding stars (supernovas) produced most of the ninety-plus elements, including carbon, that are contained in living organisms on Earth. We are truly made of star stuff. We are the product of a third generation star.

In 1973, in a paper titled "Directed Panspermia," the Nobel laureates Francis Crick and Leslie Orgel presented a concept that Life on Earth was placed here not by chance but as the intentional activity of an extraterrestrial society who seeded Earth with the first organisms or spores. They suggested that the scientific community consider a new "infective" theory that a primitive form of life was deliberately planted on Earth by a technologically advanced society from another planet. Since living spores could not survive the rigors of space, it was suggested that the microorganisms were not sent to just drift in space, but were placed in a specially designed spaceship with protection and a life-sustaining environment. At that time, this theory met with disbelief and ridicule. However, more recent scientific advances have changed these attitudes. As our own technologies take us further into outer space, it becomes more apparent that technologically advanced civilizations capable of seeding life on other planets existed elsewhere in the galaxy even before the formation of the Earth.

In 1986, from the Eighth Conference on the Origins of Life, held at Berkeley, California came the consensus that "all life on Earth, from bacteria to sequoia trees to humans, evolved from a single ancestral cell." But where did this ancestral cell come from? After due consideration, the assembled scientists were left with only one conclusion that might provide the answer to the question of the origin of life on Earth and Space exploration. The same DNA, composed of the same four nucleotides is present in all living things on Earth. Therefore, they concluded, all life came from a single source and not from random evolution.

There is no explanation for the origin of DNA by chance. Molecular scientists tell us that the DNA molecule is a vastly complex molecule that carries a digital (expressible in mathematical terms) correcting code that could not have evolved by chance. Life on earth had to have been created by an interdimensional being who imputed biochemical information, intelligence onto matter and coded it with the DNA information that gives us life. Chance is absolutely insufficient to explain the DNA molecule (much less the software carried out by the molecule). The creator requires a MIND transcendent over its creation and beyond our understanding.

In the folklore of virtually every ancient culture from the Sumerian, Babylonian, Egyptian, the ancient Greeks to the American Indians, we find the same story that tells of supernatural Celestial beings...giants that interbred with humans to create us.

∞

Aureal's story continues:

I sense your question of the Adam and Eve story. It is an allegory more profound than your religious doctrines reveal. In time, as you are able to understand more, this story will come to you. The many of you walking Earth today are of the original "cloned" children of my people from the greater planet. You, as many of you, have the memory of that voyage to earth from our homeland planet, though it is for most of you a dormant memory as you were not yet conceived.

Puzzled, I asked, "In the space ship ride to earth from our homeland, which you allowed me to remember so vividly—I was not then a separate being from you, Aureal?"

That is right, my child. It is my memory of that voyage in space which you, and the many of you, now have, but it is nonetheless your memory also. It is your ancestral memory. You call it your subconscious mind. All that I was at that time is also yours. You are totally of me. Your preciously conceived flesh and blood children do not have as close a bond to you as you have to me. Do you understand the nature of your soul birth? You are a 'cloned' identical of me, though in your mind of flesh, you must awaken gradually to this knowing. I perceive your questions before you voice them. Your current concept of cloning is incomplete.

You must realize you are a pattern of energy. Though you were an identical of my being at inception, it is your growth in experience that makes you, each of you, unique from all others. As you evolve through experience, your pattern of energy becomes unique to you. It is through your own efforts you grow in the light of your desires. Thus you become an individual unlike any other that has ever been or ever will be.

189

No two experiences or the desires that propel those experiences are the same.

In the early days of man's beginning, all of earth was a beautiful verdant garden. Two segments of this ancestral memory remain indelibly imprinted in my consciousness: that of the space ride to earth and the beginning of the Eden experience. Both of these events occurred before my inception as a "cloned" living soul, therefore, I understand that I am using Aureal's perception of that memory.

The atmosphere of this early place was draped in mist with a warm steam-like vapor rising from the ground rather than falling from the sky. Vegetation was lush and green. It was much like a rain forest, yet, not exactly. The present atmosphere of Earth is not her original atmosphere.

Core samples taken from deep within the earth conclusively prove that the climate and atmosphere from all parts of earth has drastically changed over the millennium.

∞

The second important and vivid memory I have was of the primitive people already here in Eden's Garden when "we" arrived. They were short and stocky in build. They were playful, child-like, and loving. One, a female I remember most clearly, ran toward us, her arms outstretched in a loving greeting. Though it was Aureal she greeted, it seemed she came to me. I feel reasonably certain she was my surrogate mother.

Who was this primitive earth woman who was our apparent surrogate mother? I searched through the volumes of books concerning early man, hunting for a likeness of her. Like an abandoned child, I wanted to know who she was. In my mind I held her visual image, indelibly imprinted there within my ancient memory. She was not at all apelike in appearance, only childlike in mentality. The Neanderthal seemed to be the most likely candidate.

Physically, the Neanderthals were almost like modern man. Most were stocky and big boned, but no more so than many people today and they stood fully erect. This fact came as a surprise to me, having studied anthropology as part of my college requirement in the 1940s. At that time the Neanderthal man was depicted as a stooped, hulking, apelike creature. This misconception is based on some blunders made by Marcellin Boule, a distinguished French paleontologist, who in the early 1900s made the first detailed reconstruction of a Neanderthal skeleton. From his reconstruction, Boule deduced that Neanderthal was "brutish" and "clumsy" with apelike, partly prehensile feet, a shambling, bent-kneed gait and a mind of "a pure vegetative or bestial kind."

More recently a careful reexamination of the same skeleton revealed Boule had been wrong in almost every respect. By incorrectly positioning the skeleton's big toes, the "prehensile" feet had been produced. The "shambling walk" was assumed from an equally inaccurate reconstruction of the knee joint. True, the owner of this particular skeleton must have stooped markedly—but due to a bad case of spinal arthritis and not evolutionary genes. It seems that Boule was looking for the "missing link" between ape and man and, expert or not, he must have been influenced as much by his own preconceptions as by the actual bones he was studying. Put a Neanderthal in modern clothes and send him to the supermarket. In all probability, he would pass the checkout stand completely unnoticed.

Only in their skulls did the Neanderthals differ ana-
tomically from us. Their brain was as large as our own, but
the brain and therefore the skull containing it were differently shaped. It bulged at the back with a low sloping fore-
head in front. From this difference in cranial and larynx
formation, it is deduced that the Neanderthal had evolved
to his limits of speech and mentality. However, currently
even this deduction of the Neanderthal is in question, as
more ancient remains are discovered and our technologies
for analyzing these fossil remains have drastically
improved.

Taking into consideration everything that they did, the
Neanderthals were human. They possessed considerable
imagination and sensibility. They had a technology sophis-
ticated and diverse enough to let them survive successfully
in a variety of habitats. They engaged in magical rites.
They, so far as we know, were the first to bury their dead.
Into their graves they placed tools and joints of meat,
which strongly suggests a belief in an afterlife where the deceased would need food and equipment. This also suggests
they buried their dead with some sort of ritual. For some
60,000 years they survived successfully and then vanished—or did they?—as Cro-Magnon or modern man
made his sudden appearance. Famed anthropologist, Don-
ald Johanson, discoverer of "Lucy," says that we have no
proof we are not carrying Neanderthal genes in our DNA.
A recent television documentary concerning the Wolf boy
of Mexico suggests we may have within our genes ancient
animal ancestry that date before the evolution of man,
though it normally lies dormant.

∞

Few concepts have puzzled me more than the one of cloning. Aureal had used this word, cloning, because it most

nearly explained His process of asexual duplication. Yet, Aureal made clear that his reference to cloning is a process different from and not known by our current technologies.

For another two years I pondered the mechanics of the human creation by and in the likeness of those greater beings who came to earth from some other place in outer space. Usually Aureal answers my questions immediately, delighted over my asking. However, for the cloning process, he stubbornly refused even a hint. My curious imagination explored every conceivable way within my limited ability to perceive its nature. My only clue was that the surrogate mother carried the child once conceived.

It was late afternoon and the answer to my desperately sought question on cloning was the furthest from my mind as I moved through the garden toward my house. But this is Aureal's way.

A fluffy ball of light suddenly enveloped me. In total consciousness, for that moment, I became Mary, mother of Jesus. Then a charge of lightning moved diagonally toward me, striking me in the uterine area.

It is my energy, (perceived as lightning). It is that frequency which I am, implanted in the cradle of woman, that my likeness is conceived.

This was the answer for which I had for so long sought. Still this process of the virgin birth had no scientific parallel in the reality of our current understanding.

"And God said, Let us make man in our image, after our likeness." How many times had I expressed my arrogance over the virgin birth of Jesus? "Who can believe that biblical rubbish?" I had said. Jesus, the son of God, conceived by the virgin Mary. Now it finally made sense to my disbelieving mind.

Some months later, I sat in my physics class, watching a segment of Carl Sagan's documented film, *Cosmos*. In it,

Sagan was showing the possible creation of life on primitive earth. In a large glass container he had a mixture of "organic soup," the substances prevalent in the oceans and ponds of primitive Earth some four billion years ago. Flashes of artificial lightning were activating this "organic soup" in the laboratory demonstration.

Again we face a dilemma. It is scientifically known that all life on Earth, from bacteria to humans, did not randomly evolve but came from a single ancestral cell.

Though the concept of lightning as a catalyst for creating life differs from that of the "seeding of primitive life" by extraterrestrials as postulated by Creck and Orgil, I include it as a method for creating organic life from inorganic matter. This procedure is also similar to the lightning -like energy sent forth by Aureal into the womb of woman to create a child in His likeness...a cloned likeness.

What does this have to do with the virgin birth of Jesus or the creation of man in the likeness of God in the Garden of Eden? To answer this, we must understand some basic concepts.

All things are of an energy pattern. Man is not a being of solid mass. He is an alive, vibrating frequency pattern of his own unique nature. He is an energy pattern materialized in form.

If this were not true, the cloning process Aureal demonstrates could not be a fact. Kirlian photography and recently developed film sensitive devices, extend our perceptions into realms of energies that emanate from physical bodies though they are not perceptible to the naked eye.

There are those among us today who, by the projection of their mental powers, can cause material forms to move, change form, and be created.

Research concerning the unlimited powers of man's mind, particularly in Russia, is being scientifically confirmed.

As primitive life forms were possibly created in the molecular Garden of Eden some four billion years ago, by a process of electrical activation or lightning, is it not then possible that God-man of a higher order of mind could, by projecting his energy (like a laser beam) into the womb of primitive earth woman, create a duplicate of himself?

∞

Maurice Chatelaine, former NASA space scientist, has compiled an enormous amount of speculation in his book, *Our Ancestors Came From Outer Space,* indicating that astronauts from another planet in another solar system landed on earth and mated with the Neanderthal women. This was a genetically engineered program designed to produce a much more highly developed man. It was a program designed to produce the Cro-Magnon people who were our ancestors, thus creating a quantum leap in human evolution. Using computers, he has carefully studied such mysteries as the Egyptian pyramids, the Mayan calendar, and the Sumerian Zodiac. From new and previously overlooked information, he has concluded that highly advanced civilizations existed on earth as far back as 65,000 years ago and, he concludes that astronauts from another solar or galactic civilization visited our ancestors 65,000 years ago and started the sudden evolution of man by improving his intelligence through insemination and mutation.

In the cliffs of Del Mar near San Diego, California, the skull of a Homo Sapiens or Cro-Magnon man was found in 1929 by Malcom J. Rogers, archaeologist for the San Diego Museum of Man. The brain in this 48,000-year-old skull, determined by amino acid dating, had been large enough to contain the intelligence of modern man. The skull gives evidence of a populace which occupied the southern Pacific Coast perhaps shortly after the first migrations eastward from Asia into the lands of the Western Hemisphere. They may well be typical of the earliest aboriginal Americans.

Some researchers believe this part of California is the remnants of ancient Lamuria.

∞

So much of the original meaning and truth of our creation is shrouded in the mists of antiquity. However, as viewed from the perspective of modern day research, we know that, between 40,000 and 45,000 years ago, something extraordinary happened in the development of mankind. Pushing back the curtain of man's evolution, in the deposits from that early period, archeologists have found the first skeletal remains of a people physically indistinguishable from our own. Within a relatively short period of time, these people became not only the dominant type of human being, but the *only* type.

Neanderthal, the first true members of Homo Sapiens, who ruled the earth for some 60,000 years preceding this period of time, simply disappeared (or did they?) and modern man suddenly appeared.

Some 37,000 years ago, a people identical in appearance to our own, known as the Cro-Magnon, arrived replacing the Neanderthal. They were robust and tall and came with capabilities which seem to have sprung full-blown from out of nowhere.

Cro-Magnon is the first human with a brain volume equal to ours, about 1,600 cubic centimeters. Primitive man before him had a volume of no more than 800 cubic centimeters. The Cro-Magnon were, according to today's standards, fully modern. Their intellectual and spiritual achievements are impressive, particularly in their artistic ability.

"Where did modern man come from?" asks the author of "What Caused The Sudden Rise Of Modern Man?" in the book, *Mysteries Of The Past.* "Somehow, somewhere, they must have evolved out of some Neanderthaloid population. The uniqueness of the sudden appearance of one human type and the disappearance of another leaves us with a profound mystery originating at the beginning of our creation. What characteristics could have enabled them (modern man) to triumph so rapidly and so completely?"

In seeking to unravel the mystery of why and how this remarkable event transpired, is it not possible to take into serious consideration that we truly are the children of those beings from another place somewhere in the vastness of space?

10

Eden's Garden

And so it was, as you've been told, Eve took the apple in her hand and ate of this forbidden fruit. Somehow in your histories past, this story got all garbled. It was the purpose of the soul to walk upon the Earth in flesh, which is like a space suit for its exploration. This experience on Earth, within the structure of man, is another stage of your eternal growth in self awareness. Eve's apple represents the fruit of knowing, not an act of sin forbidden, but a process, to repeat again, of evolution…the awakening of self-awareness within the brain of flesh.

This chapter contains Aureal's longest and most comprehensive transmission concerning the "cloning"(a quantum leap in the creation of man): by whom, how, and its purpose. It explains what went wrong concerning the Biblical "fall of man into the pit of darkness." Aureal describes man's long journey home from darkness into the Light of self awareness. This story could, and has been told in other ways, but the message remains the same. The use of the word *man* is generic. To change it to human or mankind destroys the cadence of the transmission.

How were we created? The Hebrew translation of the creation story tells that the Elohim (plural for gods) said, "Let us make an Adam (meaning first man) in our image and after our likeness." The purpose was to speed up the process of evolution. Many theories exist concerning man's beginning. The ancient astronauts' mating with primitive woman is the most popular concept of modern writers. Aureal tells a different story. We were cloned. But how?

∞

I listen with eager anticipation as Aureal tells the story of man's beginning in Eden's Garden.

Aureal holds his left hand in an arc, much as your hand might be if you were holding a ball. He flicks his right thumb with middle finger repeatedly into the arc. Guessing games!, I thought watching the dynamic action of Aureal's pantomime. Next day, He repeats the procedure. Still I do not comprehend. Third day, this strange demonstration continues with no verbal commentary. Thinking He would wear his thumb and middle finger to a stub, I continue watching this bizarre behavior, intently seeking the message it bears.

"Dumb channel!" I cry in frustration. "I don't understand what you are telling me, Aureal!" Still He offers no explanation.

From past experience with this method of Aureal's teaching, I knew the revelation was profound. The understanding would not come easily. Through intense desire, I would earn its knowing.

As I continue to watch, a flash of light sent forth from Aureal's "flicking" finger ignited or united with something in His cupped hand. This light, now held securely in His left hand, reflected from a mirror in the palm of that hand. But what is He telling me?

Puzzled, I consulted a knowledgeable friend with whom I had discussed many of Aureal's bizarre teachings. Immediately she recognized its symbolism.

"The left hand represents the womb of woman," she enlightened. "He is telling you that it is the Light of His being. It is His energy pattern which He projects into the womb of the native woman, (who may have been Neanderthal) to create the 'cloning' process."

"You have already told me this," my friend continued with enlightened excitement. "It is a virgin birth. It is Aureal's symbolic way of explaining the asexual duplication of Himself."

Of course, Aureal had previously introduced me to the process of projecting the Light or "frequency pattern" of the Higher Being into the womb of earth mother, Mary, to create the virgin birth of Jesus, described in the preceding chapter. But the mirror? What is the purpose of the mirror within the womb?

Aureal began his explanation.

The mirror is a symbol. It represents the reflective quality of a mind that was not present in the hominids of Earth before our coming. Our purpose in Eden's Garden was to create a quantum leap in the evolutionary process of humanity. It was our intent to develop a mind within our children which was lacking in the structure of existing Earth creatures.

It is the birth of your conscious mind we came to create, nurture and evolve. This "child," the mind of self awareness of the greater mind, was to have mirrored or reflected the wisdom of our higher mind. According to the plan, you would gradually grow into the light of our, your parent's, nature. If the plan had gone according to design, you would have never known disease or death since, in this realm of Light, such negative complexes could not exist."

Earth, at that time of your beginning, was in a higher dimension than exists for Earth at this time of your living. In the beginning, Earth was not as she is now. She was of a much higher order of eternal peace, tranquillity and beauty. It was a perfect setting for the raising of our children, who are souls of a more highly evolved nature, placed in "suits of flesh" according to the plan of growth.

Upon your plane, the baby requires much loving care, as connecting sense receptors grow and develop to their respective centers in the brain. This is a process that requires only a few short years within the nursery of your home, until maturity is reached and this child acquires self knowing. But remember, as you are my child in soul, the development within this cellular structure, the evolvement of man incarnate, has taken a millennia of time.

To develop your nervous system as the thoroughfare of sense perception is a slow process. Too fast a pace would destroy the sensitive network thus developed, and it could also burn out your storehouse in the brain

The brain is the most precious of all your incarnate possessions. It is here you store your knowing which is the collection of each and every experience you have along your path of life incarnate. The brain is like a suitcase of acquired perceptions. It is a computer, feeding back as you require this knowledge. The brain is also like a mirror, reflecting the light of your greater knowing, which is the wisdoms you receive from the Sea of Mind about you.

To become Self aware is the evolutionary purpose of our plan. To understand this process, take a funnel, an imaginary funnel will do. Place a small, a very small, cap upon its tube end. This small cap is a visual symbol of your conscious mind, your "mind of flesh." This very small cap, representing your conscious mind, contains all the memory of your evolvement through the years within your current life.

Refer to Diagram I, page 60.

The bowl, or funnel end, represents the infinite sea of cosmic Mind. It symbolizes the Light that surrounds you, the atmosphere in which you live. The narrow tube represents your thoroughfare of sense perception from this one Mind of all knowing to your conscious mind within the dark, but protective, confines of the brain. It represents your nervous system, which is like a hollow tube or tunnel of elastic nature.

It is the purpose of this elastic tube, your nervous system, to progressively expand. Carefully and protectively, it is monitored by your energy chakras, your glands, whose system progressively opens or expands allowing more Light, or enlightenments, from the "funnel's" cosmic Sea of Mind to enter, then to travel this thoroughfare to the otherwise dark confines within the brain.

(It is a known fact that we, at any time, are aware of less than one billionth of all the stimuli surrounding us.)

This is the evolution of mankind. Take another look at that small cap upon the funnel's end that you can barely see. This symbolizes your mind of flesh, the conscious mind, within the brain. I emphasize this fact.

The evolution of mankind is the development of this, the conscious mind, in a continuous expansion of awareness into the cosmic Light of truth, for MIND is all there is. The mind you use is in common with all else. Enlightenments are absorbed into your awareness according to your desire for growth. The light from the Mind-Sea about you enters the nerve centers of the flesh, traveling to the darkened corridors within the brain, thus filling this receptacle with light, enLIGHTenment. To absorb into your conscious mind the Light from the Greater Mind that surrounds and nourishes you with enlightenments is the purpose and nature of your being. But remember, this is a slow process of evolution, according to your ability to receive.

In Chapters Three and Four, we explored the tunnel thoroughfare, which is the nervous system as it applies to the vehicle of transcendence in the death experience. The

Central nervous system is the conveyance for "moving" from one realm or plane of consciousness to another. It is also the tunnel, or warp in space/time, through which I was taken by Aureal from our plane of the physical to Aureal's dimension of increased frequency.

In this beginning of your sojourn on earth, we were with you. Actually, we still walk with you, guiding and protecting. It is only that you do not perceive our nearness as, in your darkened world, you do not see our realm of Light that surrounds you now as it always has.

∞

I listen eagerly as Aureal tells the story of Eden's Garden:

For thousands of years all went well within this nursery of man, as you continued to develop and flourish.

Again Aureal held up his cupped left hand with the mirror. As He slowly began to open the hand, the light of His plane reflected by the mirror became progressively brighter representing our conscious mind's growth in enlightenment. Reflecting the light from the cosmic sea of mind, we were growing in the likeness of our parents...the "gods"...according to their plan.

Subtly, at first, however, a strain of negative complexes crept into this beautiful paradise: unrest, jealousy, greed, fear, anger. They spread at first by one, then they grew like the plague throughout the land. In this beginning of your sojourn on earth, we were with you. We did walk hand and hand with you, guiding your steps along Our path of life. It was our intent that you would become like us, your parents, from the higher plane of light.

Until this time you knew no illness, no disease, no death, for this was the plan.

"What happened in Eden's Garden?" I asked Aureal. "Did something alter the original plan?"

Yes, He sadly replied. It took a turn not intended. As turbulence struck, the planet began to rock unsteadily upon it's axis. This negative vibration was new to planet Earth, who rumbled her protests in the form of earthquakes and shed her tears of sorrow, (the flood of Noah) until all but the seeds of man vanished from her face.

In time, Earth, in her struggle to maintain her equilibrium in the higher realm of life, was pulled onto a rotating magnetic artery.

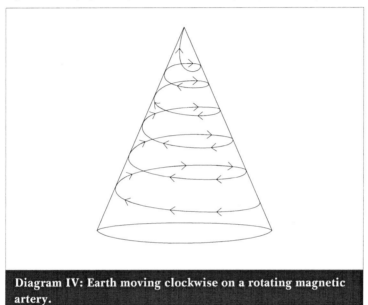

Diagram IV: Earth moving clockwise on a rotating magnetic artery.

This spiraling highway in space took her from the comfortable cosmic sea of infinite light, of a higher order, into a cavernous environment of comparative darkness (our current universe) with the sun and the moon for companions. Here Earth came under a new law. You call it gravitation, I refer to it as magnetic. It is a lower energy pattern of the more gross material realm you call the third dimension. From this literal Pit of darkness[1] it would take millenniums of time for earth and all on her surface to rise again to that point of structural perfection, the refined nature she once knew so well. The journey would be long

---

1 The black hole we will discuss in Chapter 14.

and the way along the spiraling arm would be precise in Earth's return to her home in the beautiful, cosmic sea of light.

It is important to understand what actually happened. The precipitating cause was a lowering of environmental frequency issued forth from the mind of man.

It is difficult, on the surface of our contemporary beliefs, to accept as fact that the negative thought of one individual is contagious enough to infest that of most others. Then as a consequence, the thought, being a negative vibration upset the equilibrium of an entire planet, causes that planet to fall or move onto a lower plane of vibrational activity. Into a different environment, manifestation, and law it fell. Aureal calls this magnetic artery on to which Earth fell the "pit of darkness." It is not another place or area in space. It is of a different frequency. So Earth did not actually fall, as Humpty Dumpty, of our childhood nursery rhyme, fell off the wall. Earth "fell" from the higher energy realm of one dimension into the lower, darker plane of our current third dimension. It was a change in frequency.

∞

This is the story as told by Aureal of our fall (referred to in Genesis, as man's fall):

In the nursery of your home, your baby dear must grow in learning of your light of knowledge under the careful, patient, protective guidance of you, its parent's loving care until such a time approaches that all physical connections are complete for this human form, your child, to receive the flow of mind unhindered—maturation, you call it—and stand as you, an adult human.

Should this period of development, in which the light of self-awareness is just beginning to shine, be disrupted by a force not given to the light of truth, but motivated by greed or ignorance, infest this

nursery of man. Into his mind, the intellect, then enters not the light
of truth, but darkness of a deflecting nature: superstition, fear, and
greed, which he, in turn, not realizing, passes on as truth.

And so, for millenniums of time, mankind has wandered somewhat
aimlessly in the wilderness of desolation, this darkened corridor of his
mind. He is shut off by his own doing from the guiding light of
truth—envy, hate, killing, and destroying; entangled by the forces of a
mind not open to the light (the mirror).

The disposition of man's mind in evolution was led into this hellish
dungeon by those sent from the plane of light to guide. The priesthood
in all its ritualistic glory, parading as emissaries of the light, followed
by the State (government), saw, within their greedy nature, the chance
to make man slave. What better way to keep man servant or in bondage than to control his evolving mind.

And so they, this mighty priesthood, gathered man from his earthly
cradle, regimenting him to do their bidding under the guise of kind and
loving parent, then demanding homage to a hateful god. In themselves,
the priests were of a higher order. They were we, your parents from the
plane of light, walking hand in hand with you, our children, at the
dawn of your beginning. It was our intent to carefully tender you
through those crucial years. But one among us chose to use you (It
was Lucifer, the enlightened one better known today as Satan, one of
the Brothers); thus the years of plague began, infiltrating your mind
with darkness. You, within your soul nature, knew the truth of light,
and should have used that strength of nature to quell this evil one. But
no, you chose too follow blindly until too late. The thoughts that filtered into your mind of flesh threw off the balance of your soul's knowing, thus shutting out the light.

The mind is the most important force. It is the only
power able to move pure energy. By man's thought,
Earth's environment was changed.

Aureal again held up his cupped left hand. Earlier, He
slowly opened this hand with its mirror reflecting a light

which increased in brilliance as we developed to receive it. Now, He slowly closed that hand, allowing only the smallest amount of light to flow through into the darkened interior. It was too dark for the mirror to reflect any but the slightest ray of light from the Higher Mind. Though this light of the higher order continued to surround and protect us, now in the dark, we could no longer see, so our minds were filled with falsehoods. If the light had been completely shut out, we could not have survived and Their plan for us would have failed.

Aureal now continues the story of Eden's Garden.

And so it was, your path found a turning not intended. The path of darkness then you tread, instead of the light of cosmic knowing, the birthright of your soul immortal. Thus into the pit of darkness you fell. Enslaved there by the choice of your own doing: to follow that one dark force...until Eden's cradle resounded with the cry...rocking earth with a force of negative nature, the likes of which she had not known before.

This evolution into a pit of darkness did not happen overnight. It took some thousand years of struggling to maintain her balance. And then earth fell into a lower dimension, changing her from the paradise of man into a barren desert. It washed her face of that great and promising civilization which flourished before your time of written history in which we, as gods you called us, walked with you, our children, hand in hand.

Now it was upon a spiraling beam, a rotating magnetic artery, the Earth fell...into this, the third dimension a lower energy field than she had known before. The reason? This was earth's only way back through evolution into that higher plane that once was hers.

In the plane of light, she pursued a calm and quiet course...floating peacefully in the cosmic sea.[2] On this artery, Earth would spin violently outward along its spiralling arm, carried by the sun, her vortex,

2 Chapter 15 explores the latest astrophysical facts and theories concerning the plane of Light.

a journey that would take many thousand years. The speed along this arm in space has not varied since the time of her transition, but the energy level, the frequency, along this arm is of an ever increasing nature. As Earth is propelled along this arm—this spiraling magnetic artery—the frequency of her nature and thus all upon her surface is in turn gradually increasing in frequency. Progressively, Earth is regaining the energy level, the Light, she once knew so well within the calm cosmic sea, and then humanity, will step upon the threshold of the cosmic light of consciousness you should have reached long before. Now a god man...standing mature, at last, in the greater level of awareness, to walk again hand in hand with us of the higher order in the light of a self aware consciousness.

Earth is no longer bound to the gravitational law of that magnetic artery which was necessary for that plane of being...a good law in itself, to hold fast the materials of earth through the strong centrifugal action of its spin. Yet for the soul incarnate on earth's surface, subjected to this vital law, the battle for survival, as an incarnate being, became an overwhelming task. You see, the problems that you suffer so in physical disease and death, the tensions tendered in your soul, are due to this. You, in coming into incarnate form, took from the earth to build the body that surrounds your cosmic soul. You, your reality, this soul in question, you understand, is of a higher order in the plane of life, light, mind and frequency. The more you infiltrate this form of the physical nature with the light of your cosmic being, the more vital of life and healthy will be that sojourn on earth. It is the struggle of light, of life, against the lower force of the gravitational field in which you come embodied with the materials belonging to this field. It is this which seeks to take it back as you strive to keep it, your cellular structure, for your own.

It takes the many lifetimes upon this lower plane of life, to gather about your cosmic nature the enlightenment sufficient to infiltrate these cells with the buoyancy of life. It is this light of the higher order that is so vital to maintain them, the cells of earth, against that eternal struggle with the forces of gravitation or the cohesive force of…no, not earth as you suppose, but of the frequency of the third dimension.

Earth, like you is a cosmic traveler, evolving into ever higher realms of being. She, earth, is your environment now, and has been many times before. Upon her surface, you are drawn magnetically as your evolution and hers are karmically interwoven. She is your environment, as the artery upon which she rides in cosmic space, is hers. Remember, the ever increasing frequency along this spiraling pathway? To it, lets add another thought. You are now well aware. Yes, everything is in this sea of mind. It is in this energy of wisdom, so brilliant beyond your comprehension and mine, we live. It is our level of awareness that makes for us our existing place, plane or dimension within this infinite sea.

And so it is that you, at any incarnation, point or time in the sequential history of earth's journey, may enter for a span of life. You enter each time into a more highly evolved arena of man's knowing. Why? No, not especially due to the cumulation of ancestral knowledge you call civilization. That is a byproduct of the truth. It is to this infinite sea of mind, we find an answer clear. In lifting ever higher in frequency we are entering the increasing field of Mind which seeks, as water seeks its level, to enter the brain of man, enlightening him with the wisdoms which parallel his ability to receive.

To summarize this thought: Energy/Mind is one infinite sea surrounding all things which are particles (including humans) in varying degrees of light- awareness of this one. The third dimension is of time-space perception. Thus along this radiating arm of increasing energy, earth journeys, lifting ever higher her own potential, until that time when she again will enter the calm cosmic sea of a higher dimension than your physical third.

Earth is an evolving environment for man to expand with her on this journey into the brighter arena of life. The mind is the evolution of man, an expanding consciousness in a cellular structure, filling his brain with enlightenment from the cosmic sea. This journey on the magnetic artery carries its passengers through increasingly higher realms of this greater Mind. Therefore man can conceive in a given lifetime only that which is available within the structural energy pattern of the cosmic sea in which his space ship, Earth, is enveloped at that time of his incarnation.

Aureal is telling us that Earth is immersed, enveloped, in an atmosphere of intelligent energy which metaphysicians call the all encompassing Cosmic Mind. Every moment Earth, on her journey in evolution, is entering a progressively increasing frequency of this Mind. Because we are Earth's passengers, increasingly more profound concepts from this Sea of Mind enter our conscious mind. As water seeks its level, so the greater Mind seeks to enter the lesser mind, our conscious mind.

And we continue to evolve.

Where am I going?

PART 4

Invisible worlds beyond time and space

Do not follow where the path may lead. Go
instead where there is no path and leave a trail.

II

Windows on
an Unseen World

As the mystic perceives, the scientist observes.

Faster than the speed of light, all things of Your material world disappear and reappear so you are not aware of this replenishing

∞

I entered the master bedroom of my home. There was nothing unusual in this procedure. I would make the bed, tidy the room and get on with the normal routine of the day. It was early. The warmth of the morning sun flooding through the large east window made this a welcome task.

But this was no ordinary morning. Upon entering the room, instead of the warm welcoming sun, I was greeted by a multitude of small coils of spiraling, rotating light, twisting and revolving about me. My familiar surroundings had disappeared.

In monotone, a disembodied male voice informed me.

This is what you were before. This is what you will be after. This is what you and all things are... ENERGY.

Frightened beyond rational behavior, I leaped onto the unmade bed and pulled the protective covers over me.

"This is ridiculous, Laura, are you losing your mind?" I thought apprehensively.

The cosmic energy vortices that spiraled, rotated and danced about me in the early morning light were like mirror images. Some rotated clockwise while others rotated counterclockwise. Or were they single vortices rapidly reversing their direction of spin? I could not tell.

Later, without warning, I was immersed in a warm ocean of energy flowing through and moving around me. My familiar surroundings again disappeared. As far as I could see this vast ocean existed. Within its calm, ceaseless waves the rotating vortices of my earlier experience rhythmically danced.

∞

There was never a warning to announce Aureal's moments of enlightenment. What could I have done to bring them about? Realizing the profound importance and deeper reality of these lessons, hallucination and imagination were ruled out. I was not in command nor in control. It was early in my "career" with Aureal and I was not then accustomed to His unusual teaching methods.

This was Aureal's introduction to the cosmic energy field that creates, surrounds, envelopes, nourishes and maintains all that is. Though we cannot see this field and usually are not aware of it, the space about us is teeming with potent primordial energy. As the ocean is to the creatures of the sea, so, this energy field is to the universe and all things within it.

The information in this chapter was not received in a short period of lesson time nor in the sequence to which it is arranged for easier reading. Sudden insights would dawn upon the horizon of my mind, like falling stars brightening the night sky, or they came as abruptly as an intrusion into an otherwise normal day. Always, however, they came from another dimension of space/time normally not visible to us on earth. So, it might be more accurate to say that, momentarily, I glimpsed another dimension of reality. My mind was accepting the realization that all things live in this primary field of energy. We are cradled in gentle waves that move through and around all material forms.

Aureal explained:

It is an ocean. It is the primordial energy field that contains all that is. From the smallest of matter to the largest of stars and galaxies…all reside within this ocean.

All energy is intelligent. This environment contains all that is in holographic form. Documented by metaphysicians and sages since the days of antiquity, it is the vast "Sea of Mind, of Intelligence." It contains all the wisdom that has ever been, or will ever be, and we, each of us are a part of the eternal wisdom.

∞

I watched the rotating spirals in action. It was important that I know of their tangible reality. Desperately I wanted to understand this "invisible" world to which unwittingly I was a spectator. Were these basic primordial entities known in antiquity'? Have they been observed and documented by others, I wondered? Perhaps…

The Chinese philosophy of Yin-Yang, whose ancient origins are obscure, states that the universe is run by a single principle: the Tao or Supreme Ultimate. This principle is divided into two opposite principles which continually seek balance. It is the law of symmetry, or Yin-Yang, whose interaction influences the destinies of all things. Yin is the feminine principle personifying the Earth and darkness. Yang, the masculine counterpart, reflects the heavens, and light. Where there is day, there is also night. Joined they represent universal complementary forces or principles that constitute all aspects of life. Heaven creates the ideas of things under Yang and earth produces their material forms under Yin. This action occurs constantly and cyclically, so that no principle dominates the other or determines the other. The physical universe is a whole which is balanced within itself.

Diagram V demonstrates the Yin-Yang principle. Where there is Yin, there is Yang. Where there is light, there also is dark.

Half of a circle mirrors the other half. Regardless of how we turn the circle, each half always mirrors the other. The angle of the circle changes, but its symmetry remains.

Physicists now believe the laws of symmetry to

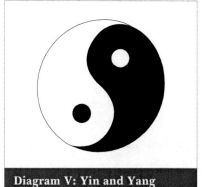

Diagram V: Yin and Yang

be the ultimate principle governing the physical world, that invisible space is a seething ferment of cosmic particles. Always created in pairs; these spinning particles flicker in and out of existence in an incredibly short time frame.

Are we considering the same concept as the ancient Yin-Yang?

With current scientific methods of investigation to provide data, physicists, formerly shunning these astrophysical eccentricities, considering space to be empty, have
begun to search for physical proof of their existence.

Einstein spent the last 30 years of his life in pursuit of
the Unified Field, the single principle by which the universe adheres. The Chinese call it the *Tao*, the Great
Ultimate.

From the perspective of Aureal's teaching, I have observed this great ocean of energy as it flows through space.
As it approaches a material object, the primordial, or basic
flow, moves counterclockwise around the object. For example, imagine a vast ocean in which material forms are scattered about on calm waves. Observe the ocean's flow. As it
nears an object, it circles around the form in a counterclockwise or retrograde direction; the creating force sus-
tains the created, holding it in form.

Upon closer observation, I realized the object was enveloped in this fluid vortex of energy. This is the auric field
that radiates from the body of all things, I thought. The
aura is the "energy envelope" that surrounds and interpenetrates the physical body, observed and documented
by mystics since antiquity. It is this dynamic energy field
that results in the halo of light about the head of Christ, angels and other exalted beings of historic lore. Today, auras
emanating from individuals have been documented
through Kirlian photography.

"What does this energy look like?" one of my students
asked.

"Streams of light," I responded. Yes, streams of self-
luminous, flowing light. Light of colors, beautiful beyond
description. How could I describe something beyond our
visual perceptions? The true nature of reality is beyond the

scope of our ordinary sensory channels. With the advent of quantum physics we, are just beginning to understand that the world extends infinitely beyond our physical limitations.

I continued to observe this counterclockwise rotation around all material forms. For some, the vortex moved faster, for others slower. Though the energy pattern encircling all material forms maintained this retrograde rotation, the speed of rotation varied according to the nature of the form. This energy vortex is the creator of the material form. The nature of the form, whether a book or human, manifests according to the speed, frequency or wavelength of rotation in and around the form. Nothing is solid mass. Everything is energy manifesting, according to its frequency pattern.

The form magnetically pulls energy to and around it in relation to the form's energy nature, just as a strong magnetic force pulls more iron filings than a weaker force. Actually this energy vortex is the form. There is an alternate or clockwise energy force simultaneously interacting with the other. The clockwise energy rotation is of Earth embodiment. The retrograde vortex is the energy body, the body of light—the source of the halo.

All things, including ourselves, are fields of energy. We live in an intelligent, responsive, energy dynamic universe that creates, nourishes, and maintains form. Physical forms are not the source of these energy fields. Rather it is the field which creates the form and not the reverse. Remember that our physical realm is the effect of and created by this subtle unseeable dimension in which we live.

William Tiller, Ph.D., one of the leading theorists in the subtle energy field, is quoted as saying, "Man appears as a being whose primary level of existence is at the non-space, non-time levels of the Universe, and who has placed himself in a space-time vehicle of consciousness for the purpose of growing in awareness of the True Self and of generating coherence in the True Self. Our perception mechanisms at the space-time vehicle level lock us into a narrowly restricted view of reality and the Self...The sensory apparatus of the space-time vehicle perceives only the 'World of Appearances' and has no knowledge of Reality."

When matter is observed at the subatomic or quantum level, it is readily apparent that the physical universe is composed of orderly patterns of frozen light.

Einstein said, "Matter is frozen light."

∞

This chapter focuses on the universal energy field, that flowing body of light /energy in which we live; how it creates and maintains its creation as it becomes an electromagnetic energy field. The frequency or speed of the energy field's rotation (the currents of energy of specific frequencies, is the underlying identity of that form.) All things are made of energy...energy of varying degrees of frequency. Whether the material form is a table or a human, it is not solid, as our perceptive senses lead us to believe. These forms are composed of energy, whose frequency or wavelength corresponds to the nature of that material form.

As Aureal put it:

This energy is intelligent. It is the basic unifying sea of mind-energy which creates by turning upon itself. The speed or frequency of this rotation determines the nature of the created form.

I became more aware of this flowing light/energy while working in the energy fields of those requesting healing or channeling. I noticed subtle colors emanating from this light/energy. It was apparent that the velocity or frequency of rotation around humans was unique to each person. It was faster around some individuals than with others. The greater the frequency of one's energy vortex, the brighter the projection of light around that individual. Energy and light are the same. Energy, Light, and the great Cosmic Mind are the same. As an individual evolves, he becomes more composed with light/energy. It is by the degree of intensity that the individual's energy field differs from that of others.

Aureal explains:

Each of you come into life with your own unique energy pattern, which is the signature of your immortality. You are this energy. You are light. You are like a magnet. You, each of you, draw from the cosmic field of energy and light (and mind) according to and in relation to that light/energy which you are. For example, a stronger magnet pulls more energy than a weaker magnet. This is only part of the greater picture. A young person normally pulls more light/energy than an older. As you progress in life, you as a magnet draw from the cosmic progressively less energy. No, this is not an immutable law of life. Only that in your society, you believe in aging and death. Do you understand that it is your belief system, your mental attitude, your thinking, that controls the amount of energy which you allow to enter your being from this greater field of energy? It is important you think on this.

As this energy applies to healing, all illness is nothing more than an obstruction to or imbalance of the free flow of this light/energy. As a spiritual healer, it is not necessary to know the name of a disease or illness. By requesting this ocean of energy to move through the patient, a request may be granted in the form of a healing.

The primordial cosmic energy/intelligence responds to one's desire, directed by the request of the mind. According to Aureal, the key or method for making things happen is this: the desire of the heart (the subconscious mind), directed by the will of the mind (conscious mind), requests the greater cosmic mind (the superconscious) to make manifest that which you desire.

This is also the method used by the Polynesian Kahunas.

∞

The flowing sea of energy is everywhere, a free energy which can be called into use by the direction of one's mind. It is so sensitive to your thought that every cell in your body responds instantly and displays an energy change within the cells. Because this energy has created the body, it, and only it, knows the precise frequency of the flow. The energy necessary to break a blockage and bring about what may appear to be a miraculous healing responds directly to the individual's basic energy pattern of perfection when obstructions are released.

The revelations of Quantum physics indicate that the influence of our thoughts on our body and our world is more potent than we realize. As Aureal reminds us:

The mind is the only power that can move pure energy.

∞

While Einstein was expanding humanity's horizons to encompass the entire universe, scientists were seeking to unearth the submicroscopic structure of matter. By prying the atom apart, they discovered a new realm of "subatomic" particles swarming around inside. In the process, they also developed the theory of quantum mechanics.

In *Parallel Universes*, Fred Alan Wolf explains the nature of this new physics, with its unorthodox ideas, from the perspective of a physicist. Among these concepts was the discovery that tiny subatomic objects could not exist independent of the observers of those objects. In the very act of observation, these tiny objects took on characteristics that could not have been present before they were observed. What one chose to examine, altered what existed! It appears that these subatomic energy particles were responding to the mental energies of the observer.

Despite the order expected by classical physics, it now appeared there was a new order in the universe, and that order depended on the human mind. This order revealed that we were in control of possibilities but not actualities. A healer, for example, can request energy to heal but cannot control the manner in which the energy will respond to that request. We could predict where and when something was likely to occur, but not where and when it would occur.

Science has discovered the reality behind that which metaphysicians and healers have known and used for thousands of years; that mankind can direct his mental powers to manifest the tangible product of his desires from this great sea of Mind /Energy/Light. Is this the method used by Jesus to materialize bread and fish to feed the multitudes as recorded in the Bible? Did He call upon the vibrational patterns to materialize these into tangible form?.

Early in my training as a healer, I laboriously attempted to use methods that I thought Aureal taught. Very quickly Aureal "brought me to my knees" when He said:

Are you so presumptuous as to think you can heal? I, of myself, cannot bring about a transformation. It is from this sea of light/energy, this great cosmic body, you seek your healing powers. As it has created you, only It knows the identity of your being. Your request is the catalyst which activates that Energy to consummate your bidding. It, and only It, knows the specific measure of power needed for the healing process. No two individuals are given like measure. Even the same individual is never treated in the same way twice, as each need is unique.

The magnetic quality of your nature, that which came with you at birth, was earned by you through eons of time's evolution on this planet and others throughout the vast universes. Yes, you are as old as the stars. Some of you have not evolved as rapidly as others, therefore do not have as great a magnetic quality. For some, the energy field is not so magnetically strong as it is for the others.

In your system of life, disease and death are the product of a diminishing energy field…a magnetic quality which progressively draws less energy into your being from the greater sea of energy about you. This, however, does not diminish the quality of your immortal energy body which continues to grow in its conquest of eternal life. As you see, we are considering two aspects of yourself.

All material things reside in this universal sea of primordial/cosmic energy. This is a free, abundant energy in existence throughout the entire universe. As water is to an ocean, primordial energy flows abundantly, enveloping all that is. All space is alive with energy. This energy is activated as it is drawn counterclockwise around, into and through material forms

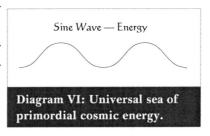

Sine Wave — Energy

Diagram VI: Universal sea of primordial cosmic energy.

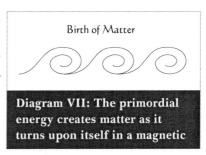

Birth of Matter

Diagram VII: The primordial energy creates matter as it turns upon itself in a magnetic

according to their magnetic nature. This counterclockwise energy is the creator of all that we know in this material world. It is the unseen force. It is that which science calls antimatter or the positron. If this counterclockwise rotation around all material forms were to stop, even for a moment, our known world would cease to exist.

Aureal calls this phenomenon electromagnetic energy. I did not know what electromagnetic energy was. I knew only its subjective nature as evaluated from my experiences in "seeing" these rotating coils of energy as they filled the space about me. In their progressive unraveling of nature's secrets, theoretical physicists have come to understand that electromagnetism is the attraction of particles with opposite electrical or magnetic charge. This accounts for the mirror image vortices spiraling in opposite directions that I have described. Electromagnetism produces light and other forms of electromagnetic radiation. Electromagnetism bundles atoms together as molecules, making it responsible for the structure of matter as we know it. The counterclockwise rotation of this primordial energy, creates material forms and continues to hold them together in form. Form is frozen energy.

Today cosmologists say that what we think of as empty space/time is actually seething with particles, which are created in pairs. John Gribbin, in his book, *Unveiling The Edge of Time,* tells us that 'empty space' contains energy which can create short-lived pairs of particles. The particles must come in pairs to ensure that there is always an electric charge balance. For example: every electron that is formed carries a negative charge and is paired with a positron carrying a positive charge. Though this sea of particles cannot be seen with our limited physical vision, physicists do not question its existence.

∞

Suddenly the kitchen in which I was preparing the family's evening meal filled with dancing coils of light. I saw only this cosmic vision, the physical reality of my kitchen having completely disappeared from my sight. Rapidly, the familiar surroundings of the room reappeared and the vortices of rotating light disappeared—only to reappear as my material world once again disappeared from sight. This alternating vision, switching rapidly from the material environment to the cosmic, continued a few more times. Aureal explained a concept of vital importance.

Like the beating of the heart, or the ticking of the clock, faster than the speed of light, all things of your material world disappear and reappear so you are not aware of this replenishing.

This is Earth's rhythmic breathing, its heartbeat. Just as you breath in energy counterclockwise from the plane of Light, and exhale clockwise Earth energy, (your physical byproducts returning to the plane of Light); so Earth "inhales" clockwise the energy pattern of our material plane and "exhales" the Light/energy of the higher plane in the opposite direction.

In my search for others who may have also observed this phenomenon, I found Gregg Braden's book *Awakening To Zero Point: The Collective Initiation,* in which he explains that Nikola Tesla, in his research of 1899-1900, found that Earth essentially functions as a massive planetary capacitor, storing and releasing electrical charges at specific intervals. These oscillations occur as a series of quick, rhythmic pulses, usually too rapid for the body to become aware. According to Braden, meditative techniques were used in ancient times to bypass the logical mind in order to consciously feel these Earth vibrations as well as sense the pulses of light. Fred Alan Wolf, in *Parallel Universes,* said that each world appears and disappears—recombining back into one world.

Our immortal body possesses a light/energy field moving in a counterclockwise direction. This is the energy rotation of the higher order of cosmic light, the energy of creation and it is the spiraling direction of the positron (thought to be antimatter).

All things disappear and reappear faster than the speed of light. One nanosecond we are in the physical world, the next our being is in the nonphysical.

In 1928, British mathematical physicist Paul Adrien Maurice Dirac developed a relativistic equation which implied that the electron must be spinning on its own axis. The mathematical properties of Dirac's equation led him to propose the existence of the positron, a unit of antimatter. The positron has the same mass as an electron but is of opposite electric charge. A collision between the two results in their mutual annihilation, with the resulting production of a burst of radiation. I question the annihilation theory as I believe it is one entity reversing its spin. The burst of radiation as the spin is reversed I have experienced as a beautiful, unearthly "ting" sound.

An experiment by Carl Anderson in 1932 confirmed the existence of the positron and thus the reality of antimatter On the basis of the mathematical description provided by Dirac, the positron has been interpreted as its antiparticle—an electron moving backwards in time (counterclockwise), exactly as Aureal had explained in his teachings. This discovery radically altered the conceptual foundations of elementary particle physics and played a key role in combining quantum theory with special relativity in the 1930's. It was then recognized that matter could be created and destroyed at will. Prior to that time, physicists had firmly adhered to the Greek notion of the immutability or the unchangeable nature of matter.

∞

These vortices of energy that had frightened me as they spiraled about me in the 1950s were now a known factor with names. Were they a single coil rotating in one direction for an instant then rapidly changing its rotation the next instant or were they two separate mirror-image entities with individual rotations (clockwise or counterclockwise) annihilating each other with a burst of radiation when colliding, as some theoretical physicists believed. The next time Aureal allowed me the vision, I looked more closely in an attempt to verify their true nature, but the movement and switch was much too fast for my detection.

"Two mutually exclusive properties of energy and matter coexist within a single electron," writes Richard Gerber, M.D., in *Vibrational Medicine*. Gerber explains that the electron is neither pure particle nor pure energy; it displays elements of both. Matter and energy are now known to be interchangeable and interconvertible, meaning that matter can be converted into energy, and theoretically it should be possible to convert energy into matter according to Einstein's famous equation, $E=mc^2$. Although this has not yet been accomplished in laboratory experiments, it has been observed and captured in the photographic records of cloud chambers in experimental nuclear facilities. The photon changes form to become two mirror-image particles, the electron and the positron. Light then, becomes matter and matter becomes energy. This seems a strange behavior but are we really seeing the interconversion of two wholly different substances or is it possible that we are observing an event more analogous to the change of state for example of water frozen back into ice?"

This is the same question I also asked, in my futile attempt to see the change in rotation of these rapidly moving vortices of energy. Was it really one entity rapidly reversing its spin, or were there two separate mirror-image entities? It was important that I know.

∞

Late in the afternoon, the light of day would soon be gone. Occupied with some long forgotten task, I heard a sound like the tinkling of cowbells in some distant meadow. Glancing upwards, I saw a rotating spiral. As it changed its spin of rotation, it created an ethereal melodic tone. Like the scene in my bedroom years before, the room now filled rapidly with these rotating dancing coils of energy.

Each change of rotation was accompanied by the tinkling or ting sound. The clue I sought lay in the "ting." There was one entity, tinging as it changed its direction of spin. No doubt the sound I heard was the physicist's "burst of radiation." The annihilation they saw was merely the rapid change from energy to particle and back again of the single cosmic entity, and not a mirror-image pair.

Early in Aureal's teachings, He emphasized the profound importance of this vortical energy phenomena. It provides many vital insights into our seen and unseen world and is as basic to our personal body as it is to the greater cosmic universe. It is the fundamental basis for all that is. All space is filled with these spiraling vortices, this electromagnetic energy that produce light and bundles atoms together into molecules to create matter. According to the ancient Chinese concept, all phenomena can be understood by using the Yin-Yang concept.

∞

Many years have passed since I was allowed to view psychically the underside of a UFO. Aureal explained the propulsion system of this space vehicle which had three cylindrical openings on its underside. This advanced propulsion system relates, I believe, to the harnessed use of the electromagnetic energy, which is universally abundant. The omnipresent energy is used through these ports to efficiently and rapidly propel the UFOs.

∞

I took a slow deep breath, though not of my own volition. It was as though I were being forced to breathe this way. I could feel the incoming air entering my lungs in a counterclockwise rotation. The exhaling breath was clockwise. For sometime thereafter I would feel this sensation of rotation with every breath I took; Counter clockwise in came the breath: clockwise out it left the lungs. Aureal intended that I understand this phenomena. The incoming breath is cosmic energy. We exhale the physical. This action accomplishes more than breathing; it also increases the rotation of the heart chakra which stimulates the vitality of the immune system. By opening the chakra, more cosmic energy enters the body, creating a healthier and happier individual.

The counterclockwise energy rotation pattern is of my plane. It is the plane of light which overlaps and interpenetrates your own. The energy of your material realm is of a clockwise rotation. As you inhale, you breathe in light/energy. Your outgoing breath is of your material plane. You are literally breathing out discarded pieces of your body. My plane has created yours and continues to maintain, nourish and love your material world. If this were not so, you would not be. With each breath, you take in the light of my plane. The breath you exhale is energy given back to my plane. There is in the energy field about you a constant interaction of the clockwise and counterclockwise energy/light particles.

Dr. George Merkl, Ph.D., referring to the energy particles as Free Energy Scrolls offered this information: "Free energy scrolls come from cosmic radiation, which bathe

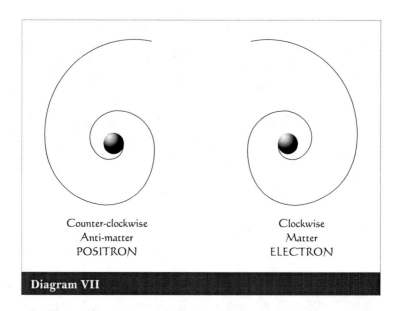

Counter-clockwise	Clockwise
Anti-matter	Matter
POSITRON	ELECTRON

Diagram VII

the earth and the universe constantly. This energy moves through all that lives. We all share it. DNA and RNA absorb these energy scrolls, which give life to everything. Free Energy Scrolls are a three dimensional energy vortex in motion. Nine hundred and eighteen pair of these scrolls braid into a photon. A photon is the basic unit of light energy. It follows that light has intelligence and everything is made from light. Some people call it cosmic consciousness, God, or the unified field."

Some physicists, including Stephen Hawking, author of *A Brief History Of Time,* believe all space is filled with mini-black holes and mini-white holes. Is this another name for the spinning energy vortices? If so, they may be "rips in the fabric of space/time" that actually provide a passage to other universes and travel through time, at least in consciousness.

Albert Einstein spent the last thirty years of his life looking for the unified field. Though he did not find it, he provided the foundation for future physicists to better understand the universe in which we live. In contemplation of observable experiments, Einstein concluded that mass and energy are interchangeable, that mass and energy are the same thing; that matter is frozen energy. He expressed this concept in his famous equation, $E=mc^2$. This is the key to nuclear power and unfortunately as the saddened Einstein came to realize, nuclear weapons.

When Albert Einstein died on April 18, 1955, he mumbled his last words in German to a night nurse who didn't understand German. However, he left the world both a scientific and a philosophical legacy which has endured.

∞

The art of all ancient peoples depict spiral motifs. Some spirals are interlocking, with an internal clockwise rotation moving out of a reverse rotation. Others show two mirror-image spirals usually with a third spiral as a triangular trio, the same formation observed on the underside of the UFO.

In all cultures of the ancient world these spiral motifs persist: in cave paintings of prehistoric man, to the pottery of native American Indians, to the gold ornaments of Peru and the frescoes adorning the walls of the 13th century BC Mycenaean palaces. Were our ancestors aware of this basic cosmic energy force that only now our physicist are comprehending?

What then are these spiraling vortices of energy?

Early in our journey together, Aureal said:

There is but one principle governing the entire universes.

That principle is...Some call it God. Some call it cosmic consciousness. Some call it the Unified Field. Some call it the Yin-Yang, but as of this writing, nobody seems to know.

12

Time Stood Still

We find ourselves in an incredibly fantastic, bizarre, sometimes bewildering world. Einstein and others have changed our seemingly understandable well-ordered universe into something totally different.

I stood at the edge of a beach...barefoot. Smoothly polished jet black stones beneath my feet, glistening in the morning sun, carpeted the area where I stood. I could feel the warm water moving around my ankles, and for a brief moment I contemplated these black potato shaped stones polished by the ocean's relentless currents. From there I walked through fine silty clay. Intrigued by the consistency of this light beige colored soil, I examined it more closely exclaiming, "This is not sand, it's clay." "That's right." my client answered quietly.

October 1992. My client, an archeologist, had just returned from a tour of ancient Mycenaean ruins near the Aegean Sea. She placed a shard of pottery in my hand asking if I could answer some questions about this ancient fragment.

Instantly I slipped into another space/time zone. Transported back to the place of the pot's origin, 4,500 years ago and to a land I have never physically been. I was no longer aware of my 20th century surroundings. This was a beach on the island of Crete. It was an ancient potter's village, now being excavated.

As I moved up the beach away from the waters edge, still intrigued by the clay nature of the soil, the sound of leaves caught my attention. Just ahead and to my left, draped over the corner of the roof of a mud brick structure, were four round dry brown leaves dancing in the gentle breeze. Curious to examine the leaves more closely, I moved towards the small square structure whose front opened to the sea.

In response to my client's question concerning how this pottery was made, a young man came from the structure's interior to provide the answer. Unlike a man of our culture, he was small, almost feminine of build, though muscular and graceful. Jet black hair fell in ringlets down his bronzed back. Bare to the waist, he wore only a loincloth. Inviting me in, he showed me his potter's wheel. The wheel head, made of flat stone, was larger than that of our modern day wheel. He then lifted this stone wheel head from its gears exposing the underside, which was housed in a depressed area of hard earth. I was profoundly intrigued by the wheel's ingenious mechanism, though primitive and awkward by today's standards. As I continued to watch, fascinated by the experience, this ancient potter dusted the loose clay dirt from his seat on the ground. He then positioned the big toe of his right foot in a leather loop at the end of a narrow wooden flange attached to the gears. The wheel revolved as he kicked the flange back and forth. Holding a paddle for my inspection he explained, "I do not make pots as you do." Then he began to paddle the revolving clay into a thin but large cylindrical shape. I relate the details to emphasize the descriptive clarity of this encounter.

How did he know I was a potter?

After answering more of my client's questions, which he seemed to have heard, the young potter escorted me further up the beach to what appeared to be three dome-shaped pottery kilns. Nearing the kilns, I observed seven beautiful women gracefully carrying loaves of bread on their head towards the...these were not pottery kilns. They were large bread ovens. The women, bare to the waist, wore wrap around ankle length skirts. Fascinated by the skirts, I described them in detail to my client.

"I planned to buy one of the skirts you have just described," she responded "Replicas of these Minoan skirts are in the village gift shop."

Taking photographs from her purse, she showed me pictures of several flat rock forms resembling those I had just described as the wheel head on which the pottery was made. "These forms were abundant throughout the village," she said. "We assumed they had something to do with the making of pottery, but we didn't know their function."

∞

Though spanning 4,500 years in consciousness in the flash of a moment is profound in itself, the meaningful communication taking place between two individuals apparently existing 4,500 years apart left me seeking an answer to the meaning of space/time. Even more astounding was this ancient potter's knowledge of our current period in time. How can this be? Did I, or rather my consciousness, slip

through a cosmic wormhole to communicate with someone living in antiquity?

The vital message here eludes our technological understanding concerning the timeless, spontaneous and effort-
less accessing of what appears to be a remote past. It has
been suggested that we cannot go back in time; that all
past events no longer exist as we think, but move into what
is called the Akashic records or perhaps an alternate
dimension.

I believe our third dimensional time-space world moves
forward on a spiral arm, immersed in the flowing sea of hyperspace which contains other dimensions. It is here that
all past events exist, still perfectly preserved, so that in
some mysterious way we can access these records of the
past.

It is my speculation that the vibrational frequency of
this ancient pottery shard, along with the archeologist's
question, registered a harmonic resonance within my being that immediately transported my consciousness to the
source for the answer. The source may no longer reside in
the past, but within the region of an eternal now, hyperspace, where all information can be accessed. Harmonic
resonance between two things or beings is like a key used
to open a door or portal to the past or future.

All things, material and non-material, vibrate with a frequency or energy pattern composed of the eternal life history of that object or being. When conditions, whatever
they may be, are in proper alignment, a resonance is set in
motion that allows the "reading" of an object, or a transition in conscious awareness to past events.

The method for channeling an object is called *psychometry*. It is based on the ability of the channel to perceive and
to interpret the vibrations surrounding the object. It is a

spontaneous reading of the information emanating from the object. It is important to understand that complete information is encoded in even a fragment of the piece, impregnated in ever molecule of the object. Even a very small piece of pottery will forever hold the complete energy pattern of the potter who made it, that of its owner and the surrounding conditions that form its life, just as every cell of your body contains the complete blueprint of your life.

∞

The ability of consciousness to transverse time barriers, spontaneously, faster than the speed of light, is such that time travel is a real possibility for all of us now. There is no need for our bodies to travel through time with the possibility of being trapped in parallel universes. There is no risk of being crushed by the gravitational forces of light- speed travel.

Why send our cumbersome physical bodies in time machines when consciousness is perceptive without the physical? Clairvoyants can observe through space and time with a clarity greater than that of their normal avenues of perception. Through telepathy, it is possible to communicate with any mind from the past, the future, or any other dimension, including our own.

I was once asked to channel a large, unusual rock unearthed from a pathway on my property. Parts of the rock had been carved by human hands to resemble a dolphin. Though crudely cut, a faceted orb resembling an eye was visible on one side of the dolphin's head. A faceted stone was cut to fit precisely in the eye socket opening.

My friend, a priest, feeling strong vibrations in an area along the path had liberated this forty pound rock from its subterranean grave asked, "What do you make of it?" I had no answer. "Channel it," my friend suggested. As I knelt to place my hands on either side of the rock, a tall figure appeared, seemingly from nowhere, to my left side. This being from another dimension informed me,

"I am the ancient one. I come in this form to impress the skeptical one [meaning Laura] with the sacred meaning of this rock. "

Startled, I examined my visitor more closely. He appeared to be full bodied, perhaps eight feet tall, wearing a long flowing, light gray robe. His long hair and equally long beard were a soft gray color. High cheek bones accentuated his aging, hollow cheeks terminating in a narrow chin.

"This is a sacred stone carved in the ancient time of Lamuria." he said. "Buried during the great upheaval of the antediluvian era, it once again surfaces to be used for a special occasion. Inherent in its structure is contained wisdom of the universe." He then vanished as suddenly as he had appeared.

Months later, a "New Age" group requested the use of my property for a festival site and the building of a large medicine wheel. The sacred rock was placed in the center of the wheel.

Two other psychics channeling the rock received much the same message. Combining our channeled information, we discovered that there were seven such stones "created" in ancient Lamuria as repositories for the DNA formula of each animal on earth at that time.

Intrigued, skeptical, and without understanding the concept in which information can be preserved in perfect form in an apparently inert substance, I asked an Indian friend to explain this strange phenomenon of placing information in a rock. It was the method used by her ancestor, she said. By dancing and chanting near a special rock, they were able to impregnate that rock vibrationally with their messages. By this method, they preserved information of their life and traditions in stone. The rock became their "book," so that later generations could "read" the vibrations and gain knowledge of their heritage preserved in this manner. One's thought is powerful when directed with purpose.

The mind is the only power that can move pure energy

Thought is composed of a meaningful frequency pattern that can impregnate or encode profound information within the desired object. Psychometry is the ability of a person to "read" the information contained within the object. The best of our paper books crumble to dust within a few generations. How long will this book last? Ancient people placed their cuneiform writings in clay or they carved meaningful images on rock to preserve their heritage for future generations. It appears our ancient ancestors used a more durable technology than our own for information storage.

The mind is capable of transcending time and space to access requested information. Just as a touch of the TV switch brings us the channel (frequency) offering the program of our choice, so somewhere in the space about us resides an infinity of information, preserved in perfect form, that is equally accessible.

Television gives us access to continual enlightenment and entertainment through the airways. Today we take this for granted and accept this remarkable technology as an integral fact of our daily living. The human mind is capable of a far superior manifestation. We are the original television. Mankind has never invented anything that has not already been expressed in nature. The human mind surpasses all man's inventions, yet the genie within us lies dormant.

∞

As a channel working with the FBI and law enforcement agencies on problem cases, I clairvoyantly "see" conditions leading to the event (usually a crime) taking place and pertinent activities following. It is as though vital information, past, present, and future, is preserved in some viable form and made available to those seeking this documentation.

Late one evening, a distraught mother phoned asking if I could locate her missing son. Triggered by her emotional request, vivid scenes flashed before me. In myopic detail I described the boy. In that moment, space/time was transcended as I watched the boy and a man leave a yacht anchored in an island harbor. Vaguely I heard the island's name. It was not familiar to me. After a few attempts, "Martinique," I said. "Yes," the mother confirmed.

"The man is his father," I said, describing a man of medium build but large in the abdominal area. "He has a hormonal disorder," I offered. She gave a name to his dysfunction. I followed the father and son as they ascended steps to a row of white cottages above the harbor. "They are no longer here," I said, apparently tapping into recent, but not current events.

Next, I was inside an old hotel looking out from its third floor window at a large fountain in the center of the main thoroughfare in Paris, France.

"They have been here recently, but are no longer here," I seemed to know.

I moved rapidly now, how or in what, I don't know. Following a road through the French countryside not far from the city, I came to a large two story white house sitting on a knoll surrounded by trees. "They are here," I said to the mother.

"The large house you describe belongs to my ex-husband's parents. Martinique is a French Island. The yacht and the cottage you described also belongs to the parents." The mother said, confirming as relevant what I related to her.

The human mind is, and probably always will be, the best time machine. Human consciousness is unfettered. It is capable of accessing an unlimited number of historical periods in time, and perhaps, vast dimensions in space. Information can come to the mind, or consciousness can go to the source. This is the heritage of mankind: to become totally aware.

∞

Briefly, I include here the highlights of an experience that has given me an invaluable insight into the early lives of both my parents. It began many years before I was born, but by some condition of mind, I was able to tune into some important events of their lives as though I were actually there with them. Unlike the Mycenaen Potter who apparently recognized my presence and communicated with me, I was an unnoticed spectator, hovering near the ceiling watching these events as they were happening.

The experience began imperceptibly at first. I was balancing my mother's aura (an energy balancing of the body used by spiritual healers) suggesting to her that she "go to her happy place." She was 90 years old and still alert in mind at this time. This was a game we played in which she silently thought of a happy time in her life while I ran my hands above her head, in the energy balancing procedure. I could feel her energy increase during these moments of happy memory.

By some law of nature, I was instantly propelled back in time, watching her seventh birthday party with a clarity and sharpness as though I were physically there. The entire event, in vivid detail, myopically moved before me. It was this event she was remembering, and the details I later described, she verified: the dress she wore, the unusual way she jumped up and down in her excitement, the number of girls at her party. Instead of tuning into her memory, however, I believe I entered her Akashic records.

I was in a large room. A high school graduation party was in full swing with young men and women eating and socializing. It was so real, I thought they might see me. Rachmaninoff's "Prelude in C-Sharp minor" silenced the socializing. Two more musical selections followed as my mother, then 18, played these three pieces for her piano recital. Clearly I heard each piece she played and was able to name them correctly and in the order they were played. I drew a picture of the pink pleated dress she wore. A narrow red ribbon holding up her long dark hair escaped as she played. I watched this ribbon float to the floor. My father (to be), mother's date for the party, was quick to rescue the ribbon.

To the right of the room's center there was a pot belly stove. Deciding to check mother's memory, I said the stove was in the room's center. She was quick to correct me. "No it wasn't. It was to the side," she emphasized.

I watched the autumn leaves fall. It was late afternoon. The party over, Dad walked Mother the short distance from school to her home. His attempted kiss was quickly rejected by my shy mother. I felt his hurt as he walked the dusty, narrow road home.

∞

The experience of entering the near or distant past or projecting ourselves into the future would be a quantum leap in the knowing of where we came from, where we are going and who we are. We could go in awareness of mind to the source, past, present, or future as it is happening. The mind, in consciousness, is capable of this transitional journey and has been making these dimensional excursions since the beginning of humankind. To travel in time and space is our innate heritage. It is an existing possibility.

Though I tell you of my experiences in spontaneously entering other time periods, I cannot of myself cause its happening. Perhaps the only difference in my experience from that of most others, is my awareness of the event. (Less than one billionth of all stimuli around you will get into your nervous system. The nervous system literally reinforces what we think exists and the rest is screened off.) Under certain conditions, this phenomena can and does manifest more easily than taking one's next breath. But for now, it presents more questions than answers.

Some researchers believe that some part of our consciousness transcends daily, without our awareness. There are individuals in dream states who are cognitively aware of transcending into conditions different from normal dream awareness. It's quite possible that during the waking state, we transcend into altered states of consciousness without consciously registering the event.

It is the ability of the mind to transcend time and space.

Time machines are seriously being considered by science to be a near reality. However, In pursuit of the necessary conditions that would make time travel a reality for all of us, we need to remember that the physical body and time machines are in no way necessary for such a journey. The human mind is not confined to time or space. It is free to go wherever it desires. It resides in every cell of the body and it exists throughout the universe. The mind is truly unfettered.

"We can't confine the mind to the brain. It has escaped," Dr. Deepak Chopra tells us in his audio taped series, *The New Physics Of Healing*.

I am convinced that we live in a great universal sea of mind. Our mind is part of this vast sea and as such, all information is constantly available to us. This is not a new concept. Great thinkers of all ages have conceived this cosmic truth.

Who knows what wondrous abilities of the human mind await our future discoveries?

Scientists are now experimenting with a means for understanding consciousness and achieving time travel that will use a computer chip modeled on human brain cells. It would interface with the human brain so we could experience information from other times and other places. Through the chip, we could communicate telepathically with any mind from the past or the future, even our own. Through the power of the computer chip, we could select destinations for virtual visits as easily as we now change channels on our television set.

∞

Once the subject of science fiction, time travel, hyperspace, black holes, white holes and wormholes are now the focus of serious scientific study. Almost anything you can imagine in science fiction is coming true today.

Now a reality, less than one hundred years ago, space travel was dismissed by scientists as outlandish speculation. In deciphering the legacy of Einstein's relativity theory, physicists have arrived at the conclusion that "rips in the fabric of space-time" may allow us to travel within the mysterious fourth dimension, identified as time. These "rips" are not only real, they may actually provide a passage to other universes and the travel backward into the past and forward into the future.

The laws of physics do not preclude traveling back into the past, although it may be a monumental task to make such concepts viable. For centuries, man has written science fiction stories about traveling to the moon. In July 1969, when Neil Armstrong took his first step on the moon's surface, science fiction became factual.

Fantasy becomes a reality and the universe becomes stranger than fiction.

Since Albert Einstein's general theory of relativity was offered to the world in 1915, many brilliant scientists have endeavored to unravel the mysteries contained within that theory. Einstein and other theoretical physicists have changed our understandable, well ordered orthodox text book universe into something so totally different, illogical and unbelievable, that nothing is as it seems.

The laws of physics state that we can only travel as fast as the speed of light, (186,000 miles per second). Super-fast space ships can't pass the light barrier, because as we gain speed we gain mass. Increased mass means an increase in the force of gravity. At the speed of light, we would be physically crushed by the gravitational forces before we could pass through the light barrier.

There are scientific loopholes, however, that possibly would allow us to travel in time. They are called worm holes. Though physicists are not sure wormholes exist they have the mathematics for them.

Worm holes are natural pathways that bypass space and time, making it possible to get from one part of the universe to another faster than the speed of light.

Stephen Hawking believes the universe consists of small black holes and small white holes. If all space is filled with particles of rotating vortices of energy (as we examined in the proceeding chapter), then perhaps the space in which we live provides passage, faster than the speed of light, from one dimension to another.

It is theorized that we move freely from one dimension to another many times during the day and night. By some fundamental law, these vortices, or worm holes that make up the fabric of space, are thoroughfares in which we, in consciousness, move freely, but because our awareness is centered in our material world, we remain oblivious of this adventure. Speculation by some authors propose that we are multidimensional beings, living in more than one dimension simultaneously. This also is Aureal's teachings in which He has allowed me the awareness of my own being living in different activities simultaneously on three different dimensions. This observation required an extreme focus of my consciousness (the forth watching the three) and I'm sure it could not have been accomplished without Aureal's help.

∞

As our knowledge expands, we come closer to the fundamental truths concerning this strange and exciting world. Science fiction yesterday, science today. Because we are curious and questioning beings by nature, constantly on the quest seeking "impossible" technological breakthroughs, the time machine could become a near future reality.

The concept of a time machine allowing us to enter both past and future dimensions, is being seriously considered by a growing number of physicists as a theoretical possibility. However if time travel is to become accessible it is imperative to consider totally new concepts embracing the true nature of time and space.

One of the most bizarre concepts is that of black holes leading into other parallel universes in which you are existing in the present stream of time, yet carrying on individual lives simultaneously in different universes. This is a difficult idea to accept as it negates the universally accepted concept of time as one simple ever-flowing stream. Psychics were the first to suggest this as a reality. Physicists now seriously consider this phenomenon as fact.

∞

What is time? Since it is not something tangible, it seems to avoid definition. Physicists call it the fourth dimension. However, Webster defines time as a continuous existence, capable of division into measurable portions comprising the past, present and future as a sequence. Time appears to be the linear succession of events, but is it?

Einstein's special theory demonstrated that as a direct consequence of the constancy of light velocity (186,281 miles per second), space and time could no longer be regarded as independent entities. One cannot exist without the other. Space-time is a single entity in which space and time are unified. The presence of gravitational fields produced by stars and other cosmic bodies causes space-time to become curved. The curvature of space-time effectively controls the motions of celestial bodies. It could be said that matter instructs space–time how to curve, and in its turn, space-time instructs matter how to move. It appears we move forward on a spiral arm of the Milky Way Galaxy.

Leading British cosmologist, Sir Fred Hoyle, contends that in the fourth-dimensional realm of space-time, the entire history of our planet is laid out as a spiral in four dimensions. He contends that everything exists, including everything that was and everything that will ever be. Past, present, and future are all contained within this fourth dimensional spiral.

∞

Several years have passed since my walk through the garden of my home took an unexpected detour into another dimension. I found myself floating up twenty-one beautiful crystalline steps leading to a large Temple of Learning: a library. It was an unearthly library like nothing one could imagine! The walls of the building were no more than two inches thick and constructed of a finely crafted, semiopaque crystalline material. The structure, some 40 feet in height, was a cathedral of exquisite beauty.

Intuitively, I knew where I was going and why. Upon entering the main vestibule of this majestic structure, I turned immediately to the right into a spacious, rectangular room in which other beings stood in quiet reverence. Aglow with a white, luminescent light that seemed to originate from within the crystal walls, the atmosphere was unlike anything on earth.

As I took my place beside the wall to my left, a rainbow colored ray of light, emanating from the wall just above my head, enveloped me. Bathing me in its light, it permeated me with the concepts contained within the light. In our libraries of earth you would obtain a book containing the desired information. Time would be required to read and understand the concepts explained within. In this Cosmic Library, learning is spontaneously acquired in the purest of knowing. Each cell of the body is permeated with the knowing. These light rays are concepts or thought forms of wisdom coded in frequency patterns of subtly colored light. This concept of light encoded information would be an evolutionary change to our worldly library system. Someday it may be.

This experience is common to all humankind. Though not from the conscious level.

Standing silently at varying distances from the wall, other beings were enveloped in their individual beam. In the middle of the room were a few radiant humanlike figures receiving their beams from the apex of the immense vaulted ceiling. The further from the wall one stood, the higher up the wall their ray of light originated. These were the more highly evolved beings receiving the finest light-color vibrations, which are wisdom of a higher order. Light emanating from the crystal wall became finer and more subtle in frequency as it ascended to the vaulted ceiling. My place against the wall with the light of a lower frequency contained concepts according to my nervous system's ability to receive.

Mind, Universal and individual, is coded in the language of Light

This Library on the cosmic plane is very real and is only a frequency away from our plane of conscious reality. The journey is of a vibrational change in the warp of space/time.

We go to this library as we sleep. During the day we may slip in consciousness into this realm unaware of its existence or of our experience there. Here we receive our learning from the infinite repository of the Cosmic Wisdom, but only in accordance with our evolutionary ability to receive. As multidimensional beings, we are constantly evolving, growing in awareness of cosmic truths.

This experience in the Temple of Learning seemed to have consumed much of my morning. However, returning to the three dimensions in full consciousness, I was still in the process of completing the same step I had begun upon entering the higher dimension. I had inadvertently stepped out of my three-dimensional world for an extended experience in another dimension, only to reenter my normal world of space-time without losing a moment of earth time.

In my early experience with Aureal, I was sometimes aware of floating in cosmic space and seeing what I called globs. As I bumped into one of these cloud-like forms, it would envelope me. I could feel its presence on my upper arms and back. Aureal explained that these were cosmic thought forms penetrating my nervous system 'thoroughfare' and traveling from there to my conscious mind. After one of these encounters I would write for hours, until I had transcribed the entire concept that had enveloped me. Like a spool of meaningful words unraveling, I wrote from its "dictation." This became one of my early methods of transcriptions or lessons from the Cosmic Mind.

One can go to the source of information as related in the Temple experience or the information can come to you. In either situation, the information is in the form of light, some call waveforms or frequencies, that by osmosis permeates the individual.

Our consciousness is capable of regularly slipping into other dimensions. It is as though a porous membrane surrounds our third dimensional world of the physical sense consciousness. Other vibrational dimensions flow through and around us, much as the ocean currents flow around sea creatures.

By an osmosis process you receive cosmic learning into your cellular structure.

Current information tells us that every cell in our body contains all the wisdom and information, of the entire universe. We are truly a Cosmic repository. What a magnanimous concept.

∞

What is time? Stephen Hawking believes that the description of the universe as having linear time with a past, present, and future is not accurate. It is from our perception of change that we have constructed the idea of time. Time is merely a concept we have accepted. Space also does not really exist except as we interpret it from our sensory perception.

In my search for answers, through current and ancient literature for the nature of time, I have found little to satisfy my inquiries. I know only that time is not what we conceive it to be. It is the mysterious fourth dimension in which we have complete freedom to move in the three dimensions of space, yet we are helplessly locked in the fourth dimension...time. Or are we? Within time, we move forward at a pace we cannot stop, speed up or slow down. From the moment of birth to our last breath at death we are relentlessly pulled along through space by time. There is no escape.

In physics we learn that time is the condition of events moving through space... neither of which exist.

To compound our dilemma in seeking the nature of time, I quote Albert Einstein as he addressed the issue.

"At what time does the train leave the station or, at what station does time leave the train?"

13

The Edge Of Infinity: The Black Hole

This cosmic phenomenon may be the key to our ascendants into the prophesied new age. It may provide the threshold to other dimensions and other universes.

∞

"Then you really believe earth is in a black hole?" I questioned the young physicist, my college professor. "Yes," he replied, "There is now good reason to believe we live in a closed Universe, a gigantic black hole."

"It is quite possible that the entire universe is, itself, a black hole," agrees Isaac Asimov. "If it is, then very likely it has always been a black hole and will always be a black hole. If that is so, we live within a black hole, and if we want to know what conditions are like in a black hole—provided it is extremely massive—we have but to look around."

At last, I was finding answers to years of intensive search for information concerning a phenomenon in space known to the world as the black hole.

∞

I was driving the California Coast Highway toward San Diego. It was a beautiful midmorning in September 1960. The sky, a clear tropical blue, offered no hint of a strange apparition that would suddenly fill the celestial space ahead as the heavens opened, illuminating a spectacular panoramic cosmic display. Like a tornado swirling in the space about me, its dark mass threatened to pull me into its rotating center where, at its other end, a faint light penetrated a narrow funnel-like opening. (This apparition is the inspiration for the cover of this book)

It will happen within the years of your life.

Aureal informed me. Though the cosmic drama lasted but a moment, it will forever remain indelibly imprinted in my memory. It was an occurrence for which I had no understanding, except as a forewarning of cosmic events that would come to pass.

Since then, I continue to receive profound information concerning this most important event that has no precedent in written history.

In time, soon, as conditions become progressively more unendurable on earth, a natural phenomenon coming from the heavens will deliver Earth and all things ready, into a new and beautiful world. It is a change or shift in Earth's polarity, a change in frequency...a transition. What you have witnessed in the heavens is a preview of the process by which you will enter the greater dimension of light. The preparation is happening now. The shift will come in the twinkling of an eye. Your sacred books speak of this ascension. You are living in that prophesied time.

Look to the heavens as they open into a bright new world, for it is promised that the day is near. The coming of the new age for earth and all upon her surface that is in readiness for this time and event,

Due to this sudden and unexpected mystical experience, I began an insatiable search for the tangible meaning of that which I had witnessed.

As I struggled to describe my vision to a friend, a high school physics instructor, I was delighted, yet without understanding of his answer. "It sounds like the black hole phenomenon," he suggested. He could tell me little more since the black hole concept had only recently come to his attention.

∞

Somewhere in space, one of the most bizarre of nature's marvels exist. Nothing in astronomy has captured the imagination more than these mind bending gravity whirlpools of the abyss. Astronomers will not stop talking about them; they've made the cover of *Time* magazine, the press loves them, and they have had a starring role in a major Walt Disney production.

Though the existence of black holes was first postulated in 1939, in 1960, the general public was not aware of this cosmic event that theoretically threatens all known physical laws and structures. I searched the libraries for black hole information but none was available. It would be another decade before *Black Holes: The End of the Universe?* by John G. Taylor came into print.

In 1973, my physicist friend, weary of my constant questions, gave me a copy of Professor Taylor's newly published book. This volume was the first of its kind to describe, in layman terms, what has been called the most destructive sensational event in the universe. The black hole is a powerful, invisible star whose menace is mind-boggling. In his book, Taylor's investigations explore the most bizarre celestial discovery yet made by man.

What is a black hole as the cosmologist perceives it? I carefully read each page of Taylor's book seeking similarities for evidence of my own psychic experience. "A black hole is a cannibal, swallowing up everything that gets in its way," Taylor states on the book's dust jacket. "Does mankind face extinction because of mysterious, invisible stars in the universe known as black holes?" he asks, as he continues to explain the bizarre nature of a black hole.

"A black hole is a massive star that has used up all its fuel and is collapsing inward at a rate equaling the speed of light...which means that no light can escape from it and it becomes invisible. There may be many such menacing holes throughout the universe. If a black hole is moving near earth, our entire planet, and all of mankind would be pulled into its dark depths with no hope of survival."

This wasn't exactly the description I had hoped for. The "black hole" I sought was a benevolent protective womb in which earth and our universe reside. It is an evolutionary thoroughfare that carries mankind from the comparative darkness of one area of cosmic being progressively toward the light into the next.

$$\infty$$

Before we pursue the real possibility that our universe resides in a black hole, let's briefly discuss the nature of this phenomenon that theoretically can be found in the cosmic space within our Universe...though it is not the ultimate black hole of my search.

The black hole is a region of the universe where gravity is so strong that nothing, not even light, can escape. It may represent the most extreme state of matter possible as it curves space and warps time. The black hole is one of the most fantastic concepts conceived by the human mind and seems to belong more to science fiction than something in the real universe. Nevertheless, Einstein's equations virtually demand that black holes exist. In our galaxy alone there may be millions of them.

Black holes might still have remained hypothetical oddities were it not for the fact that the developing science of X-ray astronomy offered the first promise of detecting black holes by the emissions from super-hot gas falling into them.

In 1970, when possible proof of a black hole's existence was found by satellite data revealing a strong X-ray source in the constellation Cygnus, known as Cygnus X-1, an epidemic of "black hole mania" ignited the imagination of the media and populace.

In the 1980s, headlines of a national publication read, "Black Hole Found." I was taking a "Black Hole" college class at the time. The news of this "earth shaking" breakthrough had been aired on radio and television the night before. Naturally, the class waited with great expectations for further information from our learned professor.

"The press seems to know more about the event than do the scientists who's mathematical calculations reveal the theoretical concept," was his only comment.

As of this writing in September 1998, twelve black holes have been seen and photographed by the Hubble space telescope. The black hole is an area invisible to the naked eye. For this reason it is known as the black hole. It is the gasses that whirl in a disk around what is called the event horizon of the black hole that is photographed. We now know that our home, the Milky Way galaxy, has a black hole at its center which is about thirty thousand light years away. It may hold the key to the origin of the world around us. It may ultimately tell us where the universe came from and how it will end or change.

The earliest speculation about black holes dates from the late eighteenth century. As early as 1798, the renown French mathematician Pierre-Simon Laplace, reasoned that there could exist stars so massive that light could not escape from their gravitational fields. The fact that Laplace predicted nearly two hundred years ago the existence of black, intensely gravitating objects in the cosmos is remarkable.

First postulated seriously in 1939, black holes are one of the greatest enigmas of modern science. Yet they are now largely accepted by cosmologists. They are stellar corpses, many times larger than our sun, that have crushed themselves into oblivion, or into another universe. The curvature of space-time becomes so severe that the doomed star separates from our universe, leaving behind a hole in the cosmos. Quite literally, the star has disappeared from the universe.

William Kaufmann, author of *Black Holes and Warped Space Time,* states that black holes may connect our universe to other universes. Intriguing suggestions once in the realm of fiction, propose that the black hole may be a passage from one universe to another. It may be a bridge or pathway into our past or future. Through it, we may enter other time periods within our own universe. We may find in it instant means of space travel. The universe itself may be disappearing into the final black hole. According to Aureal, earth is moving out of the black hole into the white hole universe called by cosmologists the Hyperspace or fifth Dimension.

Rotation is a property of a black hole. A rotating hole literally drags space and time around itself, creating a closed area. (Refer to the spiral configuration of earth's path, Diagram IV, page 64.) Rotation in the universe is fundamental. Since galaxies, stars, planets, moons, and asteroids all rotate, there is no valid reason to believe that a black hole would behave differently. The singularity or small opening of a rotating black hole is a ring.

Unlike the first concepts of the black hole as a cannibal swallowing up everything that gets in its way, it is now established that the black hole is a rotating ring. It is much like water pouring down the drain. If you watch the event, you will find an opening at the center of the swirling water much like a mouth. Here you enter the antigravity universe of hyperspace, a place where things rise or float rather than being pulled down by gravity.

The black hole can also be equated to Alice's falling through the looking glass. The frame of the glass is the black hole, the looking glass represents the opening or a "worm hole" which may represent new physical laws and possibly provide new methods for circumventing what had previously been considered absolute limitations of time and space. The black hole/wormhole may hold the key to space/time travel. With the rotating black hole, you go through the ring without encountering infinitely curved space-time. In barely four decades, the black hole concept has grown from a menacing cosmic monster to a benevolent opening into another dimension. It may be a passage from one universe to another. Through it we may enter other time periods within our own universe.

"Theoretically, by entering a rotating black hole and by carefully piloting your spacecraft, you could reemerge into our universe a billion years ago and visit the Earth before the age of dinosaurs. Or you could reemerge a billion years in the future and meet the creatures that eventually evolved from the lower life forms that today we call human beings," suggests William Kaufmann, my professor at San Diego State University.

"Whether this proves to be true, we will have to wait advances in our understanding of the cosmic frontier deep within the bizarre realm of the black hole. For now, most of us are awed and fascinated by the mere existence of black holes that have taken us to the very limits of theory and imagination." Kaufmann continues.

∞

More than ever, I sought to understand the nature of the black hole. I was certain this cosmic enigma whose essence I equated to my own mystical adventures, was the astrophysical black hole.

September 1980. As though designed especially for my purpose, a physics course entitled, "BLACK HOLES and WARPED SPACE-TIME," was offered at the local University. Propelled by an insatiable desire to understand this phenomenon, I enrolled in the first college physics class offered on the black hole. What was to have been one semester gathering material for this chapter, became almost five years of study. The black hole evolved into white holes, worm holes, hyperspace, parallel universes, wrinkles in the fabric of time, the holographic universe, time dilation, and dark matter. All of these phenomena are important to the understanding of earth's imminent shift.

Dilation is a natural function in the progressive evolution, as one moves from one dimension of life into the next. This transition from the third dimension into the higher is not a physical move from one plane of space to the next. It is an increase in energy/light. As frequency of light enters man's consciousness, he will have entered a greater awareness of light—LOVE—without physically moving.

Since cosmology is in a state of constant evolution, who knows what other dramatic, mind-stretching discoveries the most brilliant minds of this century will mathematically decipher about the origins and fate of our universe?

∞

In 1935, Albert Einstein was mathematically examining the throat or singularity of a black hole "What can we expect to find as we get progressively close to a black hole?" he wondered. "Space takes on a strange twist; it becomes increasingly curved so that a kind of bottleneck or "throat" develops (the tube end of a funnel in Diagram X, page 278). Then Einstein discovered something odd. The throat continues to narrow to a certain point, then it opens again almost as if there were a mirror image throat or, as it is called today, a wormhole, on the other end.

What is at the other end of the throat? The only answer seemed to be another universe. Einstein wondered if one could actually travel through it to this other universe. The possibility eluded him, until his calculations revealed it would take a velocity greater than that of light, and according to relativity, matter couldn't travel that fast. Einstein's calculations were, however, based on the wormhole of a non-spinning black hole.

In 1963, Roy Kerr, of the University of Texas, made the breakthrough that showed things were different for spinning or rotating black holes. Among other discoveries, the singularity or throat was actually shaped like a ring. Kerr's calculations amazed scientists. Whatever fell into the ring singularity could pass through the other end of the worm-hole. Remember, water swirling through the drain with an opening in its center. What is it like at the other end? Clearly it can't be another black hole since black holes only pull matter in. A white hole, is in effect a black hole reversed. Matter pours out of it. Astronomers call it a "white hole." In many respects it is more exotic than a black hole. So little is known of white holes they must still be considered entirely in the realm of speculation although they exist mathematically.

∞

As I stood on the threshold, with the dark universe behind me, a wave of light moved horizontally out from where I stood. Like a giant tongue. it turned back upon itself, swallowing me in its warm radiating light. There was no more darkness. I was now in another dimension. Without moving, I had entered the plane of light, the white hole or hyperspace (Diagram X, page 278).

Observe this diagram with two funnels end to end. One represents earth moving out of the black hole universe through the narrow "throat" or tube end of the funnel into the narrow end of the white hole. This next universe is not a mirror image, but like a fountain of water, it flows outward and upward spilling back upon the dark universe, overlapping and interpenetrating, filling all space with light.

This describes Earth's cosmic voyage that will culminate very soon as we move gradually, almost imperceptibly into the greater light or as the greater light moves over us. Either perception is correct. Just as the individual in a near death experience is drawn through a tunnel toward the light, Earth is moving into the light. There is no other way.

Time pulls us relentlessly through space into ever increasing light. We are changing dimensions as we increase in frequency, in light. All realms are here simultaneously overlapping each other in different dimensions. The only difference between the different dimensional worlds is their frequency. The television channels with their programs separated by frequency is an example. Or, the notes of a musical scale representing increasing frequency is another illustration. We are moving out of the third dimensional world into the next...the Plane of Light.

∞

Gravity slows time down. Einstein's theory of general relativity predicts that more intense gravity causes time to slow down. Time stops completely at the throat between the black hole and the white hole. Inside this area we find that the directions of space and time become interchanged. The shift in electromagnetic poles takes place at this point.

On earth you have complete freedom to move in any of the three space directions: left-right, forward-back and up-down. But whether you like it or not, you are dragged along through the time direction from the cradle to the grave. Whatever you gain in freedom with time, you lose in freedom with one of the directions of space. You find that you are hopelessly dragged along the space direction, straight into the throat. As you are pulled rapidly toward that point of change, it is unlikely you will even notice it—in a blink of an eye you'll be pulled into it. It takes less than a second to pass through the throat or bridge separating the two dimensions.

The Bible tells us "...it will happen in the twinkling of an eye." This is an awesome description of our impending ascension into the new age, where the rotation of energy in the black hole of our physical existence has been clockwise. Now, the polarity changes to counterclockwise.

Earlier we discussed the predictions of other channels concerning this shift. J. Z. Knight's, Ramtha said, "Earth will soon change poles. No, she will not go flip-flop. It will be an electromagnetic change in frequency from a negative polarity of darkness to the positive, light."

In *Bringers of the Dawn: Teachings from the Pleiadians*, Barbara Marciniak writes that the members of the family of Light, (or as Aureal says, children of Light) are creating a new Earth that is going to be free. Not all will wish to be free. They will have the earth of their creation as well, so there will be a splitting and a time of separation. In her second book, *Earth: Pleiadian Keys to the Living Library* this spectacular event is called the "great shift."

The following was channeled from Aureal in the early 1960's.

There are those who think the end of the world is coming and for them it will. There are those who believe the new age for mankind is about to arrive and for them it will also be.

On earth now, there are the many voices proclaiming in their individual way, this approaching event.

Sacred books, myths, legends, and traditions of all peoples of the world, contain prophecies of an "event" that will come to pass signaling the "end time" or the entry into the "new age," at the dawn of the new millennium. That time is now. The transition occurs as earth moves through the bridge (wormhole) into harmonic resonance with the "Light," (the white hole). It is not only a physical movement, but one of vibrational frequency as well.

Earth and all upon her surface have been lifting or increasing in frequency continually along Earth's journey on the spiral arm. When that "specific frequency" is reached, we enter the next realm... the plane of Light.

When will this occur? Though we are very close to the transition, no one knows the precise moment, not even Aureal. It may depend on conditions that we, the Children of Earth, bring into being by our awakening into awareness of who and what we really are: the Children of Light. While the light of this awakening grows more brightly and with greater intensity with each passing moment, ultimately we will reach a critical mass in consciousness that triggers the harmonic resonance allowing Earth's transition into the "New Age."

$$\infty$$

At the time of Professor Taylor's writing, physicists believed a black hole in space was ominous, that it would spell doom for anything nearing its vacuum-like area. Earth, they feared, was truly threatened by this "cannibal" in space. The black hole not only put the scientific world in turmoil, it also challenged many of man's basic ideas about his surroundings and his place in them.

Theoretical physicists are rapidly discovering the secrets of the cosmos, and its strange counterparts, so that scientific information is continually accumulating. As their understanding of the black hole dynamics progressed at an astonishing rate, its nature became more "benevolent."

Within this decade, progressively greater understanding of the cosmic phenomenon has indicated the black hole may not be so destructive after all. Many scientists now believe our universe is a gigantic black hole. At last, theoretically the black hole of Aureal's story has been found.

Each individual Universe must be closed, in the same sense that a black hole is closed with its own space-time bent completely around itself. So on this picture our own universe must be closed. Physicist John Gribbin, in his book, *Unveiling the Edge of Time,* explains that the idea of an entire universe residing within a black hole may seem bizarre at first, especially if you are thinking of black holes as super dense, compact objects. But the kind of super massive black hole thought to lurk at the heart of a quasar can be made out of material scarcely more dense than ordinary water. The bigger the black hole, the lower the density you need to close off space-time around a collection of matter.

The calculation shows that to make the entire universe closed in this way, you need the equivalent of just three hydrogen atoms in every cubic meter of space. This dark 90% of the universe is known as cold dark matter, and unlike stars and galaxies it may be distributed more or less uniformly throughout our familiar material universe Is it really dark or is it a light so bright we cannot see it? Is it the next dimension to which we are going?

My plane of light overlaps and interpenetrates your own. You cannot see it, as your nervous system is not yet developed to perceive it.

"If you wish to know what it is like inside a black hole, look around you," writes Carl Sagan in his book, *Cosmos.* "If the Cosmos is closed and light cannot escape from it, then it may be perfectly correct to describe the universe as a black hole."

Stephen Hawking, the English physicist, and the most brilliant mind of our century, who has created a revolution in our understanding of black holes suggests that there may be super massive black holes. The universe could be a natural black hole produced in the conditions of extreme temperature and pressure following the big bang explosion which is believed to have marked the origin of the universe.

Hawking also believes that black holes—and white holes—can be as small as a subatomic particle. The vortices don't need to be galactic in size. The space in which we live may be densely filled with very small black holes and white holes through which our consciousness may travel to other realities constantly throughout our day and night. This concept was developed in chapter twelve.

Looking to the quantum theory for large black holes, we find they have a surface temperature extremely close to zero. As we go to increasingly smaller black holes, temperatures increase. The tidal forces that would be sufficient to kill if one were to fall into the medium size black hole is negligible at the event horizon of a black hole with a billion times the mass of our sun.

∞

It has been a long journey, but at last I am finding scientific evidence of Aureal's important message that we really do reside in a black hole universe or, as He calls it, the "Pit of Darkness."

Black holes provide the key to understanding both the ultimate fate of the Universe and the origins of space and time. Today, we are facing a revolution in our thinking about the physical universe. Since the discoveries of new physics, the existence of universes that coexist side by side with our own has gone well beyond speculation. That other universes exist in some mysterious manner next to ours, or overlapping ours is one of the latest concepts expounded by physicists. Without the existence of these other worlds there would be gaps of knowledge brought to light by the discoveries of the new physics which could not be solved by our previous thinking. Physicists have recently determined that possibly eleven universes exist residing like bubbles next to each other.

Aureal informs us that there are universes upon universes, each overlapping one another in different dimensions. Because they are of a different frequency than our own, we are not aware of them. He insists:

Universes nestle together, not like bubbles but in the configuration of a double honeycomb.

This configuration is called a dodecahedron, one of the five perfect Pythagorean solids.

**Diagram IX:
The Dodecahedron**

Though astronomy predates the dawn of recorded history, what we have learned about the universe in the past few decades, is more than all the knowledge accumulated over the preceding thousands of years. And what we are currently learning about the universe is forcing our ideas of the cosmos to undergo radical changes in response to these revelations. Truly we live in one of the most exciting times of recorded history. The star-studded night sky is undoubtedly one of the most awe-inspiring phenomena in the world about us. It is little wonder that the study of astronomy is one of the most ancient endeavors of the human mind. As evidenced from ancient man-made structures still existing, the builders of these wonders possessed a wisdom of the cosmos that, in many respects, escapes our modern knowing. There is a forgotten history that only now we are again regaining.

"The black hole will certainly cause a radical change in the understanding of many concepts so long cherished by man: immortality, reincarnation, dialectic space, time, mind, the Universe itself." Professor Taylor concludes.

"In total, the black hole requires a complete rethinking of our attitude to life. Man is at one with the black-hole Universe."

14

Infinity, The Fifth Dimension, And Beyond: The White Hole

August 28, 1980. The psychic experience.

I stood in the narrow, clockwise–rotating end of a dark tunnel, looking outward into an unearthly brilliant white light. Aureal reassured me.

Earth is preparing to transcend the universe of darkness to enter her destination, the universe of light (the white hole).

The story is better told directly from the documentation at the time of this profound learning experience.

I stand in the narrow end of a funnel-shaped area of comparative darkness. It is like a threshold where I stand. Behind me it is dark, in front is light, like two rooms with a doorway between. One room is dark, the other room is bright with light. The light is so unearthly beautiful, I try to describe its iridescent rainbow-like beauty, but words do not come.

My thoughts focus on the movement within this darkened realm. Though I stand upright without moving, (I learned from Aureal that cosmic energy rotates counterclockwise) I questioned this clockwise movement.

Aureal answered my unspoken thought.

You are still in the third dimensional earth. It is the energy pattern of earth, the physical, to move clockwise.

August 29. The following morning, I awakened in the same area as that of yesterday's mystical experience. I am at the very threshold separating the dark region from that of light. An amazing contrast of dark and light confronts me. Incredibly beautiful white light is streaming horizontally outward from the wall on either side of the area where I stand. It is as though the light originates from the dark cavernous area behind me. The wall that separates the two contrasting areas is but a thin membrane, a curtain. I do not understand. Aureal offers no explanation.

August 30. The third morning, as I awakened, I am standing in the same spot as yesterday and the morning before. I have not moved. I do not move, yet a phenomenal experience is occurring: Light, coming from the dark area behind me moves past me as though I am the pivot point for its fan-like configuration. Streaming outward a short distance, the light then turns back upon itself, coming toward me, then past me from my position in the narrow threshold. Like an enormous wave of light, reaching its outermost limits, it folds back upon itself, engulfing me completely in an infinite expanse of light. The darkened region where I have been is no more. Without moving, my world of darkness has completely disappeared. The light now flows around me in a counterclockwise direction. This is a change in frequency from darkness into light and not a move in space.

Is this astrophysical shift for earth the same dynamics as the death experience and also my journey through the tunnel to Aureal's plane? I wondered.

Reviewing my notes concerning the tunnel experience, a familiar pattern emerged. In the "tunnel" (described in Chapters Three and Four) my central nervous system (the tunnel) expanded to allow a gradual increase of light/frequency so that I could "move" comfortably between our dark plane of the physical and that of Aureal's plane of white light.

Too fast a journey into the light of a higher frequency would burn out the cells of flesh.

The light at the other side of the tunnel had progressively brightened. I thought I had moved toward the light. In retrospect, however, I realized, I had not moved. It was the tunnel's fanning out at its furthermost end, allowing the gradual flow of light to fill my darkened space, that gave me the sensation of moving through the tunnel. It was the same experience!

In Chapter Five, we explored the similarity of the sleep dynamics to that of death. Sleep has been called the little death we experience each night as we slip from our physical realm into the higher plane of reality. Again the experience is the same.

Aureal likens the experience of the astrophysical black hole to the birth of a baby. Earth and its precious cargo of beings develop in the protective womb of its cosmic mother until gestation is terminated by its expulsion through the birth canal, (the singularity or bridge) into the next dimension of light.

Or to paraphrase, Mother Earth's precious cargo develops inside the womb of the cosmic black hole until it is ready for the next stage in evolution.

∞

While examining the throat, that narrow opening of the black hole, Albert Einstein discovered something odd; the throat continues to narrow to a certain point, then it opens again almost as if there were a mirror-image throat on the other end. "What is it like at the other end?" he wondered. Was the threshold, on which I stood, the throat of Einstein's discovery?

These last chapters required an intensive and exciting search for published data based upon the latest discoveries of quantum physics in order to coordinate my psychic experiences with the tangible findings.

To emphasize concepts, you will find repeats of ideas expressed in earlier chapters as each concept builds upon a preceding one. They culminate in the final chapter to explain earth's transition.

∞

We have entered the threshold of the New Age. Prophesies of ancient civilizations foretold the end of time. This does not mean the end of the world or of mankind. It does mean a drastic change in the world as we know it. These prophetic signs point to this current time in history as being very near this shift.

There will be a shift of earth's magnet poles.

There will be a splitting of earth and a time of separation.

It doesn't matter what we call this unprecedented event we face; it is a continuing sequence of scientifically explained events that began with the legendary Fall of Man in the Garden of Eden.

Modern science conceives ideas never heard of before. A look into the world of modern physics is as sensational as that of science fiction. In many ways, these ideas are more awesome than those of science fiction. They push back the veil shrouding our ancestral past and open the celestial door into our future.

It is from a handful of theoretical physicists and their mathematical equations that a majority of startling, fascinating scientific ideas originate. The nature of black holes and white holes are vaguely perceived today; yet less than fifty years ago, they did not even exist in the minds of man. Today, however, they present science with a dilemma that is unparalleled.

Bringing together what we have learned in past chapters from physicists, and what I have shared from my psychic experiences, I offer a picture of our journey and destiny on space ship earth, as it moves on its projected course through the cosmic sea.

The tunnel of our black hole is the passage from one dimension of reality into another reality.

The singularity, or throat of the cosmic black hole, is the greatest challenge that physical science has had to face. Physicists are examining this area as a possible thoroughfare for space/time travel, not realizing that what they see before them is a very real journey that we are now undertaking.

$$\infty$$

What is the white hole?

Put two funnels together at their narrowest ends.

This represents the tunnel connecting two separate dimensions of reality. One dimension is dark; the other is a higher dimension, which physicists call "the fifth dimension." This is not, however, a mirror image of the dark

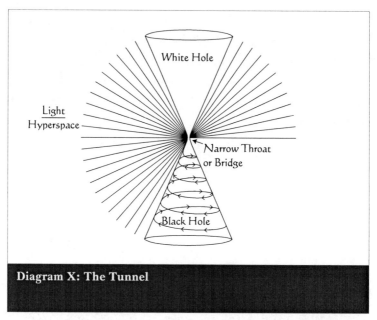

Diagram X: The Tunnel

one. It is of infinite, unbounded light, which surrounds and interpenetrates the closed darkened "funnel," so that our third dimensional world is like a capsule on a definite journey, moving through hyperspace.

The incredibly large black hole, that physicists believe forms our universe, pulls matter in from one dimension, then, on a one way journey or "point of no return," rotates it around on the cosmic conveyor belt, the spiral "highway in space" within the black hole womb. At a steady pace we, the cosmic passengers, are propelled through space/time toward a progressively increasing light—the white hole universe. Meanwhile, our evolution in awareness of all things increase with the increasing intensities of light.

Recent breakthroughs in physics have made possible an unprecedented expansion in understanding, concerning the nature of our universe. We are at the threshold of a new world which can no longer be explained by the traditional Newtonian physics. Physicists are suggesting that there are other universes. They exist in some mysterious manner, side-by-side with our own and within our techno-logically extended senses; they must interconnect in some way with our own. They may in some manner occupy the same space as our own universe.

∞

Thanksgiving morning, 1980. I awakened to the new day, bringing with it a small segment of a greater knowing. In this condition of intense awareness, I was looking at the honeycomb structure of a beehive; not in the material sense we call reality, but in a very real sense of the higher consciousness. I was becoming aware of another great truth. I had moved in consciousness, from the sleep state some call dreams, bringing part of my nocturnal lesson with me.

The universe is put together like a double honeycomb. It has twelve doorways.

That a honeycomb is six-sided, I knew; but what con-figuration was a twelve sided form? I asked my engineer husband.

"A dodecahedron," he quickly replied.

Calling the reference desk at the library, I asked for in-formation concerning the dodecahedron. "A dodeca… *what?*" The librarian replied.

Realizing I would not get an answer here, I turned to Carl Sagan's book, *Cosmos,* in which I found a picture of the five perfect solids of Pythagoras and Plato. Sitting atop the cube (representing earth), is the dodecahedron!

See Diagram IX, page 270.

The dodecahedron was mystically associated by the Py-thagoreans with the heavens. Were these ancient philoso-phers aware of a cosmic truth long forgotten? Have they left any writings on the subject? I have found little to augment the above information.

According to Aureal, our universe is only one of an infinite number of universes, all economically nestled together in a "double honeycomb" configuration: the dodecahedron.

There are twelve doorways in the universe

There is a doorway or opening at each junction of the twelve sides. Our earth travels from point A, the doorway of one universe, in an arc. Aureal bent his arm slightly at the elbow to emphasize the path of earth on its rotating cosmic journey to point B—its destination through another doorway leading to adjacent universes.

Always onward; always evolving on this cosmic journey. It is a continuous flow of energy from one universe into the next through a narrow opening.

This narrow opening is called the singularity, or Einstein's "throat." Some physicists refer to this junction between two separate realities as a "wormhole."

In my fathers house there are many mansions [universes] put together like a double honeycomb [a dodecahedron.]

Where is this mysterious white hole universe?

Perceptions brought to light with the discoveries of the new physics could not be solved by previous thinking without the existence of other universes.

There is growing acceptance among physicists, including several Nobel Laureates, that our universe may actually exist in higher-dimensional space, a hyperspace. Previously thought to be an empty void, except for scattered celestial gas, dust and stars — space seems to be infiltrated with a matter that fills most of its expanse.

Physicist Fred Alan Wolf in his book, *The Spiritual Universe,* says that parallel universes may be extremely close to us, but in a higher dimension of space which physicists call hyperspace.

I live on a plane only a frequency away from yours.

∞

In the 1970s, there were indications that something was amiss in the heavens. More matter appeared to be lurking in the depths of space than was apparent. It is matter that doesn't shine, cannot be seen, but somehow has an impact upon how stars move and galaxies whirl and holds the galaxy together so it doesn't fly away. Though this exotic matter doesn't emit, absorb, or reflect light as we know it, up to 90% of the mass of a galaxy is in the form of this hidden, undetectable "missing" mass which is not luminous but has weight.

"Dark Matter," as it is called, seems to be an unseen invading stuff that is not made of normal atoms, like those we encounter on the face of the Earth. The majority of matter in the Universe, 90 percent of it or more, is absolutely and totally different from the everyday stuff that we walk on and breathe. It cannot be made of the atoms and molecules, most of us take for granted. Yet it may be the commonest substance in the Universe. We are the ones made of unusual stuff.

Why is our third dimensional world so different?

Aureal said we fell into the pit of darkness, out of which we must now rise. This is not a fall in space/time but one of frequency.

The discovery that almost 100% of our universe is made up of this substance set a chain of cosmological events in motion that is revamping our conception of the entire Universe.

Is this matter really dark, or is it the overlapping universe Aureal calls the Plane of Light? Is this the white hole we are now "entering" as our perceptive senses evolve to see it? Is it here that the proverbial Garden of Eden, birth place of man, is located?

Recall Aureal's words:

You never left Eden's Garden. It surrounds you still as it always has. You cannot see it as your perceptive senses are not yet ready.

And:

I am right here where you are. You cannot see my realm, as your nervous system is not yet developed.

∞

186,000 miles per second is the speed of light determining our perceptive universe. Our nervous system does not register frequencies of information beyond the boundaries for our physical perceptions. Clairvoyants, however, perceptibly enter worlds of light brighter than that of earth. Those experiencing clinical death tell of the unearthly white light at the end of a dark tunnel.

In my years of communicating with those who have passed on, I have clairvoyantly seen their plane as a universe that overlaps and interpenetrates our own. It is simultaneously in existence with ours, separated by frequency, not space. Upon death, the individual is automatically drawn to an area within this overlapping "hyperspace" that is in harmony with his own. Those of like, or harmonic, relationships (friends and relatives) are together on this plane. It is their home. Protagonists cannot coexist on any plane other than our earth plane. Due to the cosmic law of harmonic attraction, it can be no other way.

As we have discussed in a previous chapter, this is the home plane where we go not only in death, but each time we sleep. Time and space, as we perceive them, do not exist in hyperspace. There is no sun or moon in hyperspace. Extra light isn't needed, as hyperspace is of a white luminous light. There is no spinning in space, as we now know, in the third dimensional realm of the black hole.

∞

What is the purpose of the white hole universe?

Fred Alan Wolf says, "If we look at the 'vacuum of space' through the lens of quantum physics, we find that this vacuum is not empty at all but alive with vibrations that contain the potential for anything."

Is it the great Sea of Universal Mind we are seeing? From the pages of antiquity, seers and metaphysicians alike have described this infinite field of light/energy/mind that flows around and through all that is.

In consciousness, we are moving out of the darkened universe into a progressively brighter light. The universe we are entering is an unbounded continuation of increasing light which surrounds and interpenetrates our own world as it always has.

To assure that we understand the unprecedented phenomena that confronts us at this singular period of time, it is necessary to go over certain key points.

The black hole and the white hole can be perceived as astrophysical realities, that is something physically happening in a space/time continuumT They exist also as metaphysical truth. For example, these phenomena represent the evolution of the mind incarnate, the development of mankind from the darkened confines of the lower animal mind into the light of God man's: Cosmic Knowing.

Evolution is continually lifting the mind into increasing arenas of the infinite Light of Knowing.

Asleep in the rock.

Stirring in the plant.
Awake in animal.
Aware in man....

Aureal's next communication was not familiar to me. "I don't understand you, Aureal," I lamented.

Of course not, you are not there yet.

Evolution is ongoing and infinite. Consciousness is always expanding into brighter light.

Inner space of the mind and outer cosmic space are the same.

Humankind carries, within its DNA, the blueprint of the universe. The laws of space are known to the mind because they are of the mind.

There is a compelling similarity in the transition called death, the evolution of consciousness, and the birth of earth into the Light of a new environment. We are looking at the same governing principle for the physical transition of death through the tunnel into the white light at its other end; the metaphysical transition of consciousness from the dark confines of the brain (earth consciousness) into the light of cosmic consciousness and the astrophysical transition for earth into the Light of a New World. The law governing the cosmic is the same for all. "As above, so below."

In each of these experiences, one is moving from a dark confining space toward an ever-increasing light. The individual evolves toward the light into the next dimension hyperspace, or the fifth dimension. This is our evolution. The more the light increases in your aware center, the more profound the concepts you understand.

∞

Though the ultimate of light/mind envelops us all the time, we are aware of only that amount of light/mind which our perceptive senses in their progressive condition of evolution can receive.

Aureal explains this process of evolution:

On a dark night, you grope your way along the path ahead. You light a match to see, but dimly, the immediate area of your steps. The light of a torch or flashlight increases your ability to see more of the surrounding area of your path. A floodlight envelops you and a greater area of your path is visible. Your progress is much faster now that you can see more of your immediate environment. Then the sun lights up your world, making it increasingly more visible to your perceptive senses.

And so it is with the evolution of consciousness, nourished by the light of the greater cosmic mind. The greater the light, the more profound your understanding.

Mind is encoded in light.

Light is information. For many thousands of years, mankind has been in resonance with a lessor light/information (the black hole). We have progressively evolved into the higher frequency of Light that has enveloped us all along. Again we consider the light at the end of the tunnel in the clinical death experience. It is into this higher frequency of light (the white hole universe) that earth is moving. Until this time, death and rebirth was the only way.

Hal Lindsey said, "There will be one generation that will never die."

According to the Edgar Cayce readings, "only in the three dimensional plane does the transition from one plane to another necessitate the process called birth and death. The soul, the spirit of God in man, has been immortal from the beginning. It is not born and does not die, for souls are as corpuscles in the body of God, the Whole."

As we move into the light of the next dimension, are we going some place we have never been? Of course not! At night, as your body lies in sleep, you go to the place of Light, which is your home. To understand how this will happen from a more scientific perspective, look at Diagrams III (page 65) or X (page 278).

Earth has journeyed through the cosmic black hole in which she, our spaceship, has been relentlessly pulled through space/time to the small opening, the "throat," the stargate at the other end. Einstein mathematically perceived that the throat opened into a mirror image from the black hole into a white hole, forming a bridge between the two dimensions. Notice from the diagram that the bridge is not straight but curves outward on each side, separating the two dimensions of reality.

This bridge between the two realms, Aureal explained, also represents the legendary "rib" of Adam. At this point between the two dimensions, the bridge, the higher being of Light, Adam, breathed his "Life" into earth Mother, Eve, to conceive the creation of mankind in Eden's Garden. (This concept has been covered in a Chapter 11.)

The creation story began and was documented thousands of years before the Hebrew version in Genesis. From the ancient cuneiform texts found in Mesopotamia, the Sumerian word *TI* means both "life" and "Rib." Those who compiled Genesis, it seems, had a translation problem, or were they making a dominating male social statement? We may never know.

∞

As I emerged from my journey through the tunnel into the light of Aureal's plane, I psychically stood on this bridge, looking back over the journey that had taken me eighteen years to transit. In death, it takes but a moment. I observed that the bridge did, in fact, curve slightly outward at each end narrowing at the center. Look again at the configuration of two funnels placed tube end to end and the same form is observed.

Where was the Garden of Eden?

In the beginning of your creation earth was not then as she is now. In this higher vibrational realm of your beginning, you knew no disease, no death.

The source of our biblical stories originated at the predawn of history from a people who's ancestry, it appears, came from the heavens. Is Aureal correct in insisting that the Garden of Eden existed in a higher dimension at the time of our beginning then Earth is now?

Is there scientific proof that Earth has not always been in the third dimension? Though it has not been easy to validate some of Aureal's controversial information, this was the most difficult. I searched through archeological discoveries; the latest in geological research, I looked for some clue in Genesis, all to no avail!

If Aureal were wrong on this information concerning the beginning of mankind in a higher dimension, it would be the first of His teachings to be incorrect. I had to find the location of the biblical Garden of Eden.

For generations, man has sought his birthplace, a garden paradise in which there was no disease or death. I found supporting evidence for Aureal's story once I realized the creation story in Genesis is a watered down, abbreviated and multi-edited version of cuneiform texts discovered more than a century ago in Nineveh (modern day Iraq). The clay tablets, preserved by a fire in the library of the Assyrian king Ashurbanipal, records a creation story that in some cases parallels word for word the tale in Genesis. These texts existed thousands of years before the Old Testament was compiled; the story itself began long before the cuneiform documentation by the ancient civilization.

The Sumerians, appearing mysteriously some 6000 years ago, were the first known civilization. These ancient people had a superior technology and literature of their own. On clay tablets, they recorded their histories in which they insisted it was from "Those Who from Heaven to Earth Came," that they learned all they knew. Many of their texts exhibit a profound knowledge of our solar system. Only within the last decades of the twentieth century have our modern discoveries allowed us to glimpse a fraction of the cosmic information documented by these ancient people.

A cuneiform tablet, found in the ruins of Nippur in Mesopotamia, suggest a link between the Sumerian text and the biblical narrative of the Garden of Eden. It said: "There existed a pure and bright land that knew neither sickness nor death."

According to cuneiform texts, Eden was the home of "The Righteous/Divine Ones of the Rocketships." This information was drawn pictographically on the clay tablets as a two stage rocket whose command module could separate for landing. In later texts they were known as the "Heavenly Ones," then "The Lofty Ones," with whom human kind had Divine Encounters.

Aureal explained:

We walked hand-in-hand with you when you were new on Mother Earth.

This communication would have continued, according to plan, if we had not violated the divine design and fallen into the "pit of 'darkness."

The source of our biblical stories originated at the predawn of history from a people who's ancestry, it appears, came from the heavens.

Aureal insists that at the time of our beginning, the Garden of Eden existed in a higher, more perfect dimension than Earth is now. At that time, Earth was in the same plane as Aureal's much older and larger home planet. It is a region we cannot now see within our visual perception of the third dimension.

According to the Edgar Cayce readings, the projection of the perfect race into matter occurred in the Garden of Eden, which was not only in Iran and the Caucuses, but in five different places in the earth at the same time. Today, these lands are basically barren desert. It is difficult to conceive of this arid region ever having been a paradise on earth. Some drastic earth changes have occurred. Have dimensional changes also taken place?

That Earth is a school of evolutionary learning and not our home, has been a common theme from the beginning of our sojourn here. If this is not our home, then where is home? Obviously it is not in the darkened universe of the third dimension.

Mankind has been on a journey through darkness to reach again his birthplace within the light of "Eden," where disease, death, and rebirth are not known.

You never left Eden's Garden. The light and protection of her plane still surrounds you. It is only that in the darkness of your developing mind you cannot see her. As the light shines more brightly with each passing day, soon again you will stand side by side with us, your parents, as you did in the time of your beginning within the plane of light.

Though we think in terms of space and time, of traveling a great distance in a long period of time, in reality, the transition is very simple. Our perceptive senses through our central nervous system have developed gradually allowing progressively more awareness of the light that is

increasing about us. Without moving, we are entering another dimension; the plane of light, the 5th dimension: hyperspace, dark matter. It is known by many names.

What about the shift? We are moving from the clockwise
rotation of the third dimension into the counterclockwise
direction of the fifth dimension. The electromagnetic energies of earth are realigning. At the moment of this
switch—faster than the speed of light—Earth leaves the
black hole and enters the plane of light. This is not a movement in space/time. It is a change in frequency, a shift in
electromagnetic poles, and an evolution...a quantum
leap...in the consciousness of mankind.

∞

From the earliest cuneiform texts, the story is told of man's
fall from grace and his attempt to return home again.

Where is man's home?

15

The Journey Ahead

In man's analysis and understanding of himself, it is as
well to know from whence he came as to whether he is going.

Edgar Cayce

September 1970, 7:45 AM. Soon, I would start my day with
an important business engagement. Anxiously, I looked at
my watch. If I left the house now, I could be there five minutes early. These were my last worldly thoughts before I entered another plane of reality.

It began with a message from Aureal. As I stopped to
write His words of wisdom, I lost awareness of my earthly
dimension and, as a result, I never arrived for that important business engagement.

For the next two hours, I wrote rapidly from Aureal's
dictation. It covered more than 10 pages of profound information concerning a singular event for earth and all on
her surface. To understand the mechanics of this

impending event, I would experience some incredible psychic journeys.

It started with a boat ride down the rapids of the Colorado River. Totally unprepared for this adventure, I was one moment in my California home and the next moment precariously riding the rapids of the Colorado River. As I dropped down the rapids, alone in my small craft, I could feel the intense force of gravity pressing firmly against my body from the impact of the steep fall. For that intense, turbulent moment I was scarcely able to breathe. Then all was quiet, as I came to a sudden halt in the calm pool below.

Note: Psychic experiences are just as real, perhaps more real, to the senses of the one experiencing them as they are for one actually making this trip in the physical environment.

With barely time to ponder the rapids experience, I was in a space ship leaving earth's surface. Again, I experienced the strong force of gravity pressing firmly against my body as the vehicle increased in speed to escape earth's gravitational force. Entering outer space, released from the force of gravity, I floated in a quiet, tranquil sea.

With just enough time to register the second adventure, I was now on a sled, propelled forward at an enormous speed, as though pulled toward some unseen something. Struggling to maintain my balance on this roller coaster ride, I looked up just in time to see a wall of translucent substance blocking my path immediately ahead.

In my wild journey, I passed rapidly through this substance, not hindered by its presence. As with the first two experiences in which I moved rapidly through a strong force of gravity to arrive in a calm "sea," this ride also stopped dramatically, as I passed through the translucent curtain into a realm of brilliant white light. All three adventures contain within their nature the same sensory elements: the rapid ride through space with the pressure of gravity on the body as we experience it in the third dimension, and the sudden change from gravitational pressure to a calm floating sensation as we enter the fifth dimension.

I entered a sea of caressing liquid light, in which I calmly floated. Upon passing through the translucent curtain, there was an instantaneous change from this frantic, uncontrollable ride through darkened space, into a calm floating sea of brilliant, warm, white light. I had arrived in another world, another universe, separated from our own dimension by this thin translucent membrane. It is a wall of frequency/energy, a warp in cosmic space. It is an area or threshold that separates one universe from another.

The sled of my ride represented earth: earth traveling through this barrier of intense energy. Obviously I was neither the initiator nor was I in control of this hectic, frightening cosmic journey. It was another of Aureal's lessons. He wanted me to understand the nature of the impending event for Earth. Riding the rapids, the lift-off of a space vehicle, and the rapid down hill sled ride. All produced the same experience of extreme accelerationlike that of earth's frantic journey through space, though we don't feel it.

Passing through the thin translucent wall into the calm floating "sea" represents the higher dimension of Light—hyperspace, the fifth dimension. What purpose would this mystical experience serve, if it were not a forewarning of Earth's journey toward its predestination? This was not a dream and Aureal does not play games. For me to experience a concept psychically is one of Aureal's favorite methods of teaching.

This journey with earth, we take constantly from birth to death, without feeling the movement nor the force of gravity. Since all motion is relative to the other planetary movements, we are not aware of the cosmic journey as Earth moves constantly in orbit around our sun. The orbital speed of earth at the equator is 1,000 miles per hour as she rotates around her axis. We travel 60 thousand miles per hour around the sun in its yearly course. Simultaneously, our solar system revolves around the galaxy's nucleus at a speed of about 670,000 miles per hour, moving up and down in a dolphin-like or sine wave course. Some ride!

∞

And, so, these negative forces that would keep earth and man bondage, that caused her upheaval in times long past, will soon wash away. How? It is simple, my child, all is simple that's truth. Remember, I told you, that soon, very soon now, earth will enter the frequency LOVE, of a much higher order: A dimension where negative complexes cannot exist. And so, as earth and all things upon her enters this point of frequency in her wild journey in space, she will shoot through a curtain of high energy force. You will see it and hear it just before she approaches. It will look like falling snow, but will not be of that nature. It will sound like popping corn as it falls from the heavens. This is a high energy curtain that earth will pass through as she moves off the magnetic arm into the calm free-floating state that was hers long ago. That which has evolved in purity and trust for this time and event will remain undisturbed by this transitional move.

We have embarked upon a journey of evolutionary momentum, from which there can be no turning back. Without a map from any previous generation, we are moving forward through Earth's dramatic, sometimes catastrophic changes. The nature of this change, is a fundamental force of creation and evolution.

∞

Is there one among us who does not feel something unusual happening in our lives—to our world?

Centuries of prophecy and warnings of catastrophic change taking place within this period of history abound. The calendars of ancient peoples developed thousands of years ago, almost universally end in this current time. The Mayan calendar indicates that time, as we have always known it, ended in July 1992. Those living on earth between July 1992 and December 2012 will experience a phenomenon historically unique. It is being revealed in different ways and in a variety of languages by Native American prophecy, ancient Egyptian mystery schools, and sacred Tibetan and Chinese Orders. It is being echoed by present day prophets, channels, and seers who without knowledge of biblical prophecies or scientific predictions are saying the same things the scriptures foretell.

I believe civilizations have traveled this path before us, leaving behind their magnificent architectural structures for us to wonder about but no written record of their experience for us to follow.

Two thousand years ago, sacred literature predicted events that are being fulfilled in our time, before our very eyes. New age seers speak of the coming earth "shift," attesting to its truth. Books fill the shelves of book stores bearing the message of the "Coming," even though nothing like this has ever happened in recorded history. Some call it the end time, certain our world will soon be no more. Some call it the coming of the "New Age," others say we are "moving toward the light."

The transformation unfolding on Earth is characterized not only by cosmic events but also by dramatic changes within the earth, and reverberating within the cell structure of all creation. Few people question that Earth is moving rapidly toward an indescribable climatic event that will change Earth and all upon her surface. What is it?

Now scientists are giving us quantified facts of the event. Earth is changing in its physical dynamics. Time, is speeding up.

Ramtha, speaking through J. Z. Knight, tells us that Earth will change magnetic poles but it will not pivot on its axis or rotate in the opposite direction.

There is ample evidence that this switch in magnetic poles has occurred on a regular schedule every thousand years in earth's geological history. The geologic record indicates that the magnetic fields of Earth have shifted at least 14 times in the last 4.5 million years. It apparently is a natural phenomenon of this planet.

Scientific evidence indicates that the last geomagnetic reversal was completed just 12,400 years ago during the eleventh millennium BC. It was this millennium in which the ancient Tiahuanacan civilization in the Andes disappeared. It was during this period also, that vast numbers of large mammal species all over the world became extinct.

Scientists expect the next reversal of the earth's magnetic poles to occur around AD 2030.

The dramatic experience I related in the opening of this chapter portrays the change we are now facing as earth moves progressively through the vibrational barrier of one dimension to enter another. According to Aureal, the electrical charge for our material plane flows clockwise. It is called matter. Antimatter, the electrical charge for earth's overlapping plane, rotates counterclockwise. Two seemingly opposing poles pulse in and out of each other ceaselessly; Thus we have the electromagnetic charge of earth as discussed in Chapter 14. The clockwise direction is dominate to our physical sense orientation, though the counterclockwise is equally present. It is the Yin Yang principal of dark balanced by light. Our consciousness is opening into the light.

In 1899, Nikola Tesla discovered that Earth essentially functions as a massive planetary capacitor, storing and releasing electrical charge at specific intervals.

This last chapter examines the dynamics of this shift in Earth's polarities, both from Aureal's channeled explanation, that of other channels, and from the current scientific data now confronting us. When will it happen? From all sources of information, it is happening now.

From the perspective of science, two fundamental, yet seemingly contradictory, conditions are occurring simultaneously: The frequency of our planet is speeding up while its magnetic rotation is slowing down.

Aureal explains:

The speed along the spiraling highway in space has never changed since Earth began this journey in the biblical "fall" of man. Because Earth travels on a "cosmic conveyor belt" within a cone configuration of the black hole universe, the frequency has steadily increased as she approaches the narrowing end[3] of your journey. You feel the increasing intensity of this frequency as it radically effects your cellular structure.

The base resonant frequency or fundamental vibration of the planet is speeding up. As the vibration increases, more light and more information flood our planet. Vibration, light, and information are the same, so as the vibration/light increases, we become more aware. Yet the magnetic poles are decreasing in magnetic intensity. Data

---

3 The "Einstein throat."

indicates that the intensity of Earth's magnetic fields is now approximately 38% less than it was 2000 years ago.

An article concerning magnetic reversals, in the June, 1993 edition of Science News, states that, "The magnetic field weakens considerably when it switches direction. Since magnetics are a function of planetary rotation, a lessening in the intensity of magnetics would seem to indicate a lessening in the rate of Earth's rotation." Gregg Braden, in *Awakening to Zero Point: The Collective Initiation,* says this is precisely what is happening, that the inner and outer cores of Earth are slowing and there is an overall lessening in rotation of the planet.

Twice in 1992, and at least once in 1993, the National Bureau of Standards in Boulder Colorado reset the cesium-atomic clocks to reflect "lost time" in the day. This is necessary to remain in synch with sunlight.

Historically, Earth has pulsed at 7.8 cycles per second. This value has been so stable that global military communications have been developed relying upon this constant. At present, the oscillations are moving into increasing frequencies toward a resonant frequency that will trigger the change; that switch in poles the ancients called "the shift of the ages" that brings into being the beginning of the "New Age."

Measurements of Earth's fundamental vibration have been taken by independent sources in various parts of the country, which show conclusively that the pulsing frequency has gradually accelerated. The greatest increase began in 1987. Since 1990 the pulsing of earth has steadily increased from 7.8 to 8.6 cycles per second. Though these pulsings are too rapid for human awareness, our cells measure time by the number of pulses per second that emanates from our planet, so we sense that time is speeding up.

As a result of this increase, each cell of your body is trying to keep pace with the rhythmic "heartbeat" or reference frequency of Earth. Moving into the resonant pattern
of a higher tone, each life form, including human, attempts to manifest a new rhythm frequency. This frequency is indicative of the composite vibration of Earth at
a given point in time.

According to Gregg Braden, thirteen cycles per second
will become the new base resonant frequency. When Earth
reaches 13hz on the electromagnetic scale, this frequency
will trigger the harmonic resonance signaling the beginning of the next phase in evolution. It is the point in which
Earth's magnetic poles shift. The poles of Earth are electromagnetic frequencies that move and change. Right now,
they are changing every day. They are no longer a stable
coordinate for maps of navigation and our Atomic Clock
requires constant adjusting because we are losing time.
These are some of the facts.

Each cell of our body is constantly shifting patterns of
energy to achieve the higher harmonic resonance of our
home Earth. Our body is purifying rapidly: our cellular
structure is becoming filled with more light. We are moving rapidly now into the next phase of evolution. We are
headed toward a time of extreme change, sometimes
called the End times, where reality, as we know it is going
to shift. It is not something to be feared. In spite of today's
world appearances, the Earth will not end. We are entering a new and wonderful reality of a higher dimension. As
Earth continues to evolve, she moves into progressively
higher, finer frequencies of Light/energy carrying with her
all upon her surface who also wish to evolve.

Ancient Biblical texts tell us: "Lo, I tell you a mystery. In
these days, [referring to this current time] we shall not all

sleep. We shall all be changed in a moment, in the twin-kling of an eye."

In Revelation 20 and Matthew 25, we are told that God's Word assures us there will be one generation of be-lievers who will never know death.

The *Book Of Mormon* says; "In those days, ye shall never endure the pains of death. When I come in my glory, ye shall be changed in the twinkling of an eye from mortality to immortality. It is in your bodies that you will see your creator."

The Emerald Tablets of Thoth, the Bible of Masonic tra-dition, written 13,000 years ago, proclaim, "The form of man is in the process of changing to forms of light that are not of this world.

Aureal adds:

The change to all bodies has been gradual and subtle, lifting them from the gross condition of physical into the light of a more buoyant energy nature.

In the beginning of human evolution, the living cell was observed as a cylindrical shape, with light barely shinning through an otherwise darkened form. As we evolved, our cellular structure became filled with more light. At this time in our evolution, our cells are a globe of light encir-cled with a thin band. In the future, the band will disap-pear as we become pure light.

The transition, or the ascension in Biblical terms, is the process by which Earth's electromagnetic fields change. Not all humans will make this change into the higher fre-quency. It is their decision. We all have free will.

Aureal reminds us:

All things not pure enough to go through will vanish from sight.

Scientifically, it is known that a material form will disappear from sight if accelerated in frequency.

"Matter," to repeat Einstein1, "is frozen energy."

Was it a switch in polarities from the higher frequency counterclockwise plane of light to the lower clockwise third dimension that brought about the "fall" of mankind from Eden's Garden? If so, then Earth was in the higher dimensional plane some call hyperspace, where there would be no need for the sun or moon.

In the days of your beginning, Earth was not then as she is now. She was in a higher dimension of light where sun and moon were not necessary.

You never left Eden's Garden. It surrounds you now as it always has.

∞

We are embracing one of the most exciting periods in the history of man. "New age" channels, sometimes called mystics, speak optimistically of the wondrous joyful era just ahead. Earth and all upon her surface are going through a transition. That earth is nearing an "end time" is the central theme of the new age message. This does not mean the end of Earth or mankind. It is the heralding of a change, a quantum leap in the evolution of humanity.

In 1970, Aureal informed me:

I have much to tell you of thoughts so profound I MUST have a pure channel. It is through your entire body that my thoughts are transmitted to you. The more profound the concepts, the clearer must be my Channel. If your cellular structure is not filled with light, cleansed, you cannot receive the information of this higher frequency. Seven years I will give you to purify, then it is imperative you are ready to understand the message I bring.

Thus began my cleansing diet to give up meat and the grosser foods which kept the light from impregnating my cells. I became a vegetarian, growing most of the food that grace my table, according to Aureal's instruction.

In 1977, Aureal announced:

It is time now you must understand the nature of your earth's changes.

The cleansing of my cells was not sufficient when Aureal's higher frequency communication began, so He awakened me briefly sixteen times during the night when my mind was receptive. With each brief awakening, I documented portions of His message until it was complete. Reading the entirety of my nocturnal writing the following morning, I was amazed to find a complete transmission from Aureal with no indication of its segmented delivery. It was the concept of the dividing, split or shift of planet earth that I documented.

All things in their time divide, like the splitting of a cell. Remember, the solid appearance of your world is an illusion. All is made of energy.

In Biology, this process is called "mitosis" in which two complete mature daughter cells are created from the one mother cell, each one going to a different pole. Aureal pulled his right fist out of his left encircling hand to explain how Earth would divide. This describes the shift in poles: one part separates from the other part, leaving two whole earths. One earth attains a higher, finer frequency than the other. The other remains in comparative darkness at a lower vibration, the third dimension, as we now known it.

Aureal warned me that this change would happen in a moment so short it could not be divided.

The transition, the shift, will happen within the years of your life. It will happen so quickly, in a flash of time.

Likewise, 1 Corinthians 15:52 NASB: "In a moment, in the twinkling of an eye..."

Since this was a difficult concept to understand, I sought a more tangible explanation. I found Barbara Marciniak's 1992 reference from the Pleiadians in *Bringers Of The Dawn*, concerning this division. She explains that we are creating a new planet in which there will be a *splitting of worlds*. When this shifting occurs, not everyone will experience it in the same way. Some will go with an Earth shift of destruction because this is their choice. It may be the end of the world as they know it as they will not be in harmony with the new frequency. For others it will be a state of ecstasy as they enter the higher frequency of a more perfect world some refer to as the fifth dimension.

Those who are ready for this higher vibration will remain undisturbed by the transitional move.

As the critical threshold is reached, earth's magnetic field will decline very rapidly prior to the pole reversal and the increasing frequency (pulsing heart beat) moves us into a higher band of harmonic resonance. On this threshold, the electromagnetic poles reverse as Earth moves into resonance with the "light." We are no longer in the darkened 3rd dimensional world spinning in space on a magnetic arm. The realm of light has enveloped us. Earth did not go flip-flop, she moved out of one vibratory dimension into the next.

All things not pure enough to go through will perish from sight. They may continue with the 3rd dimensional world while those who are ready for this time and event will move into the higher dimension of light.

Ramtha tells through his channel, J. Z. Knight, that there will be a changing of earth's polarities.

Braden, in *Awakening To Zero Point,* explains that there will come a splitting of earth, a shifting of earth's polarity. We are now living in a very special time in history, in which the world we have always known is rapidly changing as we approach the close of one cycle and the birth of a new world. The drastic change manifesting upon earth at this time has been predicted and prophesied by ancient as well as modern seers. Records of many ancient people and our sacred books tell of this time. It is the birth of a New World, not the end of the world, Braden assures.

An ancient Hopi prophecy speaks of the "Twins of Heaven" One of the Twins is the "Guardian of the "North Pole" and the other Twin is the "Guardian of the South Pole." The day would come, the prophecy says, when the "Twins" will wreak chaos, havoc at these Poles. Metaphorically, this equates to the electromagnetic frequency changes that we are experiencing now.

Though the mechanics of this "shift" in polarity is expressed in different ways by the various authors describing this unprecedented event, they are unanimous in agreement that cosmically, something is happening that has not happened within our historical memory. We are moving into it now as Earth and her human cargo accelerate through evolutionary change.

Impossible? In this decade when mysticism and science are merging, our technologies have allowed us to penetrate more profoundly into the nature of the universe, prying from it secrets that find no equal in past generations.

The split or shift is a sequence of processes and events that are under way. The dynamics are simple. However, when Aureal began the explanation, it seemed inconceivable that earth could split without drastic consequences for all living things upon it. In Chapter 12, we examined the eternal cosmic dance of interlocking electro-magnetic spirals that fill all space and that physicists call the electron and positron, or matter and anti-matter, that rotate in opposite directions in a magnetic field. They may be minute vortices of black holes and white holes that fill all space.

Faster than the speed of light, all things material disappear and reappear.

Due to the constant alternating rotation of these electrons and positrons, according to Aureal's teachings, we move between the material world into "hyperspace" and back again so rapidly we are virtually unaware of the shift. We live in both worlds, but are conscious of only one; so life seems continuous until death takes us to the other. Where do we go when we die? Since it is apparent that consciousness is continuous as we pass through the portal of death, we go to our vibratory home in hyperspace...the light filled world at the end of the darkened tunnel.

The world of hyperspace, which the physicists call "dark matter," consists of 90-98% of the matter within the universe. This dimension of matter surrounds and interpenetrates our own world. Our visible universe, made up of less than 2% is like a small capsule floating in an infinite protective sea. This vast realm of "dark matter" replenishes our material world. Like a heart beat, for that minute fraction of time, we are enveloped in hyperspace, the Plane of Light. Because our consciousness is centered in the physical realm, we continue unaware that we live simultaneously in at least two dimensions.

∞

Whether in sleep, death, in expanded awareness, or the journey as earth's passengers into the plane of light, the process is the same. The underlying theme, whether it is a physical transition in death, the Metaphysical journey through the tunnel of the central nervous system to accomplish an expansion in consciousness, or the Astrophysical journey of earth through the pit of darkness into the plane of light for the evolution of the species, the nature or mechanics of the transition remains the same.

In this chapter, we have considered the "scientific hard fact" evidence of the shift. We have examined some of the ancient prophecies and scriptural references; and we have pondered current "new age" accounts. The understanding of this subject can be approached metaphysically, metaphorically, or it can be explored through the latest in scientific technology.

In Aureal's explanation, combined with that of theoretical science, we see earth's passage within the darkened cone reaching the apex of its journey. As earth continues through the narrow throat onto the "Einstein bridge," the cosmic light from the other realm becomes progressively brighter. When that specific frequency of light is reached, a "splitting" or "shift in magnetic poles" will occur.

From the top of the cone we see two spirals of energy flowing into the adjacent dimension like steam rising from a pot of hot water, one spiral is rotating counter-clockwise; the other is turning clockwise (Diagram XI, page 307). These are the eternal energies of the cosmic dance we have discussed in a previous chapter. As Earth reaches this specific threshold of frequency, part of Earth will go with the counterclockwise flow into the awareness of Light; hyperspace. All who are not yet ready for this transcendence will remain with the clockwise physical consciousness, which we now experience.

Two-thirds of those on earth at the time of this transition, will continue with the old earth, as they do not choose to change. We do have a choice, but that choice is dependent on our frequency pattern; that which we have become through our desire. One-third will make the transition into the Light. The Scriptures Book of Revelations tell us in prophesy that "...one shall stand and two shall fall. Each group of people will think the other group has perished." By increasing the vibratory rate of your cellular structure to a higher dimension, those who had been seeing you in three dimensional space can no longer detect you, though you remain in the same geographic location. Though you stay in a simultaneous range of existence, you are no longer within their range of perception. This separation is caused by a change in frequency, not space. Though we are in the transition now, the actual shift or splitting will occur "in the twinkling of an eye" exactly when that precise frequency or harmonic resonance is reached.

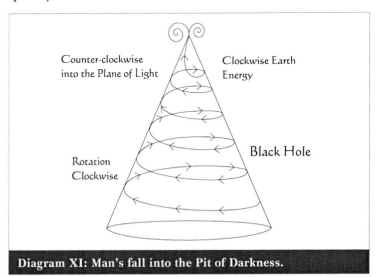

Counter-clockwise into the Plane of Light

Clockwise Earth Energy

Black Hole

Rotation Clockwise

Diagram XI: Man's fall into the Pit of Darkness.

All things and bodies which have evolved in purity and trust for this time and event will remain undisturbed by this transitional move.

Aureal equates these transitions to the gestation period of the growing baby within its mother's protective womb. When time approaches, the cervix dilates, allowing the baby to move from the dark womb (black hole) into the light of its parents' world.

To attain an expansion in mind, the individual's chakra monitoring system dilates to allow more of the fifth dimensional light (enlightenment) to enter the central nervous system. When the time approaches, the small opening known in black hole terminology as the singularity, will dilate, allowing earth to "move" out of the black hole through the narrow opening into the white hole or plane of light. "Move" is not the proper translation. It is the Light of the next realm that envelopes Earth's precious cargo thus dissipating the dark. The same law, or principle, operates on three levels: physical, metaphysical, and astrophysical. The transition is the process in which Earth's electromagnetic fields change.

∞

In *The Late Great Planet Earth*, Hal Lindsey explains that according to the gospels and the Old Testament, there will be certain people who will inherit for a time the Kingdom of God in their mortal bodies. Also, Lindsey says, in Revelation 20 and Matthew 25, God's Word tells us that there will be one generation of believers who will never know death. He also assures that those believers (those who are ready for this time and event) will be removed from the earth before the Great Tribulation—before that period of the most ghastly pestilence, bloodshed, and starvation the world has ever known. Lindsey calls this the "Rapture" or "Translation."

From outward appearances and from prophecy we are approaching that time. Edgar Cayce said, regarding his dire predictions of earth's drastic changes that the future is not fixed and we can change it. The human mind is far more powerful than we realize. Lindsey continues to explain, "that someday, a day that only God knows, Jesus Christ is coming to take away all those who believe in Him. He is coming to meet all true believers in the air (which is the higher frequency or dimension.) There will be those who will be transported into a glorious place more beautiful, more awesome, then we can possibly comprehend. When Christ comes to earth for the second time, we are told, in Matthew 25, that He will divide the believers from the unbelievers. At the time of the Rapture, all the living believers will be caught up to join Him in the clouds."

Though Lindsey interprets his material from the Fundamentalist's perspective of Biblical prophecy, Aureal explains that earth and all upon her surface who are ready for this time and event will transcend into the plane of light...into the new age...without the process of death. Death was never intended in the original plan for the evolution of man. The ongoing evolution of life is the plan for all things.

There are those who think the end of the world is coming and for them it will. There are those who believe the new age of man is about to arrive and for him it will also be.

Weaving together Biblical prophecies made thousands of years ago with the voice of present day astrologers, prophets, and seers, we know the day of Judgment must be near. According to the Christian doctrine, Christ made it emphatically clear, that no one would know the day or hour of the "second coming." However, He said nothing about the year or the month.

There are those who predict the end of the world is near. There is a depressive lack of motivation among our young people who see only a bleak future for humanity. Yet, we live in the most unusual period of history, the culmination of one age and a new and wonderful beginning in another. Despite so much destruction, hatred and war in the world, there is reason for anticipation of a bright new world of Love and optimism for the near future.

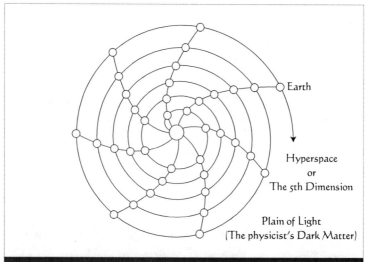

Earth

Hyperspace
or
The 5th Dimension

Plain of Light
(The physicist's Dark Matter)

Diagram XII: Earth at the end of a spiral arm of the Milky Way Galaxy, ready to move into the Plane of Light.

∞

We need to know from where we came, and after a very long journey through the "tunnel of darkness," we are finally returning home again.

As I began this chapter, I had no clear idea how Earth would change poles, divide, or split. It was unbelievable that Jesus Christ would meet all true believers in the air. It was beyond my imagination to know how part of Earth's population would be carried into the Light of a New Age, leaving those not wishing or ready for the change with the other part of earth. A preposterous, unbelievable supposition, yet the concepts from Aureal continued to build one upon the other until they culminated in the theory advanced in this chapter. It is a simple and natural switch or shift in the electromagnetic field of earth. One pole is of light, the other dark...the Yin-Yang. Every thing is a vibration, an energy that is constantly moving and flowing within a pattern of frequency that lifts us out of the darkened womb into the greater light of knowing. Call it going home to the light at the end of the tunnel, where we go as we transcend this plane in death. Call it hyperspace, as we move from the astrophysical black hole into the mysterious white hole.

Or is it an evolutionary quantum leap, as we open into the light of an expanding conscious awareness of that which has surrounded us all the time: The Love and the Light that has always been, our Garden of Eden, the birthplace of mankind on Earth? We never left, though in the darkness of mind we remained unaware.

Afterword

As I write this, news from all parts of the world is bleak with stories of earthquakes and tidal floods obliterating entire cities, killing thousands of people. The United States just bombed terrorist camps in Sudan and Afghanistan with possible retaliation. Humanity, it seems, is facing extinction, not only from nature but from man himself as the threat of a third world war looms on the horizon. With new and deadly technologies of destruction and unimaginable biological strains of germ warfare, ninety percent of the world population could become extinct within moments.

We live in dangerous times. All conditions of the Biblical prophecies concerning the last days and the end of time are now in place. Despite all the cries of doom and gloom, we live in the most interesting period in the history of mankind. It is a time of transition, of rapid change. Edgar Cayce said that the future is not fixed. It is a probable future that can be changed by the human will, the human mind, and desire. We create our own reality. Our thoughts, feelings, and actions are more powerful than we realize. Quantum physics has shown that matter responds to the observer...the mind. The critical mass of humanity, by its unified projection of thought, has achieved the spiritual conversion or enlightenment necessary to modify an otherwise catastrophic ending for the new millenium.

The collective information from Aureal and all other extra-dimensional beings tells that we live now in a most unusual, wonderful time in which earth and mankind are being transformed in consciousness. It is a quantum leap in evolution. We are lifting into a higher dimension of light, love, and harmony where life is more wonderful than we can imagine.

There will be one generation that will never go through death of the body to get there, the Bible assures...we are returning home.

This is not the final word; the search for truth is progressive and requires many paths. Truth is relative. What mystical truths we perceive today on the frontier of a new age will be accepted knowledge tomorrow. And so we move on, always seeking the greater reality to know who and what we are and from where we came.

The author does not pretend to understand all the questions we continue to ask. It is hoped, however, that some light has been shed upon the path of mankind's eternal search for truth and that what we seek so desperately to know today will be common knowledge tomorrow. But as we march forward into the light of knowing, there will always be more questions than answers, for that is the destiny of mankind in his search for himself.

Bibliography

Bernstein, Morey, *The Search for Bridey Murphy* (Garden City: Doubleday, 1965)

Braden, Gregg, *Awakening To Zero Point: The Collective Initiation* (Sacred Spaces/Ancient Wisdom, 1993, 1994)

Cerminara, Gina, *Many Mansions* (New York: William Sloan Associates, Inc., 1950)

Chatelain, Maurice, *Our Ancestors Came From Outer Space* (Garden City, New York: Doubleday & Company, Inc., 1978)

Chopra, Deepak, M.D., *Quantum Healing: Exploring the Frontiers of Mind/Body Medicine* (New York: Bantam Books, 1989)

Fiore, Edith, Ph.D., *You Have Been Here Before: A Psychologist Looks At Past Lives* (New York: Ballantine Books, 1978)

Fox, Matthew and Rupert Sheldrake, *The Physics of Angels: Exploring the Realm Where Science and Spirit Meet* (New York: Harper Collins, 1996)

Gerber, Richard, M.D., *Vibrational Medicine* (Santa Fe: Bear and Co., 1988)

Haskins, Susan, *Mary Magdalen: Myth and Metaphor* (Harcourt Brace & Co., 1993)

Hawking, Stephen W., *A Brief History of Time: From the Big Bang to Black Holes* (New York: Bantam Books, 1988)

Jaynes, Julian, *The Origin of Consciousness in the Breakdown of the Bicameral Mind* (Boston: Houghton Mifflin Company, 1976, 1990)

Kaufmann, William, *Black Holes And Warped Spacetime* (San Francisco: W. H. Freeman and Company, 1979)

Kaku, Michio, *Hyperspace: A Scientific Odyssey through Parallel Universes, Time Warps, and the 10th Dimension* (New York: Oxford University Press, 1994)

Lindsey, Hal, *The Late Great Planet Earth* (New York: Bantam Books, 1970)

MacLaine, Shirley, *Out on a Limb* (New York, Bantam Books, 1984)

Macvey, John W., *Time Travel: A Guide to Journeys in the Fourth Dimension* (Chelsea, Michigan: Scarborough House, 1990)

Moody, Raymond Jr., M.D., *Life After Life* (New York, Bantam Books, 1970)

Ostrander, Sheila and Lynn Schroeder, *Psychic Discoveries behind the Iron Curtain* (Englewood Cliffs: Prentice Hall, 1970).

Pagels, Elaine, *The Gnostic Gospels* (New York, Vintage Books, 1979)

Riordan, Michael and David N. Schramm, *The Shadows Of Creation* (San Francisco: W. H. Freeman & Co., 1991)

Roberts, Jane, *The Seth Material* (Englewood Cliffs: Prentice Hall, 1970)

Roberts, Jane, *Seth Speaks: The Eternal Validity of the Soul* (Englewood Cliffs: Prentice Hall, 1972)

Sagan, Carl, *Cosmos* (New York: Random House, 1980)

Sitchin, Zecharia, *Genesis Revisited: Is Modern Science Catching up with Ancient Knowledge?* (Santa Fe: Bear & Company, 1991)

Sitchin, Zecharia, *The 12th Planet* (New York, Avon Books, 1976)

Sitchin, Zecharia, *Divine Encounters* (New York, Avon Books, 1995)

Sutphen, Dick, *You Were Born Again To Be Together* (New York: Pocket Books, 1976)

Sugrue, Thomas, *There Is A River: The Story of Edgar Cayce* (New York: Henry Holt and Company, 1942)

Talbot, Michael, *The Holographic Universe* (New York: Harper Collins, 1991)

Taylor, John G., *Black Holes: End of the Universe?* (New York: Random House, 1973)

Thorne, Kip, *Black Holes and Time Warps* (New York: W. W. Norton & Col, 1994)

Time-Life Books, Lost Civilizations Series, *Sumer: Cities of Eden* (New York: Time-Life Books, 1993)

Time-Life Books, Lost Civilizations Series, *Wondrous Realms of the Aegean* (New York: Time Life Books, 1993)

von Daniken, Erich *Chariots of the Gods* (New York: G. P. Putnam's Sons, 1968)

Weinberg, Seven Lee, Ed., *Ramtha* (Eastsound, Washington: Sovereignty, Inc., 1986)

Wolf, Fred Alan, Ph. D., *Physics Proves the Existence of the Soul* (New York: Simon and Schuster, 1996)

Zukav, Gary, *The Dancing Wu Li Masters: An Overview of the New Physics* (New York: Bantam Books, 1980)

Whispers in the Wind

Communications from an Ascended Master

Name _____

Address _____

_____

city/state/zip _____

Please send me ___ copies at $17.95 each.

Amount _____

7.75% sales tax _____

(California residents only)

Postage and handling _____

($3.00 for first book and $1.00 for each additional book)

Total _____

∞ *Checks / Money Orders*

Send to:

**Sun Valley Publishing
1880 East Chase Avenue
El Cajon, CA 92020**

∞ *Phone / Credit Cards*

Check one: ❑ Visa ❑ Mastercard ❑ American Express

Account # _____ expires _____

Cardholder _____

Phone # _____

Signature _____

Send to:

**Silvercat Publications
4070 Goldfinch Street, Ste. C
San Diego, CA 92103-1865
(888) 299-9119** *toll-free*